A WINDOW ON EUROPE

Cover illustration

The 'Valley Section' stained glass window, illustrated on the front cover of this book, was made for an early advocate of European co-operation, the Edinburgh biologist and polymath Sir Patrick Geddes (1854–1932). It shows a city and its region and illuminates, through word and symbol, the interdependence of human beings and their environment.

Geddes' recognition of the historical, geographical and ecologocal inter-relationship of the cultures and peoples of Europe and the world is of central relevance to the citizens of today's Europe; interdependence and cooperation between European nations is a constant theme of the Lothian European Lectures 1992.

*The Lothian European
Lectures 1992*

A WINDOW ON EUROPE

*Edited by Geraldine Prince
with an Introduction by
Neal Ascherson*

CANONGATE PRESS

*in association with
Lothian Regional Council*

First published in 1993 in the United Kingdom by
Canongate Press Ltd, 14 Frederick Street, Edinburgh.

The publishers acknowledge the support of Lothian Regional
Council in the publication of this volume

British Library Cataloguing-in-Publication Data
A catalogue record for this book is available on request
from The British Library

ISBN 0 86241 453 9

Typeset by
Hewer Text Composition Services, Edinburgh.
Printed and bound in the United Kingdom by
the Cromwell Press.

Contents

ERIC MILLIGAN
Foreword   vii

Acknowledgements   x
Editorial note   xii
Biographies of contributors   xiii

NEAL ASCHERSON
Introduction   xix

The Lothian European Lectures 1992

1 **WILLIAM E. PATERSON**
*Europe undivided: from spring in winter to winter
of despair?*   I

2 **JAN EGELAND**
Europe and the global challenge of 20 million refugees   16

3 **JULIET LODGE**
*European Union: working together towards a Europe
of the Regions?*   30

4 **DAVID EDWARD**
Nations, states, people and commerce   46

5 **EDWARD SAID**
Imperialism and after: Europe, the US and the rest of us   64

6   PETER PALUMBO
    Vision of a new Europe   90

7   JOHN SIMPSON
    Politics and the new Europe   99

8   ADRIAN BIRD
    Understanding the human genome –
    Scottish science in Europe   117

9   JOHN SMITH
    Europe and the world: preparing for the 21st century   130

10 DAVID MARTIN
    Beyond 1992 – a deeper and wider Europe?   143

11 GENNADY GERASIMOV
    Russia as an integral part of Europe   157

12 HELENA KENNEDY
    Europe and our rights   168

13 CRISPIN TICKELL
    Europe: the environmental dimension   184

14 EDWARD HEATH
    At the heart of Europe   205

15 MURDO MACDONALD
    The 'Lothian in Europe' Lecture
    Patrick Geddes: Visual thinker   229

16 JACQUES DELORS
    Address to the University of Edinburgh   256

    Notes and further reading   263
    List of European terms and acronyms   268

Foreword

AS THE LOTHIAN EUROPEAN LECTURES UNFOLDED OVER THE
autumn months of 1992, it became clear that, although the domestic political agenda was dominated by the Maastricht Treaty, this
would not be the case in Edinburgh. While others might become
fixated on the technicalities of subsidiarity, the 15 speakers in the
Lothian European Lectures programme preferred the richer territory of the ideals, values and aspirations of a Europe irrevocably
changed by the fall of the Berlin Wall. For many of the speakers,
that was the starting point for profound analyses of Europe in flux.
It was given particular relevance by Edinburgh's role as the host
city for the European Council of Ministers 'Summit' in December
1992. This was to be the last major European meeting before
the Single Market completed further change in the relationship
between European neighbours.

Throughout the six-month period of the UK's Presidency of
the European Community a number of public and private bodies
throughut Edinburgh and Lothian Region orchestrated a range
of European events which constituted an extraordinary display
of intellectual and civic energy, all engaging in their various
ways with the compelling issue of 'being European'. As a
local authority with a long history of involvement with EC
programmes Lothian Regional Council had wished to enhance
this local sense of 'Europeanness' by fostering a responsible,
well-informed, constructive debate embracing Scotland's, and
Lothian's, role in 'Europe of the Regions' and extending to
Europe's interdependence with the world beyond the European
Community. The Lothian European Lectures brought to the

city speakers of outstanding quality, several of whom were professionally involved with European decision-making at the highest level; others spoke of ways in which their political, cultural, intellectual or academic concerns were acquiring new and urgent European inflections.

This initiative, conceived as part of a long-established 'Lothian in Europe' programme, was rewarded with the achievement of three key objectives. First, the committed support offered by the partnership of institutions established to manage the series – an arrangement unique in the United Kingdom – allowed Edinburgh's European stature as a centre of excellence in learning, research and culture to be demonstrated. Pooling resources, the Lectures Committee constructed a programme at the highest level, thus enabling the realisation of a second objective – the facilitating of a debate which addressed the ideological, rather than structural, underpinning of Europe.

Most crucial were topics fundamental to Europe's future: the moral and strategic problems posed by refugees; European identity and nationalism; the rights and freedoms of European citizens; the potential for the strengthening of bonds between European states and with the world beyond Europe. This allowed the Edinburgh 'Summit' to be viewed against the backdrop of a city, and a nation, which acknowledged that the technicalities of subsidiarity, important though they might be, were not as significant as the broader questions of how and why the UK could and should be 'at the heart of Europe'.

Neither overly technical nor obscure, and certainly jargon free, the Lothian European Lectures drew vast and responsive audiences, allowing the lectures to achieve their third objective of full public participation. Formal, and sometimes contentious, responses to lectures were matched by spontaneous comments or questions from audiences. They contributed their own optimism, scepticism, knowledge or opinions as participants in a two-month long 'conversation', identified by one commentator as a demonstration of 'an independent civil society at its international best'.

The publication of these lectures is evidence of a belief that in the 'battle for the hearts and minds' of the citizens of the new Europe, much can be gained from the vitality and subtlety of reasoned and informed discussion. In this respect, the greatest debt is owed by Lothian Regional Council and its partners to the speakers whose contributions honoured the city, making this project a memorable and rewarding experience. The Lothian European Lecturers, and the distinguished Scots who introduced or responded to them, gave the citizens of Edinburgh and Lothian the opportunity to savour for themselves the experience of the city during the Enlightenment when, as one eighteenth-century observer remarked, it was possible 'to stand by the Mercat Cross [of Edinburgh] and within a few minutes take by the hand 50 men of genius'. It is a pleasure here to express Lothian Regional Council's gratitude to the men and women of genius who spoke in Edinburgh, and also to thank most warmly Neal Ascherson, whose introductory essay brings fresh insight to this edition of the lectures.

A Window on Europe takes its title from a phrase quoted by Gennady Gerasimov. He spoke of Peter the Great's image evoking the historical process of the coming together of the nations of Europe, which ratification of the Maastricht Treaty, and the widening of the Community, will help to advance still further in our own time. Primarily a journal of such ideas about European union and expansion, this book is also testimony to an important and exciting moment for Lothian. On the eve of the Single Market, the people of Lothian welcomed the European ideal with enthusiasm and style. At the same time, Edinburgh presented herself confidently and, we hope, with grace as a capital city proud of her European heritage. Lothian Regional Council is also particularly proud of the contribution to a greater understanding of the complexities of the new Europe that the reflections, seen through this 'window on Europe', make possible.

Eric Milligan
Convener, Lothian Regional Council

Acknowledgements

The Lothian European Lectures 1992 were devised and developed on behalf of Lothian Regional Council by Geraldine Prince. The Lectures were realised by the Lothian European Lectures Committee:

Chair: Norman Ireland,
Principal, EC and Corporate Affairs, Lothian Regional Council

Sheila Brock
Head of Public Affairs, National Museums of Scotland

Jill Crofts
Assistant to the Chief Executive, The City of Edinburgh District Council

Ray Footman
Head of Information and Public Relations Services, the University of Edinburgh

Maurice Griffiths
Director, External Relations, Napier University

Richard McGookin
Publications Officer, Heriot-Watt University

Geraldine Prince
Co-ordinator, The Lothian European Lectures, and Education Consultant, *Lux Europae*

Special Advisor to the Committee
Professor William Paterson, Director, Europa Institute, the University of Edinburgh

Lectures Administrator: Sybelle Medcalfe

The Lothian European Lectures Committee acknowledges the help and support of:

The Caledonian Hotel
The Herald
InterCity
Justerini and Brooks Ltd.
KPMG Peat Marwick
Royal Mail Scotland and Northern Ireland
Waterstone's Booksellers
Arthur Lodge Catering
The Georgian House (The National Trust for Scotland)

Editorial note

THE LOTHIAN EUROPEAN LECTURES WERE DELIVERED IN Edinburgh between 20 October and 9 December 1992, as official events of the UK's Presidency of the European Community. They formed part of the Edinburgh and Lothians European Programme, a series of European events staged in the period leading up to the European Council of Ministers meeting held at the Palace of Holyrood House on 11 and 12 December 1992.

The first 'Lothian in Europe' lecture, given by Dr Murdo Macdonald as part of this series of events, is included in this volume, as is the address given by M. Jacques Delors on the award of a Doctorate *honoris causa* from the University of Edinburgh.

Canongate Press and Lothian Regional Council are grateful to speakers for permission to publish their texts, which have been edited for this volume. In addition, Professor Lodge and Professor Paterson have revised their lectures for publication.

Marina Warner's lecture, 'From the Sibyls to Mother Goose: the story tellers of Europe', sponsored by Lothian Regional Council and the National Museums of Scotland, is not available for inclusion for copyright reasons. The material covered in Marina Warner's lecture, delivered at the Royal Museum of Scotland on 26 November 1992, is included in her forthcoming book, *From the Beast to the Blonde: a study of fairytale* to be published by Chatto and Windus in 1994.

This publication was made possible with the cooperation of BBC Radio Scotland who made available tapes of lectures recorded and used in broadcasts throughout the period leading up to the Edinburgh 'Summit'.

Biographies of contributors

Professor William E. Paterson was appointed Salvesen Professor of European Institutions and Director of the Europa Institute at the University of Edinburgh in 1990. He began his academic career at the University of Aberdeen and from 1970 lectured in German Politics at the University of Warwick, latterly as Professor and Chairman of Department. Co-founder of the Association for the Study of German Politics, he is currently Chairman of the University Association for Contemporary European Studies and has been a frequent participant at the Königswinter Conferences. He has published in the field of German and European politics and has been a visiting fellow or lecturer at universities and institutes in Germany, most recently at the Max Planck Institute in Cologne.

Jan Egeland worked during the early 1980s as a radio and television journalist for the Norwegian Broadcasting Company and various newspapers. In 1985 he was awarded an MA in political science from the University of Oslo for his thesis on International Human Rights Policy. After working as a research coordinator for the Henry Durant Institute, Geneva, he became Head of Information and Head of the International Department of the Norwegian Red Cross, was appointed Political Advisor to the Norwegian Minister of Foreign Affairs and was appointed State Secretary in the Ministry in February 1992. Jan Egeland has been a guest lecturer at the University of California at Berkeley, at the Truman Institute in Jerusalem and the International Peace Research Institute in Oslo. He has written a number of books and articles on international humanitarian issues.

Professor Juliet Lodge has an international reputation for her research on European integration, having worked continuously to increase awareness and knowledge of the European Community and the implications of the Single Market. Responsible for setting up the European Community Research Unit at the University of Hull, Professor Lodge promotes interdisciplinary activities and liaison with government departments, international organisations, local authorities, business and professional bodies. In 1991 Juliet Lodge was nominated for the EC Commission Jean Monnet Chair in European Integration and made Professor of European Politics at the University of Hull. Juliet Lodge is Visiting Professor at the Université Libre de Bruxelles and, in 1992, was nominated as 'Woman of Europe'.

Judge David Edward CMG QC is a judge at the European Court of Justice, Luxembourg. He was Salvesen Professor of European Institutions and Director of the Europa Institute, the University of Edinburgh, from 1985 to 1989, and was made an Honorary Professor at the University of Edinburgh in 1990. He has been a specialist advisor to the House of Lords Select Committee on the European Community in 1985, 1986 and 1987, a Member of the Panel of Arbitrators for the International Centre for Settlement of Investment Disputes from 1981 to 1989 and Chairman of the Scottish Council for Arbitration, 1988-89. Judge Edward was Judge of the Court of First Instance of the EC from 1989 to 1992 and Member, Foundation Senate, Europa Universitat Via Drina, Frankfurt-an-der-Oder.

Professor Edward W. Said has achieved wide distinction both as a literary critic and as a political commentator and activist. Educated at Princeton and Harvard, Professor Said teaches, and has taught from the beginning of his career, at Columbia University in the City of New York where he holds the title of University Professor in the Department of English and Comparative Literature. His books include *Orientalism, The Question of Palestine, Musical Elaborations* and *Culture and Imperialism*. Professor Said is the BBC Reith lecturer for 1993.

Lord Palumbo was appointed Chairman of the Arts Council of Great Britain in 1989 after distinguished associations with art institutions including the Metropolitan Museum and the Museum of Modern Art in New York and with the Tate Gallery and Whitechapel Gallery in London. He is a noted collector of contemporary fine art and also of the decorative and applied arts and a patron and champion of Modern Movement and contemporary architecture.

John Simpson CBE joined the BBC in 1966 and has served as Foreign and Diplomatic Correspondent, as Political and Diplomatic Editor and, since 1988, as Foreign Affairs Editor. He witnessed the tumultuous changes in Central and Eastern Europe in the late 1980s and early 1990s, events analysed in *Despatches from the Barricades* (1990) and *The Darkness Crumbles* (1992). John Simpson has been the recipient of numerous distinguished awards, including the BAFTA Richard Dimbleby Award in 1992. He was made a CBE in the Gulf War Honours in 1991.

Professor Adrian Bird was appointed to the Buchanan Chair of Genetics at the University of Edinburgh in 1990. His academic career has covered posts at Yale University, Zurich University, the Medical Research Council, the Mammalian Genome Unit and Clinical and Population Cytogenetics Unit in Edinburgh and from 1988 to 1990 at the Research Institute of Molecular Pathology in Vienna. His research interests centre round DNA and the genome, and are currently supported by major grants from the Imperial Cancer Research Fund and the Wellcome Trust. He was awarded the Fellowship of the Royal Society of London in 1989 and at the Edinburgh Science Festival in 1992 was acknowledged as one of the most widely cited scientists in Scotland.

The Rt Hon John Smith QC MP is Leader of the Opposition in the House of Commons. He was first elected to Parliament in 1970. Between 1974 and 1979 he served as Parliamentary Under Secretary for Energy, Minister of State for Energy and Secretary of State for Trade. As a member of the Shadow Cabinet since 1979, he has served as Opposition Spokesman on Trade, Energy, Employment, and Trade and Industry. Most recently, he has served as Shadow Chancellor. In 1992, John Smith was elected leader of the Labour Party.

David Martin MEP has been a member of the European Parliament for the Lothians since 1984. Born in 1954, he received his education at Liberton High School, Edinburgh, and took his degree in economics at Heriot-Watt University. He served as a Lothian Regional Councillor from 1982 to 1984 when he was elected to the European Parliament in Strasbourg, becoming the youngest ever leader of the Labour Group and subsequently a Vice-President of the Parliament. He has published a number of highly influential pamphlets on European institutions and politics, contributed to a number of books and, in his capacity as the Parliament's spokesman on Institutional Affairs, is the author of the major official reports known collectively as 'The Martin Reports'.

His Excellency Gennady Gerasimov was born in Kazan and studied law at Moscow University. He embarked on a successful career in journalism, starting as a contributor to *New Times Weekly* and working for *Trud* and *World Marxist Review*. He continued for many years as a syndicated columnist with Novosti Press Agency and spent almost six years in the United States, becoming finally editor-in-chief of *Moscow News*. At the start of Perestroika he was invited to join the Diplomatic Service of the USSR as spokesman for the Ministry of Foreign Affairs. In 1991 he was appointed Russian Ambassador to Lisbon.

Helena Kennedy QC was born in Glasgow. She has practised as a barrister since 1972 and was made a Queen's Counsel in 1991. She is on the Bar Council, initiated the establishment of a Sex Discrimination Committee at the Bar and is a Commissioner of the National Commission on Education. She has been a regular contributor to radio, television and the print media where she comments on controversial legal and social issues, particularly as they affect women, children and families. Helena Kennedy is the Chair of Charter 88, the citizens' movement for constitutional reform.

Sir Crispin Tickell GCMG KCVO has had a distinguished diplomatic career having joined the British Diplomatic Service in 1954. From 1970 to 1972 he was Private Secretary to successive Ministers responsible for negotiations for British entry into the European Community and was Chef de Cabinet to the President of the European Commission from 1977 until 1980. Sir Crispin also served as British Ambassador to Mexico from 1981 to 1983 and was the British Permanent Representative on the Security Council from 1987 to 1990. He has been concerned with the environment for many years, taking advantage of a sabbatical year at Harvard in 1975-76 to write *Climatic Change and World Affairs*. He is now Warden of Green College, Oxford.

The Rt Hon Sir Edward Heath KG MBE MP first entered politics in 1950 as the MP for Bexley. He was Parliamentary Secretary to the Treasury and Government Chief Whip from 1955 to 1959. From 1960 to 1963 he held the position of Lord Privy Seal with Foreign Responsibilities and from 1963 to 1964 was Secretary of State for Industry, Trade and Regional Development. In 1965, he was elected Leader of the Conservative Party and was Leader of the Opposition from 1965 to 1970 when he became Prime Minister, a position he held until 1974. As Prime Minister, he completed the negotiations for the United Kingdom's entry into the EEC in 1971. In 1992, Sir Edward was appointed Knight Companion of the Most Noble Order of the Garter, the most senior honour awarded. He contributes his vast experience as a widely respected Parliamentarian and European from his position as 'Father of the House of Commons', the longest serving Member of Parliament.

Dr Murdo Macdonald is a writer, lecturer and teacher. Born in Edinburgh in 1955, he studied painting in London before reading psychology at the University of Edinburgh where he was awarded a first class degree in 1981. His PhD was devoted to the relationship between art and science. He contributes regularly to *The Scotsman* articles on the visual arts and is the editor of a number of books on art and ideas, including George Davie's *The Crisis of the Democratic Intellect* (Polygon, 1986). Since 1990 he has been a lecturer in the Centre for Continuing Education in the University of Edinburgh.

Jacques Delors was born in Paris in 1925 and was from 1945 to 1952 Executive Officer and subsequently Head of Department at the Banque de France. He then continued with an exceptionally distinguished career in economics, administration and academe, becoming from 1971 to 1972 Chargé de Mission for economic, financial and social affairs to the Prime Minister of France. In 1974 he joined the Socialist Party, becoming a member of the Central Committee of the Party in 1979. In the same year he was elected to the European Parliament, becoming President of the Commission of the European Communities in 1985, a position he still holds. Jacques Delors' outstanding contribution to European affairs has been recognised by the award of many distinctions, including the Degree of Doctor *honoris causa* from the University of Edinburgh in December 1992.

Neal Ascherson is a writer and journalist born in Edinburgh, who is at present a columnist on *The Independent on Sunday*.

Geraldine Prince is a lecturer in the Humanities Department at Edinburgh College of Art, writer and educational consultant.

NEAL ASCHERSON

Introduction

NO OTHER EUROPEAN CAPITAL LAID ON AS ELABORATE AND
hopeful a welcome for the European Community's heads of
state as Edinburgh did in 1992, when the European Council
met there for two days in December. There will, I think, be
nothing like it until those magnificent festivals sometime in the
future when Prague or Budapest or Warsaw – national capital
of a full member of the Community at last – gains the right to
be the Council's host for the first time.

In those two days, there were (at a rough count) six rallies,
seven lectures, four concerts, something like a dozen special
theatre productions, at least ten exhibitions, two street fairs,
a 'kirking' ceremony for the Heads of State at St Giles, a
degree ceremony at the University of Edinburgh for Jacques
Delors, some five minor protest marches and a huge, inspiriting
'March for Scottish Democracy' at which 25,000 Scots amazed
themselves by uniting to call for a Scottish Parliament. There
was poetry and dancing, French and Scandinavian film seasons,
a sculpture show of 'light forms' and installations, a special
Scots £1 note bearing the Community flag, even an attempt
to rename a committee hall in the City Chambers the 'Jacques
Delors Room'.

Was it all disproportionate? The Heads of State, busy in
Holyrood House, had few moments to spare for all the functions
and delights laid out for them. But the two big days resembled
another significant moment in Scottish modern history when
in 1822 King George IV visited Edinburgh – the first visit of
a British monarch to Scotland since the Union over a century
before. Then, too, 'there was a very entertaining and ludicrous

state of bustle and expectation of the sedate and sober citizens of the Scottish Metropolis'. And then too, in 1822 as in 1992, Scotland was seized with a huge enthusiasm to display itself to 'the world' as a modern nation. The message in 1822 was mainly addressed to the rest of Britain. But the message in 1992 was sent wider: a declaration to Europe that Scotland – although a component of the United Kingdom – was in its own estimation a full partner in the project of European Union, even if it could not be a formally full partner in the Community's institutions. There was nothing, I think, disproportionate about this wish to celebrate the Council's arrival in Edinburgh as something like a rite of international recognition.

In all these preparations and reflections, the Lothian European Lectures functioned as a sort of pole around which ideas and emotions steadily crystallised. They began early, in October, and ran on through a series of fifteen addresses to culminate with Sir Edward Heath, speaking only three days before the Edinburgh Summit opened. They were held all over town, in universities and learned institutes and libraries and – four of them – at the Royal Museum in Chambers Street. They were, to the ill-concealed surprise and delight of the organisers, for the most part hugely attended. To see the Museum hall packed out and disappointed crowds queueing outside in the darkness and sleet of Chambers Street is a rare compliment for visiting lecturers in Edinburgh. A spark, an urge went round. People wanted to take part in this Europe of theirs.

The lectures were billed as a programme 'celebrating the United Kingdom's Presidency of the European Community', which was then drawing to its end. But few of them were celebratory about that Presidency, and many were angrily critical of the hesitations and inhibitions of the British Government over the project of European Union. Neither were all of them about the politics of Europe in the direct sense: Marina Warner talked about story-tellers, Professor Edward Said about imperialism and migration, Professor Adrian Bird about genome research in Europe and in Scotland in particular.

They were a diverse group of statements, in subject and in texture. But they had a number of virtues in common. None of them descended to 'Euro-guff' or 'Eurolatry'; that rhetoric of optimistic cliché and polished jargon which disgusted thousands of British audiences in past decades. None of them invoked the genial frauds of 'Euronationalism': all those dubious, legitimising discourses about the ancient unity of Western Christendom or about the 'first united Europe' supposedly brought about in an Iron Age 'Celtic Empire' – that myth which gave rise to the magnificent, thoroughly misleading *I Celti* exhibition in Venice in 1991. And none of them, rather strikingly, had anything good to say about the European policies of the British Government of the day.

The 1992 Lothian Lectures belong to a certain moment: a nervous, self-critical one. It had not been a good year. Many hopeful developments seemed to be unravelling. The Maastricht Treaty was in doubt, after a first Danish referendum had refused to ratify it, and Britain – which had been driven out of the ERM after a disastrous run on sterling in September – was leading a vigorous counter-attack against the whole project of political union. Germany was floundering, apparently unable either to transform the economy of the new eastern Bundesländer without overstraining the state finances or to deal with spreading outbreaks of right-wing violence against foreign immigrants. In Russia, President Yeltsin was no longer the hero of the 1991 barricades but a tired politician fighting for his life against his own parliament. Czechoslovakia, perceived as the most 'Western' and stable nation state in post-communist Europe, was about to break up. In what had been Yugoslavia, the killing had concentrated in an appalling communal civil war in Bosnia; the futility of Community attempts to end this conflict was already leading to bitter recriminations among EC members about past policies and to rising cynicism about the very possibility of anything worthy to be called a common foreign and defence policy.

In the first lecture of the series, Professor William Paterson evoked a 'bonfire of the certainties'. It was not just the glacial solidity of the Cold War which had gone, but the West's confidence – during and immediately after the revolutions of 1989 – that the 'democratic system' and a free-market or at least mixed economy could be installed rapidly and without too much pain in the countries which had emerged from a half-century of communism. This process was now plainly going to be a long haul, with regressions. Some of the speakers seemed to think that it might be indefinitely long or not succeed at all, and some of the lecturers who spoke about Eastern Europe were startlingly pessimistic. John Smith MP, leader of the Labour Party, thought that a new Marshall Plan for Eastern Europe was neither possible nor necessary, and suggested that the Group of Seven should appoint some lofty figure to 'galvanise' Western assistance to the East. Professor Paterson said that the Community must provide 'massive public investment' if the whole democratic project in Eastern Europe were not to fail. Sir Edward Heath bluntly stated that early admission of Eastern nations to the Community was out of the question: 'they can't be welcomed . . . their economies are in an absolutely disastrous state'. Gennady Gerasimov, the former Soviet spokesman who had become Russian Ambassador in Lisbon, implicitly agreed with Paterson when he insisted that there was a danger of nationalistic dictatorship in Russia if the West did not provide effective assistance to Mr Yeltsin, but said unambiguously that his country intended to join Europe in some sense – to become 'an equal, normal member' of the family of European nations. In spite of appearances, the ancient battle between Slavophils and Westernisers in Russia was over, and the Government and the majority of the people were irrevocably on the Westernising track.

All but three of the speakers were British, with an appropriate majority of Scottish voices. If there was a gap in the spectrum of opinion represented by the Lothian Lectures, it was the absence – Mr Gerasimov and Mr Egeland excepted – of speakers from European countries outwith the Community. Those missing voices might have added a more positive tone to the whole colloquium, and might have corrected the tendency to worry – in a sometimes unfocused way – about the post-1989 re-emergence of nationalism and to generalise about it as a source only of disorder and instability. The exception here was the lecture by John Simpson, foreign affairs editor of the BBC, who talked with directness and emotion about his own reporting experiences after the fall of the Berlin Wall, in the great revolutionary demonstrations in Prague in November 1989, and during the failed putsch in Moscow in August 1991. Simpson argued strongly against the view that Central and Eastern Europe were merely reverting to the condition of the 1930s: the Continent of 1992 was essentially a much safer place than it had been before 1939, or during the Cold War when – as he reminded his listeners – the penalties for any attempt to change national or international structures could have been apocalyptic and terminal. Appalling as the events in Bosnia and the rest of ex-Yugoslavia had been, they were not a threat to the peace of Europe as a whole in the sense that they would drag major powers into military confrontation. The nationalisms now evident in Europe were 'new' and less malign: 'an unruliness, a vat of liquid which is boiling away . . . froth on the surface of the creation of a new state'. Simpson insisted that 'the barbarians are not at the gate'. He suggested that the will to national independence could not and should not be suppressed, and he ended by recalling the national hymn sung in Wenceslas Square in Prague when Alexander Dubček stood on a balcony beside Vaclav Havel and met his people again: 'May the governing of your affairs come back to you, at last, my nation.'

I have quoted a lot from Simpson because his imaginative approach allowed him to understand events in the 'wider Europe' as components of a broad historical process, rather than as inert obstacles to the creation of some better order. But many speakers showed the same sense of process when they examined the prospects for European Union and the attitudes of the United Kingdom. These examinations seemed to fall under three headings: the need for a new 'constitution' for the Community, the leakage of authority from the old-fashioned nation state which was flowing upwards to Community institutions and downwards to the regional level, and the specific hang-ups of the United Kingdom which arose essentially from an archaic doctrine of state sovereignty.

The Community already has a working constitution, which is the Treaty of Rome. Judge David Edward, of the European Court of Justice, quoted the jurist and diplomat James Bryce to define it as a 'flexible constitution' which balanced the interests of European integration against those of the Member States and those of the peoples represented by the Parliament. The argument now, the 'Maastricht argument', was not really about federalism, which already existed to a significant extent, nor about sovereignty, which had already been largely pooled, but about power – who should exercise it and how, and subject to what checks? He was not the only Lothian lecturer to suggest that to 'oppose Maastricht' was simply to vote for the status quo and to leave the present power problem unsolved and stagnant. David Martin, the MEP for the Lothians, went into more detail. He rejected the options of doing nothing or of building a sort of 'United Nations of Europe' in which the 'Big Five' nations would monopolise the Commission and act as a 'Security Council' with hegemony over an expanded Community of some 38 members. Martin proposed a radical democratic transformation, in which the Commission (rather like a British Cabinet) would 'emerge' from the Parliament, while the Council of Ministers would be replaced by a European Senate in which seats would be distributed to regions and small states on the basis of population (one for Malta, ten for Germany and so on).

Regionalism intrigued many speakers. (Nobody except Sir Edward Heath supported the British definition of 'subsidiarity' as the right of nation states to make their own internal decisions – and he only did so in order to denounce it: '. . . in most cases, [a policy] will be better done by the Community as a whole'.) But the most penetrating remark, in my opinion, came from Professor Juliet Lodge, who observed that 'advancing the concept of a Europe of the Regions is a necessary step to creating a solid basis on which to build the European Union'. She might have gone on to point out that the converse is also true: that the movement towards stronger and more autonomous regions moves more rapidly when the progress towards central 'federal' institutions is going well, and correspondingly slows down when – as in late 1992 – the federalising process is being obstructed. Here a grand dynamic was revealed. The increase of authority at Brussels and the increase of authority at Stuttgart or Barcelona or Milan are in reality a single phenomenon: the slow diminishing of the nation state.

Here the question of sovereignty is raised with a vengeance. Judge Edward quoted his favourite Bryce again: 'The controversies which the Doctrine of Sovereignty has provoked have been so numerous and so tedious that a reader . . . may feel alarmed at being invited to enter once again that dusty desert of abstractions . . .' But it was a desert which the Lothian lecturers rightly skirted. Edward, as I have mentioned, pronounced the sovereignty problem to be over. Sir Edward Heath stated memorably that 'sovereignty isn't something you put down in the cellar and go down with a candle once a week to see if it is still there . . . sovereignty exists to be used and used for the benefit of the citizens'. It was generally agreed that obsession with national sovereignty was a peculiarly British difficulty – more accurately, an English difficulty, for several speakers made a point of recording their sense that Scotland was in many ways a more 'European' place than its southern neighbour. Jacques Delors spoke of the link with Europe as 'a constant feature of Scottish history' and went on to discuss in detail Scotland's relationship to the Community, while Juliet Lodge said that 'cynicism in the UK over European Union is largely an English problem. As one crosses the border into Scotland, one crosses into Europe.'

It was Helena Kennedy QC who analysed this 'English

problem' as the constitutional backwardness of the British state. The antique doctrine of parliamentary sovereignty, a form of modified absolutism left over from the seventeenth century, was creating in our own times both a growing deficit in civic liberties and an alarming incompatibility with the constitutional system of the Community. Her immediate objectives – a Bill of Rights, an entrenched 'right to know' to pitch against the tradition of official secrecy, a culture of human rights and a devolution of government to the nations and regions of Britain – would go a long way to 'Europeanise' the United Kingdom.

But these British divergences also illustrate, by contrast, what a strange hybrid – what an Arcimboldo face made up of the fruits of political theories from the eighteenth to the twentieth centuries – the Community is. The Rights of Man are here and so is the doctrine of popular sovereignty embodied in a written constitution, though in this odd structure the constitution came first and the 'people' who are supposed to create it through their Parliament were invented later. There is Catholic theory, but also a whiff of the American Revolution, in the idea of subsidiarity. There is both British Victorian *laissez-faire* and the neo-liberal doctrines of Friedrich Naumann in the Single Market concept; Christian Democracy in the notion of a 'social' capitalism; Marxism in the founders' confidence that industrial fusion must lead to a fusion of political superstructures. And somewhere, repulsive as the thought is, National Socialism contributed to the idea that the loss of overseas empires must be followed by a united Europe protecting its economic strength against outside competition.

The Community, like many artefacts, seems to be strictly planned but in reality is largely the product of unpredicted, organic growth. This should teach humility. Sir Crispin Tickell, in his account of how the Community developed its response to environmental threats, reminded his Edinburgh audience of the long-haul facts of life: the impermanence of this particular Europe which we inhabit at one point during its changes since the last glaciation. Professor Edward Said and Jan Egeland spoke about refugees and migrants, and Edward Said even proposed that it was no longer the settled citizens but the displaced, the wanderers, who were now becoming the subjects of European and world history with their 'unhoused, de-centred, exilic energies'.

These are among the inmost and hungriest flames which are burning away the old European certainties. The humility they imply should be used to change our view of what the European Community will finally look like. Professor Adrian Bird spoke of the Scottish contribution to genome research, recalling that the first isolation of a gene in pure form was carried out in Edinburgh in the late 1960s. The Lothian Lectures, I hope, bring their audiences and readers to the point at which they can begin to decipher the genome of the European future.

This will be no superstate of the traditional kind. This will be no gleaming imperial beast distinguished by uniformity, command of force and decisiveness in using that force. On the contrary, this Europe will be a sponge. It will resemble a huge, collective, soft-textured creature of uncertain outline, composed of countless individual organisms of different sizes and appetites. It will include nation states, autonomous regions, petty principalities, independent islands, federations, free cities, travelling communities, ethnic groups with members in every place but a homeland in none, and many millions of legal and illegal migrants swimming in and out of the sponge's gaping pores.

This sponge-Europe will be rich, and in many ways ingenious. But it will not be good at sudden decisions or painful choices. It will be united in one sense, but infinitely divided in several others. It will be impossible to kill, but at the same time it will be almost incapable of killing anything or anyone else. Nobody – none of the Community's founders and dreamers and architects – meant Europe to emerge like this. And yet this, if we are lucky, is how it will be: the negation of all the worst vices of Europeanism in habitable form. And we will be happy in it.

The Lothian European
Lectures 1992

WILLIAM E. PATERSON

1   *Europe undivided: from spring in winter to winter of despair?*

The post-war settlement

THE EUROPEAN ORDER, SOMETIMES CALLED THE YALTA settlement, that perished in the autumn of 1989, although it had appeared permanent and immovable, represented a sharp break from all its predecessors. Until then the modern international system had been incontestably Eurocentric. Within the previous system European states had also felt themselves to be genuinely sovereign; a conviction that survived the First World War and its resulting web of war debts and reparation payments. The system was multipolar with a plurality of power centres and the major European states all counted for a good deal while the influence of the two future external superpowers was much less central. This multipolarity and the effective sovereignty of European states also meant that states continued to be very flexible in their international alignments.

Yalta Europe

The post-war settlement, more evocatively known as Yalta Europe, was a victors' peace which recognised and enshrined the overwhelming military strength of the United States and the Soviet Union, and divided Europe between East and West. The new system was markedly bipolar and European states lost their freedom to change alliances. Sovereignty was most obviously lost in the field of security but the hard shell of the nation state was also penetrated in the recognition of increasing economic interdependence reflected most powerfully in the development of the European Community. European division and constraints on the exercise of sovereignty produced two German states which were highly integrated into their respective systems and rendered Germany more an object than a subject of the international system – a situation which prompted François Mauriac's aphorism 'I love Germany so much that I am glad there are two of them.'

Every international system is a mixture of costs and benefits and Yalta Europe was one in which the benefits accrued overwhelmingly to the Western half. These benefits included unprecedented and sustained levels of prosperity. Armed struggle was confined to irredentist movements in Northern Ireland, the South Tyrol and the Basque area. Within Western Europe national reconciliation was possible, most notably between France and Germany, and where border disputes remained, as between Greece and Turkey, the Western alliance acted as a tourniquet to contain the damage. A stable and liberal democratic polity, the Federal Republic, was established for the first time in Germany. The costs of meeting a perceived security threat from the Soviet Union were largely borne by the United States.

Within Eastern Europe there were also some benefits. While prosperity was not achieved, full employment and a rather grey existence was secured. Frontier disputes appeared settled and national minorities took up folk-dancing instead of arms – a development with which we are not entirely unfamiliar in Scotland.

Significant though these gains were, the costs of the system were indefensible. Throughout Eastern Europe there was a complete absence of civil rights, and governments rested not on popular support but ultimately on the Soviet military presence. The maintenance of such a system involved the suppression of civil society and the corruption of personal relations through a network of informers – a development already anticipated by George Orwell.

Spring in winter: the collapse of the system

The Yalta system finally succumbed in 1989 but it had been corroding from within for at least a decade. The election of a Polish Pope, his visits to Poland and the activities of Solidarnosc changed the situation in Poland by demonstrating just how little support the regime possessed. The Helsinki Process sustained and focused dissident activities like Charter 77 across Eastern Europe. The fundamental cause, however, was the weakness of the Soviet economy, exacerbated but not created by its response to the Western challenge of the 1980s. Mikhail Gorbachev increasingly accepted, after his advent to power in 1985, that the Soviet Empire would have to give ground and that the Brezhnev doctrine of limited sovereignty for states within the Soviet reach would have to be replaced by what Gennady Gerasimov famously christened on Gorbachev's behalf as the Sinatra doctrine (I did it my way).

A whole range of European thinkers have pointed out that autocracies are at their weakest once they begin to reform. By 1989 the Soviet Union no longer possessed the will or the capacity to suppress the increasingly vociferous mass protest movements demanding political change and access to an individualistic Western life style. There was no real prospect of a Tiananmen Square and of the local regimes only the most independent, the Ceausescu regime, attempted bloody suppression of popular revolt. It was this sudden and unexpected feeling of power by populations that had endured over four decades of powerlessness that gave the winter of 1989 its spring-like quality and produced the emblematic images of Vaclav Havel in Wenceslas Square and the breaching of the Brandenburg Gate.

Post-Cold War assumptions

It may be useful at this point to list the core assumptions held by Europeans about an 'undivided Europe' in the glad confident morning of the temporal and political spring of 1990. I use word 'European' advisedly since the rather unnuanced views associated with the Fukuyama 'End of history' school found very little echo on this side of the Atlantic. Briefly put, the Fukuyama school saw the defeat of communism and the triumph of capitalism as an historical end point. In Europe, states and nations have always played a more central role in historical consciousness and history is more often seen as being driven by their conflicts than impersonal economic forces or the clash of ideologies.

1. A central assumption focused on the changing security environment in Europe and the prospects of a 'peace dividend' in the wake of the visible decline in Soviet power. Resources and energies which had been tied up in the maintenance of alliance systems were now expected to be freed to find more positive uses.

2. It was assumed that, with the fall of the communist regimes, it would be possible to establish liberal democracies throughout Central and Eastern Europe.

3. German unity took place under a European roof and politicians in both East and West shared a common belief that the destiny of at least Poland, Czechoslovakia and Hungary lay within the European Community. Havel spoke of 'returning home to Europe' and Mrs Thatcher in her 1988 Bruges speech had described Warsaw, Budapest and Prague as being as much European cities as Bonn, Paris and London.

4. Germany was perceived as the most obvious beneficiary of the ending of European division and its role and influence was expected to increase steeply.

5. While the weakness of the Soviet Union was recognised, th   ninant assumption in Europe in early 1990 was that   s still a high chance that it would remain intact   ssion centred on how it was to be associated in   way with the changes.

     'er the breaching of the Brandenburg Gate it   to identify the determining features of the

The key building block of that future will continue to be the nation state since it remains the basic source of legitimacy and the only unit with the capacity to act, in however constrained a manner, across the entire policy range. A logical extension of this view would suggest that those states which are economically strongest and which already play the most central role in the defining European organisation, the European Community, will be the most influential. Germany, and less certainly France, would appear to be the self-evident candidates for leadership in the new Europe.

The United States, the dominant actor in post-war Western Europe and the clear victor in the Cold War, will continue to lose influence on European developments given its economic weakness, the increasingly introspective mood of its mass population and political elites and the very steep reduction of the American military presence in Europe.

Britain also looks unlikely to be at the heart of European developments.

1   Britain has retained and prized a particularly close association with the United States. 'It sometimes seems to us that for Britain the Channel is twice as wide as the Atlantic' – Hans Ulrich Klose. The decline in American interest and influence in Europe necessarily also entails a decline in the influence of the United Kingdom.

2. The end of the Cold War reduced the central importance of security issues, and power has become more obviously related to economic strength. Dominique Moisi observed of this change 'the balance between the mark and the bomb is moving to the advantage of the former'.

3. The core agenda of the United Kingdom in relation to Europe is perhaps best characterised as a cafeteria Europe where the emphasis is on offering a wide range of choice and participants can pick and choose on an *ad hoc* basis (variable geometry). This conception of Europe might best be described as 'the view from the Happy Eater'.

It is, perhaps, no accident that these preferences correspond to those of the major extra-European actors – Japan and the United States. Europe's future is, however, much more likely to be decided, in the long term, by the Europeans themselves. The dominant choice of the French and German political classes, reflecting their view that the central rationale for European integration is overcoming intra-European nationalism, is not for a cafeteria future but one which views Europe as a family. 'Membership is selective and exclusive and at least partly inherited, the organisation is hierarchical not egalitarian; the commitment is integrative, wide-ranging and progressive, not optional or selective.'[1]

The key institutional actor

Those institutions most obviously rooted to the demands of the Cold War, or even those dedicated to transcending it like the CSCE, have clearly lost some of their institutional *raison d'être*. The EC, like all other European institutions, could not fail to reflect the impress of the Cold War, but defeating the Soviet threat was never its central purpose and its institutional leaders, especially Commission President Jacques Delors, moved adroitly to defend its *acquis* after 1989. The European Community has little real endogenous political existence but reflects rather the will of its Member States who have continued to see it as vital to the achievement of welfare ends. The European Community has also always served a dual function as a vehicle for German energies and as reassurance to Germany's neighbours that these energies will be contained. A united Germany increases, rather than lessens, the importance of these considerations. The EC will, therefore, continue and expand its role as the key institutional actor but at a pace determined by its Member States.

The Soviet Union, the great loser, has collapsed and Russia has returned – a Russia with a continuing formidable military capacity but wracked by internal dissension and economic weakness and unlikely to shape the new Europe in a positive manner.

Part of the optimism of the 1989 spring reflected a relatively buoyant West European economy and a climate of euphoria about the speed with which Central and Eastern Europe could be marketised. The boom in the post-unity West German economy and its demand for imports sustained this mood for some time. The ever-rising costs of German unity, met not by fiscal policy changes but by high German interest rates, have pushed up interest rates elsewhere in Western Europe and deepened a gathering recession. Unemployment is rising steeply in Western Europe while the Central and East European economies are in a perilous state. The effects of the recession are inevitably not confined to the economy but have cut deeply into the authority of Eastern and Western governments and everywhere there is talk of an autumn of discontent if not yet a winter of despair. The European public mood is best described as one of 'morosité'.

Disappointment and despair are greatest in Central and Eastern Europe where the starkest reality is the daily slaughter and the exodus of refugees from Bosnia and Croatia and even the bedrock assumption that the end of the communist regimes would transfer the border of democracy eastwards from its proud new position on the Oder to the Bug now looks optimistic.

The checklist of woes is all too easily assembled. Liberal democratic ideas which were so potent in delegitimising communist regimes are much less powerful in creating and sustaining liberal democratic regimes in states unsupported by civil society and tortured by communal and ethnic division. The dissidents who brought about the change often find the exercise of power difficult. Timothy Garton Ash recounts the dismay of a young Dresdner during the first free election campaign of March 1990 at finding that his friends had different views from his own.[2] Only Poland, Hungary, the Czech lands and Slovenia look like very safe bets at the moment. Even in these states and in the five new German Länder the feeling of empowerment, the newly awakened sense of political competence associated with mass involvement in bringing down tyranny, has often been replaced by cynicism and despair. In many of the other states the choice seems to lie rather between authoritarian populism, continuity with sections of the previous regime, or chaos.

Economically the task of transformation has proved extra-ordinarily difficult. The collapse of the Soviet market and at least partial exposure to global market conditions has proved extremely challenging to the still largely state-owned and hugely indebted economies. Agreements were signed between Poland, Czechoslovakia, Hungary and the EC, and EC entry was mentioned as an aspiration in the preambles but appears unrealistic at present. To meet the criteria for economic convergence with the EC these countries would need to more than double their GNPs by the end of the century. The replacement of their largely worthless capital stocks to bring them up to Western levels would require an inward investment of at least $100bn every year till the turn of the century. At present Hungary, the most successful state, has only managed to raise $1.6bn.

The Europe Agreements were notably ungenerous. Despite imports from that area representing only 4% of total EC imports and the claim that the agreements offered a significant and asymmetric level of access to Western markets they were very restrictive in so-called sensitive areas, i.e. agriculture, steel, textiles and chemicals, which were precisely the areas in which these economies are competitive.

In the midst of a recession Member Governments are unwilling to, as they see it, export jobs from voters to non-voters but without more market access it is difficult to see how these economies can be ready for entry at the turn of the century, the declared aim of Western governments (reaffirmed in the Conclusions of the Edinburgh EC Summit in December 1992) or how liberal democratic governments can be sustained on a long-term basis in that area.

The national question

Even during the immediate post-communist period, concern was expressed about the lethal potential of the national question once the communist permafrost had thawed. The complexity of the national issue is perhaps best illustrated by the following Hungarian anecdote. In December 1941, the Hungarian Ambassador went to the State Department to submit Hungary's Declaration of War. The Senior State Department official was somewhat surprised and enquired as to Hungary's location and whether it was a Republic. On being informed that it was a Monarchy, he then asked the name of the King, to which the Hungarian Ambassador replied that there was no King but there was a Regent, Admiral Horthy. This prompted a further question about the Hungarian fleet. The Ambassador then replied that Hungary possessed neither a fleet nor a sea coast. Pleasantries by now over, the Ambassador was then asked about the nature of Hungarian claims on the United States. On being told that there were none, the State Department official hypothesised that the claims must be against the Polish allies of the United States. The Hungarian Ambassador replied that the Poles were natural allies of the Hungarians but that they did have claims on the Romanians. The relieved State Department official said 'So you have declared war on the Romanians.' 'No sir, they are our allies.'

The national issue has proved to be every bit as troublesome as pessimists expected. In that sense, the period since 1989 has not seen the end of history but its re-emergence. In some of the successor states ethnicity has been used as a basis for citizenship rather than more inclusive concepts, e.g. in Slovakia despite the presence of Hungarian and Gypsy minorities. The existence of national minorities means that there are any number of potential frontier disputes. Intra-ethnic tension not only affects relations between states but has led to the soft break-up of Czechoslovakia, ironically known as 'the velvet divorce', fighting in the ex-USSR and internecine warfare in what was Yugoslavia.

The agenda that is to be tackled in Central and Eastern Europe is thus truly daunting. If democracy is to be securely established or even if mass distress and flight is to be avoided, the West must endeavour to secure some real measure of economic transformation in that area. It must also seek to contribute to defusing the lethal potential of ethnic conflict and to extend what is sometimes called a pluralistic security community, an area where war between states is unimaginable, as far eastwards as is possible.

What is to be done?

In deciding how to respond to these challenges and the problems and opportunities presented by the emergence of a unified Germany and the break-up of the Soviet Union the metaphor of architects and gardeners is often invoked. The architect believes that the disappearance of the Soviet Union and 'the bonfire of the certainties' calls for a radical new design while the gardener relies on the incremental growth of what is already established combined with whatever weeding is necessary. I am not especially attracted to either image. My academic activity has lain more in the analysis of past and existing structure in the more passive tradition of the profession followed by my father and grandfather who were surveyors. As my wife will tell you, my gardening is of the low intervention variety and I simply lack the patience to be a successful weeder.

To be more serious, the images suggest a false dichotomy. Any plausible European response must involve a considerable amount of weeding and pruning of redundant institutions but the scale of the changes to be responded to and the sudden appearance of new blooms in the form of new states transcends any incremental response and some redesign is necessarily involved.

The role of Germany

At present, the lion's share of the burden is being borne by Germany. It is Germany which is the overwhelming source of investment in Central Europe and Russia, and it is Germany that has given asylum to the refugees from the conflict areas. It is, however, simply not conceivable that Germany can tackle the problems of Central and Eastern Europe on its own. Moreover, a return to the *ante bellum* system of sovereign states, described in an early part of the lecture, is neither available nor desired. Germany's own history and the history of that area preclude a major German contribution to the solution of the new security dilemmas. Even the question of German participation in AWACS missions over Bosnia in early 1993 provoked recourse to the Federal Constitutional Court. Germany will remain a civilian power.

The economic burden of the transformation of the five new Länder, of aiding the poorer Member States of the EC, while simultaneously providing aid and loans to Russia and Central Europe, is simply not sustainable. Electoral pressures will, with some difficulty, maintain the present volume of transfers to the five new Länder but Germany is unlikely to meet the costs of the structural funds in the manner envisaged in the immediate post-Maastricht period. A high German interest in moving the Community border eastwards to create a 'zone of stability' to cover the Czech lands, Hungary and Poland remains and there is no doubt that this would be the preferred solution for the German government and the Central European governments. It is absolutely central to German policies for containing westward emigration. This still leaves unanswered the question of how these economies are to be transformed.

The argument thus runs: the nation state remains the key actor in Europe after the end of the Cold War but it is beyond either the will or the capacity of Germany, the most powerful nation state, to accomplish these changes by itself. In this sense Germany is too weak, rather than the currently fashionable view that it is too strong for its surrounding environment. This leaves institutions and the key question to be tackled is whether those problems are best tackled by a battery of institutions or by a single institution.

The gardener would advocate reliance on those institutions that survived the Cold War. He would argue that there is still work for NATO to accomplish in the medium term in providing security until Soviet forces have been completely withdrawn from Germany, the Baltic States and other states in Central Europe. NATO clearly retains a role in dealing with the potential nuclear threat posed by Russia and the Ukraine. It will also clearly remain important as an insurance policy against the possible long-term resurgence of an expansionist Russia. A number of Central European states would also like NATO to offer them security guarantees. Such a policy would, of course, transform NATO from an alliance into a system of collective security.

A pluralist would also point to the institutional strengthening of the CSCE and map out a future for the institution as an umbrella organisation while the European Community would be charged with the economic transformation of Central Europe.

However attractive and necessary such a programme appears in the immediate and medium-term future, it is simply not enough. Firstly, much time and energy is spent by institutions in turf struggles, e.g. between the Council of Europe and the CSCE on Human Rights. More fundamentally, the existence of a whole range of institutions allows the nation states of Western Europe to blur their responsibilities by endless discussions about the most suitable institutions. My suggestion, therefore, is that the problems of Central and Eastern Europe would be better addressed in the medium and long term by a single institution. The CSCE played a useful role in bringing the Cold War to an end but lacks any convincing institutional capacity and is an increasingly marginal player apart from the field of arms reduction. No major state now sees it playing a central role and its most prominent apologists, Mikhail Gorbachev and Hans Dietrich Genscher, have left the political stage. NATO and the EC are the sole plausible candidates and if my argument about the declining interest of the United States in Europe is correct then NATO seems unlikely to be the most suitable vehicle. The diverging economic interests of Europe and the United States also render it unlikely that NATO could be broadened to encompass the economic dimension. This leaves the European Community. It has cut a very unconvincing figure in the Yugoslav crisis for two fundamental reasons. Its present policy instruments are purely economic and they turn out to be ill-adapted for ethnic conflict. More immediately, whereas during the Cold War every potential conflict required and usually resulted in unified action, because the threat and the risks were perceived as shared, in limited and politically confused conflicts, as in former Yugoslavia, differences in the national interests of the Member States loom large, e.g. in the disputes over the recognition of Croatia. It was, of course, precisely that collective identity, that shared perception, that helped deter aggressors and ensured that NATO was never actually involved in armed conflict. It is unlikely, however, that the Yugoslav imbroglio will be the last ethnic conflict in Eastern Europe and my view is that Western Europe must at some point be able to frame an institutional response to these ethnic crises. Moreover, an intra-ethnic conflict is not the only threat to security in that area. Other threats include environmental disaster and mass refugee movements and, in an undivided Europe, instability and chaos in Central and Eastern Europe cannot fail to have an impact on Western Europe.

The immediate priority for the EC must be to address the pressing economic issues of Eastern Europe, with more market access an obvious first step, and one which would also benefit Western Europe, as Jacques Attali has repeatedly pointed out.

Over a longer period much thought must be given to precisely which power should be given to the EC to begin to accomplish these tasks and as to how membership increase can be made compatible with institutional efficiency without creating an over-centralised colossus.

The Maastricht provisions on Common Foreign and Security Policy and the Commission's Directorate-General for International Affairs under Hans van den Broek represent the beginnings of an attempt to widen the EC policy repertoire to deal with crises in its surrounding environment. The present West European enthusiasm for subsidiarity appears attractive in the wake of the Maastricht ratification difficulties and viewed from a West European perspective. It is difficult, however, to see how an *ad hoc*/variable geometry Western Europe could summon up the political will to allow market access, far less agree to the massive public investment in East Central Europe that is urgently required on a continuing, rather than *ad hoc*, basis. Market access, in any case, probably requires some economic recovery in Western Europe and aid on the scale required will, at the least, require more imaginative leadership and a greater public readiness for sacrifice. These, again, are unlikely without an economic recovery. Agreement on a security policy, however necessary, also appears some way off.

I am, of course, aware that the immediate priority for the European Community is enlargement to include the EFTANS and that this enlargement will make redesign of the Community, in the way I have envisaged, less likely rather than more likely given their highly developed referendum arrangements and the very restricted appetite of a considerable proportion of West Europeans for cuts in their life style, changes in their established institutions in the middle of a recession, or military intervention to secure order in East/Central Europe. What I have tried to do here is to point out where the costs will fall and indicate that these will fall, as in the preceding system, on the Eastern half of Europe and that this can only be altered by a radical change in our Western institutions.

In drafting this lecture I have been tempted, perhaps unwisely and certainly uncharacteristically, to adopt the role of architect, partly by the sheer scale of the problems but also by my preoccupation with the recent death of Willy Brandt. What I have had to say here and the mismatch between problems and responses must be seen as gloomy and I want to end by repeating Willy Brandt's introduction to the North–South Report (1978) 'Situations are seldom hopeless if they are not accepted as such. And hope itself is the most important element in avoiding obstacles which might otherwise appear insurmountable.'

William E. Paterson's lecture was sponsored by the University of Edinburgh and delivered at the Playfair Library, the University of Edinburgh, on 20 October 1992.

The lecture was chaired by the Hon. Lord Clyde, Chancellor's Assessor of the University of Edinburgh, and a response was given by Joyce McMillan, journalist and writer.

JAN EGELAND

2   *Europe and the global*
     challenge of 20 million
     refugees

THE MILLENNIUM WHICH IS NOW DRAWING TO A CLOSE
has seen more years of conflict, hardship and displacement of
people than of peace, stability and protection of human rights.
Although both Norway and Scotland have been on the periphery
of most of the European major power rivalries, our histories
too have been marked by upheaval. Since the earliest Viking
raids, Scottish civilians have been forced to flee from foreign or
their own armed bands. In other periods, Scotland generously
provided safe havens for refugees from other countries. My own
countrymen sought refuge here during the Nazi occupation only
a generation ago.

As we, from our peaceful corner in north-western Europe,
witness unprecedented numbers of refugees and displaced people
elsewhere in the world, we should not forget the suffering of our
own displaced forefathers.

I have been working with and for refugees on all continents
for the last ten years as a human rights activist, relief worker
or agent of foreign policy. Few challenges are, in my view, as
important for promoting peace, human rights and development
as solving and preventing the forced displacement of peoples.
Looking ahead, my efforts are inspired by a political goal and a
humanitarian dream, but at the same time by a profound fear.

My goal is for us to reinstate refugees and migrants in their
rightful place on government agendas all over the world. While
the number of refugees doubled to as many as 15 million during
the 1980s, there was no corresponding increase in the attention

focused on the issue by decision-makers outside the regions directly affected. The fate and the future of the displaced and the homeless should be seen as part of all and second to none of the major international policy issues, including security and economic policies.

In the wake of the dramatic international developments that began in 1989, we have managed to achieve this goal for some refugees, but far from all. The situation of the Palestinian refugees has been recognised as a vital issue in the Middle East peace process. The Kurdish exodus of 1991 led to a multinational humanitarian intervention, and the present stream of refugees from the former Yugoslavia is seen as a European security crisis rather than yet another human drama. Substantial political and material resources have therefore been allocated to meet short-term needs and find long-term solutions for these European, Kurdish and Palestinian refugees. However, no similar international efforts have been rallied for the benefit of African, Andean, Afghan or the majority of other 'forgotten' refugees.

My dream therefore was, and still is, to mobilise sufficient international political and economic resources for the fate of all displaced peoples, thus enabling the 1990s to become the most successful decade of repatriation and rehabilitation in the history of man. With a total of at least 40 million refugees and internally displaced persons, there have never been as many fellow human beings waiting for help to go home as there are today.

To help these people return to their homes we must make peace and combat poverty on an unprecedented scale. Now that the Cold War is a thing of the past, the United Nations and the regional organisations have been able to embark on more and bigger peace-keeping operations in the last 20 months than in the preceding 20 years. Whether Secretary-General Boutros Ghali will be able to fund his ambitious new agenda for peace making, peace keeping and preventative action remains, however, an open question.

Paradoxically, after decades of multi-billion-dollar wars we now lack the money to realise the dream of voluntary repatriation to a record number of countries and regions, from Afghanistan to Eritrea and Mozambique. On his first day as High Commissioner for Refugees in 1989, Thorvald Stoltenberg was alerted to this situation by a small note on his desk, which read: 'We now have the chance to bring 40,000 Namibians home, but no money to do so . . .'

Recent events have done more to confirm my worst fears than to promote my goals and dreams. The world is experiencing a nightmare of new wars and new disasters. And nothing is as disruptive to our efforts to care for and help repatriate existing refugees as new, uncontrollable mass movements of people. High Commissioner Stoltenberg did manage to raise the necessary funds to help the 40,000 Namibians home. But, at the same time, we were faced with more than one million new refugees fleeing from their homes in a chaotic Liberia.

We all expected and planned for 1992 to be the year of repatriation. But in spite of the massive efforts of High Commissioner Ogata, there are now 20 million refugees, as opposed to last year's 17 million.

Two journeys through the war-torn former Yugoslavia brought home to me the full impact of the worst refugee disaster in Europe since the last world war. More than two million people have now fled their homes. The refugees I talked to all described a brutal war where producing refugees is an end in itself. 'Ethnic cleansing' is in reality as abhorrent as it sounds. If it is not stopped now it could spread to other parts of Europe where many vulnerable groups fear the aggression of stronger peoples.

However, as Europeans we should not forget that nine out of ten refugees are neither European nor in Europe. Even worse than the war in the Balkans is the crisis in the Horn of Africa. The conflict and chaos in Somalia deteriorated dramatically in the course of 1991, only to reach unprecedented proportions in 1992. Ethnic warfare and drought have caused more than 300,000 Somalis to flee to Kenya. Another 500,000 people have already sought refuge in Ethiopia and other countries. Moreover, 450,000 Ethiopians who were refugees in Somalia were forced back to Ethiopia.

Like Europe and Africa, the Asian continent is also the site of new refugee disasters. In the early months of 1992, a vast number of refugees poured across the border from Burma to Bangladesh. By the end of June, more than 270,000 Burmese refugees were registered in camps in Bangladesh. Yet another group of refugees, whose plight may be less well known, are the ethnic Nepalese who have been fleeing from Bhutan to Nepal since early 1991. This refugee population numbered 65,000 at the end of June 1992.

In recent years, Latin America has had greater success in finding solutions to the continent's refugee problems. However, the violence in Colombia has probably forced as many as 500,000 people to leave their homes. Some of them are now living as internally displaced persons in Colombia, and some as refugees in neighbouring countries.

In spite of all these setbacks we must not allow ourselves to become disillusioned, as new strategies are urgently required to solve refugee problems. I am grateful for this opportunity to discuss at this important university how we can help the world's refugees return to their homes and prevent new displacements. In this connection, let us take a closer look at five distinct refugee populations.

My first example is Cambodia. Following the October 1991 Comprehensive Political Settlement on the Cambodian Conflict, the UNHCR, the Thai Government and the Supreme National Council of Cambodia agreed on a programme of voluntary repatriation for the 370,000 Cambodian refugees in Thailand. Some 330,000 refugees have now registered for repatriation.

This repatriation operation has been relatively successful so far due to the comprehensive approach chosen. Basic prerequisites for repatriation are the establishment of peace in Cambodia, reconciliation of the political factions and reconstruction of the country. However, even though this is one of the best planned repatriation operations ever undertaken by the UNHCR, it has not been without complications. The peace process has proved to be fragile and the Khmer Rouge have adopted policies which do more to instil suspicion than to inspire trust. There is insufficient land for farming and the human toll taken by land mines will remain high for years to come. Furthermore, the quality of drinking water is not acceptable for persons who have been used to drinking chlorinated water for years in the refugee camps.

Nevertheless, by the beginning of August, more than 70,000 refugees had returned to their home countries. 'Quick Impact Projects' have been established in collaboration with the UNDP to ensure the economic viability of affected communities. The United Nations Transitional Authority in Cambodia (UNTAC) provides security for the returnees. Steps are being taken to chart land that is free of mines. Optimism is high, and there are cheerful scenes where children who have grown up in refugee camps see cows and water buffaloes for the first time. The Norwegian Government strongly supports this huge, pioneer 'experiment' in Cambodia. We have sent experts on demining, refugee protection officers and personnel to help prepare for the scheduled democratic elections.

Another positive development taking place in South-East Asia is the halt in the exodus of boat people from Vietnam, my second example. Meanwhile, an increasing number of Vietnamese refugees are deciding to return home. This repatriation is taking place within the framework of the 'Comprehensive Plan of Action' that was established in 1989 by the International Conference on Indo-Chinese Refugees. This favourable development has come about partly as a result of political and social change in Vietnam, but also thanks to concerted international assistance and political pressure during the past three years.

The Norwegian Government provides support for income-generating projects for boat people who have returned to North-Vietnam. In addition to protecting those who return by our international presence we have also undertaken information campaigns to prevent a new exodus. We hope that this integrated approach will prove fruitful.

The difficulties in planning a repatriation programme have been particularly apparent in the case of Afghan refugees, my third example. In 1988 the UNHCR prepared a detailed repatriation plan, which was rendered obsolete by subsequent developments. In 1991 a 'Pilot Repatriation Project' was established. It was only in the first quarter of 1992 that the political and military development in Afghanistan began to give impetus to the repatriation process. During a single week in July, some 100,000 home-bound Afghans crossed the border from Pakistan. Before repatriation began in 1990, there were some 3.2 million refugees in Pakistan and a further 3 million in Iran. Since then, more than one million have returned home. However, the latest developments in Kabul are threatening to reverse the repatriation trend. In fact, new refugees have already fled from Afghanistan.

The Afghan case shows how difficult it is to plan and organise a repatriation programme. Suddenly, when the refugees find that the time is ripe, there is a rush to go home. This situation places a tremendous strain on the logistics of refugee organisations and on available funds.

My fourth example is a war-ravaged country, Mozambique, where government and aid organisations work too independently of one another, lacking proper coordination. The Norwegian Government has therefore sponsored an initiative by the Norwegian Refugee Council to design an integrated regional plan for the repatriation and reintegration of Mozambican refugees, internally displaced persons, demobilised soldiers and other affected local populations. This process will involve all concerned governments, donor countries, UN agencies, regional institutions, and local and international NGOs. The UN system will now perform an integrated assessment and programming exercise. It is our hope that an integrated repatriation programme will be ready in time for the implementation of the peace agreement reached in Rome under the auspices of President Robert Mugabe of Zimbabwe.

One of the most difficult refugee situations we face today is that arising from the protracted war on our own continent in the former Republic of Yugoslavia, my fifth example. The exodus of refugees is a tragic example of the fact that a refugee crisis usually cannot be resolved by humanitarian aid alone. Until a political solution is found, the prospects of ending the war are very bleak indeed. I am afraid that, as in other similar situations, the international community responded far too late and with far too little firmness. The Balkans might have been spared this war had *prevention* been stressed when the first signs of conflict appeared in 1990.

It is now imperative that steps be taken to prevent a further escalation and spreading of the conflict. We hope that the observer teams that were sent by the Conference on Security and Cooperation in Europe to Kosovo, Sandjak and Vojvodina at the request of the Norwegian Government and the United States Government will contribute to the prevention of such an escalation. The mandate of the mission is to promote dialogue between the parties, monitor the human rights situation, and establish fora for solving problems. I believe we should avail ourselves of such preventive diplomacy more often, and commend Secretary-General Boutros Ghali for including this in his important Agenda for peace keeping and peace making.

What can we learn from our efforts to deal with the above-mentioned five refugee populations? Twenty million refugees and equally many internally displaced persons testify to the inadequacy of our present ways and means. It is time to develop new strategies if we are going to have any chance of reversing the trend of an ever-increasing number of refugees and displaced persons.

First, we must include all displaced persons and migrants in our quest for short-term protection and long-term solutions. Both as an aid worker and as a politician I have felt an increasing need to focus more attention on mass movements of people *not* covered by the traditional definition of refugees in the Geneva Convention.

Environmental refugees, people fleeing from war, poverty and starvation, and the internally displaced all have the same basic needs as individually targeted political refugees. Nevertheless, millions of homeless, rootless and displaced persons receive little or no attention simply because the UNHCR cannot cope with a further 20 million people in addition to the record number of conventional refugees that fall within their mandate. The Norwegian authorities will now initiate a series of international seminars and studies to document the needs of both internally displaced persons and environmental refugees fleeing from desertification, soil erosion, pollution, etc.

I am not advocating that we redefine the concept of 'refugees' or the mandate of the UNHCR. But we cannot ignore the necessity of examining how the UN, governments and NGOs can do more to help all displaced persons by means of short-term relief measures and permanent return or resettlement programmes.

Second, we should have a clear understanding of what we definitely cannot expect to achieve. It is neither realistic nor productive to try to create new organisations or mechanisms. Instead, we should use the methods we have differently, or combine them in new and unorthodox ways.

Furthermore, we should realise that resettlement in faraway countries will benefit only a decreasing minority of the global refugee populations. In 1956, it was not difficult to find safe havens for the relatively limited number of Hungarian refugees in other European countries. Today, however, the vast majority of the 40 million refugees and displaced persons must be assisted and protected as close as possible to their homes, with a view to helping them safely home as soon as possible.

Third, there can be no long-term solutions without a *comprehensive* package of humanitarian, political and development initiatives. As the five above-mentioned cases demonstrate, we must devise a system of coordinated burden-sharing, in which all rich countries and all countries adjacent to the affected areas participate.

At international conferences, *all* major unsolved refugee problems should be discussed. The UN can play the role of a catalyst and coordinator for comprehensive plans with goals ranging from peace building to repatriation. All concerned parties should be part of such negotiated plans and solutions.

The Yugoslavian crisis also illustrates the inadequacy of separate efforts to deal with a complex conflict in which all the issues are intertwined. To resolve a situation in which some 40 negotiated ceasefires had been disregarded, the London Conference brought together all relevant parties to agree not only on a comprehensive solution but, perhaps even more importantly, on a broad-based continuous follow-up mechanism, which has been termed the Geneva Process. 'Burden-sharing' has become an important principle in this process. Faraway countries must contribute financially to those countries receiving the majority of displaced persons. They should also give asylum to those who seek it on their own initiative or at the request of the UNHCR. Burden-sharing means that no one may refuse to take some kind of action!

Fourth, we must ensure that international action is taken to protect vulnerable communities in repressive systems. Comprehensive strategies to safeguard the human rights of those threatened by aggression and brutality should be elaborated. Few continents are discovering as many latent cultural and ethnic conflicts as our own, after the fall of totalitarian communism in Eastern Europe. In 1991 the Nordic countries proposed a series of means to help transform the United Nations into a more effective tool for 'maintaining international peace and security', to quote Article 1 of the UN Charter. A major obstacle to the achievement of this goal is the principle of non-interference in internal affairs as set out in Article 2 of the Charter. However, the interpretation of this principle is not static. In the past few years we have witnessed a growing willingness to intervene which would have been unthinkable only a few years ago. In our efforts to prevent conflicts and atrocities we should welcome 'humanitarian interventions'. But we must proceed with caution to counteract the divergence that seems to be emerging between an activist North and a defensive South.

We must continue to support the right of the UN to launch programmes of humanitarian assistance for vulnerable communities. Such actions must always have purely humanitarian goals and only be taken at the request of the Security Council. In this field we should also strive for closer cooperation between the Security Council and the Commission for Human Rights.

Fifth, to be able to provide humanitarian assistance in time, we must have the necessary organisational and material preparedness. The immense suffering of the Somali civilian population demonstrates that yet again the international community was too slow in responding to an imminent disaster. Our capacity for *early warning* has increased in recent years because of enhanced cooperation between networks of NGOs and the multilateral organisations. There was no lack of warnings that Somalia would suffer. But there was no *early intervention*. In Norway, the Ministry of Foreign Affairs has taken the initiative to create a Norwegian Emergency Preparedness System (NOREPS). In cooperation with the Norwegian Refugee Council, we can provide the UNHCR and other UN agencies with more than 100 experienced relief workers within 72 hours, anywhere in the world. We can also provide ten categories of selected relief items from stand-by relief stocks in Norway and Africa in less than 24 hours. This system has proved to be of great value in emergency situations when disasters strike far too quickly for any one multilateral or non-governmental organisation to cope with them alone.

Sixth, we should enhance the UN's ability to make peace and prevent conflict. During the last few years, we have witnessed new developments in both the nature and the content of UN peace-keeping operations. Traditionally, these operations have been of a purely military character. Today, the peace-keeping forces aim to help the implementation of agreements between conflicting parties by both military and civilian means. Their mandate has been extended to include organising free and fair elections, monitoring human rights and police conduct, ensuring public order, providing humanitarian assistance and repatriating refugees.

We have proposed that the UN should more actively send fact-finding missions to areas of potential conflict. The UN capacity to launch operations on humanitarian grounds should be strengthened. The United Nations should make more frequent use of warnings and sanctions. The modalities of undertaking enforcement actions as a last resort should be clarified. And the Secretary-General's office should be strengthened to enable him to keep the Security Council informed about potential conflicts.

Seventh, the efforts of the UN system, other international agencies and non-governmental organisations should be coordinated in order to enhance efficiency and avoid duplication. UN agencies are currently striving to improve their cooperation and preparedness with a view to providing emergency humanitarian assistance. The decision to establish the UN Department of Humanitarian Affairs and the appointment of an Emergency Relief Coordinator at the Under-Secretary-General level is a step in the right direction.

One result of the new coordinated humanitarian system is the effort now being made to stabilise and prevent displacement in border areas in the Horn of Africa. The United Nations has now developed a cross-mandate and cross-border preventive zone. This operation provides assistance to people in need regardless of their status as refugees, displaced persons, or victims of conflict or drought, and operates within the framework of local traditional ethnicities. The United Nations Development Programme, the United Nations High Commissioner for Refugees, the World Food Programme, the Food and Agriculture Organisation, the United Nations Children's Fund, non-governmental organisations and local governments all participate in this new approach.

Non-governmental organisations represent the greatest potential for future effective humanitarian action for those in greatest need. Their operational capacity and rapid mobilisation of resources make them the best tools for immediate international disaster relief at the grass-root level. We are actively lobbying the UN and other governments to give them the same status in disaster preparedness as they have in the Norwegian system.

Eighth, from our corner in north-western Europe, we may easily overestimate the effect of emergency assistance and underestimate the importance of rehabilitation and long-term development. The initial relief phase should always be followed by international cooperation and support for reconstruction. It is important to prevent refugee camps from becoming shelters in which refugees spend decades passively waiting. And it is imperative that the poverty that has caused so many refugee disasters should not be allowed to produce new ones.

Ninth, we must reaffirm our commitment to provide protection through political asylum for those in need. We should fight the tendency to close European borders to asylum seekers. I believe the High Commissioner is right in appealing to the rich countries of Europe to liberalise their asylum policies, rather than make them more restrictive. However, if possible, we should give priority to assistance in the region affected, rather than spending enormous resources on transporting and integrating refugees in faraway countries. This is the policy the High Commissioner is pursuing in all refugee disasters, including that in the former Republic of Yugoslavia. We should, however, also consider the possibility of establishing an instrument of *temporary* protection for 'war refugees', lasting as long as the conflict itself. This would enable us to reach more refugees than we are able to help today as we have no alternatives other than rejection and permanent asylum.

My tenth, and last suggestion, is a more powerful strategy to protect and promote democracy and good governance. Through a system of checks and balances, a participatory democratic order can ensure that no segment of society becomes omnipotent. A firmly embedded democratic culture is also a barrier against aggressive foreign policies that may end up creating new refugee populations. With its long-standing democratic traditions, Europe will be in a position to play a key role in the promotion of human rights and democracy as an increasingly important factor in the international debate on development and foreign assistance.

Europe's task is to assist the UN and other international organisations in teaching governments and individual citizens how a democracy functions, and how to develop democratic institutions and an independent legal system. It is equally important to advocate to key sectors that respect for human rights is a prerequisite for a democratic order. Adherence to human rights conventions is a related goal. The number of states that have not ratified or that have made reservations to the various conventions is far too high.

Some 70 years ago polar explorer and scientist Fridtjof Nansen was named the first High Commissioner for Refugees by the League of Nations. Over a period of five years from 1920 to 1925, Nansen organised the exchange of 450,000 First World War prisoners, the first massive international relief efforts for millions of famine victims in Russia and the Ukraine, and the first systematic relief and repatriation efforts for refugees. Millions of Russian and Armenian refugees were given support and several hundred thousand Greek and Turkish displaced persons and refugees were exchanged. Most importantly, perhaps, Fridtjof Nansen managed to persuade more than 50 governments to agree to allow the many refugees and stateless persons to travel under what was called a 'Nansen passport'.

I believe we should try to go back to the 'Nansen roots' of international refugee assistance. Only through bold, innovative and comprehensive action by many cooperating governments can solutions be found for large displaced populations. Only through massive involvement through humanitarian assistance, peace making and long-term development can Europe reverse the trend of increasing numbers of refugees on our own continent and in faraway places. Preventing new refugee disasters whether they are due to war, drought, floods or environmental catastrophes is a moral imperative and a vital self-interest. 1992 has taught us that no country will be unaffected if we are not able to help more refugees return home and prevent new ones from being forced out of their homes. Europe is no exception. There are many latent conflicts and disasters which will affect our own societies if we are not able to rally the political will and economic resources for massive preventive action in Eastern Europe and other disaster-prone areas.

Jan Egeland's lecture was given as *the Nansen Memorial Public Lecture* and delivered at the Playfair Library, the University of Edinburgh, on 27 October 1992. It was presented in association with the University of Edinburgh and arranged in liaison with the Royal Norwegian Consulate General in Edinburgh.

The lecture was chaired by Sir David Smith, Principal and Vice-Chancellor, the University of Edinburgh, and a response was given by Lord John McCluskey, Chairman, Scottish Refugee Council.

JULIET LODGE

3   *European Union: working together towards a Europe of the Regions?*

'Europe is conducting an experiment in continuity and change.'

Jean Monnet

'Wer in europaischen Angelegenheiten nicht an Wunder glaubt ist kein Realist.'
Anyone who does not believe in miracles in European affairs is not a realist.

Walter Hallstein

'Mon objectif est d'unir des peuples et d'associer des nations.'
My goal is to unite peoples and associate nations.

Jacques Delors

EUROPEAN UNION: IS IT A MYTH? A REALITY? SOMETHING in the process of being constructed? Or something whose parameters change with each successive generation?

In many respects European Union exists. In the European Community, we have been working together to realise the 'ever closer union' since the inception of the Communities. The current furore over the Intergovernmental Conference on Political Union and EMU leading to the Maastricht Treaty establishing the European Union arises because of misunderstanding and disinformation. However, cynicism in the UK over European Union is largely an English problem. As one crosses the border into Scotland, one crosses into Europe.

The dimensions of European Union

What are the dimensions of European Union? A political scientist might view the changes and challenges of the 1990s in structural terms. Much has been said about the creation of a new European Architecture. EC Commission President Jacques Delors has talked in terms of a Europe of concentric circles within which the EC/Union forms the core and from whose centre spread out the European Economic Area (comprising the EFTA states and would-be EC applicants) the Council of Europe, and the CSCE. The new European Architecture is seen to rest on complementary functional differentiation among the different institutions rather than competition between them. This idea of interlocking institutions also encompasses the defence and security alliances. NATO and the WEU are not only to develop a complementary and mutually beneficial relationship between themselves as well as with the Union but are expected to play a major role in maintaining security and contributing to stability within the Euro-Atlantic region, however that may be defined.

European Union itself is more than a mere feature of the new European Architecture. It is seen as its anchor, as the bastion of stability and peace founded on liberal democracy and a broad commitment to maintaining a social market economy. However, there is not yet consensus over what the European Union implies for its component units, its governments, regions and people. Disagreement persists over the meaning and desirability of supranationalism as opposed to loose intergovernmental cooperation; over subsidiarity in practice (with the UK unique among the Twelve in seeing it as meaning not devolution to the most appropriate decentralised and lowest possible level of government but devolution to the national government); and over the nature of the democratic deficit and democratic legitimacy within the EC. Further divisions occur among sub-national units in the debate over regionalism versus federalism. Clearly, European Union has many guises. It is a fluid concept, a gradualist and pragmatic process of integration, a notional territorial entity without aspirations for territorial aggrandisement but one which is nevertheless finding its territory expanding rapidly to the north, south and potentially east. Viewed as a unique international organisation based on the *acquis communautaire* of the supranational EC, its locus of political authority is obscure and contested. Its very fluidity is a source of strength however, for it gives us the chance by working together to make the European Union genuinely democratic, open, transparent, responsive and legitimate in the way initiated by the Single European Act and the 1984 European Parliament Treaty establishing the European Union. (The latter remains the benchmark for an eventual constitution for the Union.)

The Maastricht Treaty is flawed, not because it seeks to create a centralised polity but because the governments' insistence on a three pillar structure undermines the *unicité* needed to ensure that it is able to act in international affairs in a manner which will enable it to regain or at least hold its position in the international political economy, and which will affirm its role as a civilian power committed to finding constructive means of bringing states together to maintain peace and honour human rights. The Maastricht Treaty certainly widens the scope of integration. It increases the depth of integration and augments the EC/Union's capabilities and responsibilities. But it does not provide the necessary financial, institutional or political means. Therefore, care must be taken to ensure that it develops in a way that enhances its effectiveness, efficiency, responsiveness, accountability, transparency and democratic legitimacy. As Delors said, Europe must be close to its citizens.

The role of citizens

Following the initiative of the Spanish Prime Minister, the issue of EC citizenship was put on the agenda of the Intergovernmental Conference on Political Union. This raised the federal spectre because opponents of the kind of decentralised federalism implied by European Union argued that it was in line with the specious idea of European integration leading to a withering away of the state. It is true that European integration queries the role of the state in the modern world and that, within the EC today, the state is having to share its former position as the pre-eminent decision-making and policy-making body with supranational and regional bodies. But it is not the case that it has established a sense of EC nationality. The EC has symbols of belonging and identity (the flag, the anthem, driving licence, limited mutual recognition of professional qualifications and social security and other provisions geared towards facilitating labour mobility) but it has not supplanted the Member States in commanding a sense of allegiance or loyalty.

However, people from all walks of life have been working together, often unconsciously, in endeavours which bring them together and cement the Union. Sometimes, these are consciously constructed by the pump-priming efforts of the Commission's non-structural fund programmes which promote mobility, cross-frontier exchange and cooperation and which create patterns of working and thinking in an EC-wide sense. Normally, it is necessary to have three partners from three different Member States to be successful in a competition for resources under such programmes. These have enhanced mutual awareness. The Single Market programme has also increased awareness, despite the hype, of the EC.

Local actors have taken the initiative in trying to shift people's perceptions of the EC in a way which enables them to capitalise economically on the Four Freedoms but which also promotes a psychological shift towards them internalising 'Europe': the EC (and the future European Union) is not 'out there'. It has become the normal frame of reference for policy-makers at all levels.

Everyone who has the nationality of an EC state is a citizen of the European Union. This can lead to discrepancies among

the Twelve because it is up to the Member States to decide
who shall or shall not have the status of national. The basic
rights stemming from Union citizenship are: the right to
reside in any EC country; the right to move freely within
the EC; the right to participate in local and municipal (but
not national) elections, as well as elections to the European
Parliament, in the state of residence; the right to petition
the European Parliament; the right to complain to the new
Ombudsman in instances of maladministration by the EC
institutions or bodies; and the right to the diplomatic or
consular protection of any EC state when in third states.
A direct political relationship has been created between the
EC/Union and its citizens which goes beyond their obligation
to abide by EC law, and their right to invoke rights enshrined
in it. The invisibility of the source of EC legislation and the
readiness with which national governments use the Commission as a scapegoat for domestically unpopular decisions
(most of which they have agreed to in the Council) continues
to be problematic. In the context of the ratification of the
Maastricht Treaty, the difficulties may become even more
poignant.

The threat to European Union has not come from the people.
Even referendums in some Member States needed to ensure
ratification of the Treaty cannot necessarily be construed as
indicating popular discontent with the EC since they are likely
to become votes of confidence in the national government of the
day. Rather, they have become part of an armoury of devices
used by some national governments to deal with their own
unpopularity and lack of domestic credibility. Had the Danes
secured the necessary five-sixths majority in the Folketing, a
referendum would not have been necessary. However, some
states are required by their constitutions to submit any constitutional change to referendums. This is legitimate and proper.
What is less acceptable is the way in which other governments
have exploited the situation.

Delegitimising European Union?

Some governments have tried to delegitimise the goal of European Union by a variety of means including giving false signals to would-be members. The UK, the first state to leave EFTA to join the EC, suggested that European Union should not proceed in terms of a deepening of the EC's capacity to act but rather through an 'Eftarisation' of the EC. This cannot disguise its opposition to integration compared with intergovernmental cooperation. The UK has also given the misleading impression that the *acquis communautaire* is negotiable when it clearly is not: some applicants clearly think that they can seek 'opt-outs' instead of the more usual transitional periods to smooth entry and accommodation to EC norms in domestically problematic sectors.

It will not be possible to opt out of the common foreign and security policy or out of the pillar on cooperation in judicial and home affairs. Non-alignment or neutrality must be re-assessed by states seeking to join the European Union.

The UK marginalised itself during the run-up to the Maastricht negotiations and failed to play a truly constructive role in elaborating the future European Union. Its refusal to endorse a genuine democratisation of EC decision-making also undermined its credibility as a champion of parliamentary democracy and subsidiarity. Penalties flow from this. Others are setting the agenda and defining the ideal of the EC/Union as an exemplary system based on respect for liberal democratic norms and practices, human rights, and the practice of working together and fostering positive cooperation among former enemies.

Maastricht and the future of Europe

Working together means upgrading the common interest and working towards the common good. The problems entailed in realising this are known and overcome at local levels. Strategies have been developed for overcoming fear, forging a sense of common purpose, motivating and mobilising people (as through the European Weeks). Awareness rises and attitudes change as a result. Opposition to integration may decrease or rise. It may remain. Even then, it is likely to be tempered by an appreciation of the practical implications of European integration.

The new Treaty provisions can be exploited with this in mind. They must be interpreted imaginatively. The trans-European networks open numerous opportunities for further joint ventures (Germany swiftly got off the mark to see how its eight borders with other countries might benefit from this). There is a multitude of educational, cultural, scientific, technological and social programmes (such as ERASMUS, YES, TEMPUS, ESF programmes for the disadvantaged, for example) that help to create new links. The *Gesellschaft* of the EC is underpinned by cooperation and commercial endeavour independent of the EC but also bolstered by programmes like INTERPRISE (for entrepreneurs from SMEs in three regions from three Member States).

Maastricht opens doors, codifies existing practices and gives them a legal base. For instance, in respect of judicial cooperation, there is a Customs Information System and SCENT (the System Customs Enforcement Network) which was set up in 1987. Work has progressed on issues of asylum, refugees, the abuse of the Four Freedoms, illicit trading, etc. under TREVI in the context of European political cooperation. The scope of integration has impinged upon highly sensitive areas with the connivance of national governments who saw such cooperation as an essential and logical pragmatic and political counterpart to the realisation of the Four Freedoms. They had been misleadingly over-simplified and portrayed in economic terms.

All the activities of the EC and the new range of measures designed to facilitate the attainment internally of a borderless Single Market go to make up the underlying and emerging sense of *Gemeinschaft* as each generation takes up the Monnet method, reinterprets and advances European Union and leaves for its successors a flexible, democratic, imaginative, transparent and solid legacy. The result is a web of ever-expanding links and experiences at the sub-national level among the public and private sectors.

Local governments have often taken on a very active role both in initiating ventures and cooperation within the EC context and also, crucially, in implementing EC policy and contributing to the realisation of the Single Market and a European Union that is already in practice pretty close to the people. The autumn 1992 Birmingham Summit communiqué stressed the need to demonstrate EC benefits to citizens and referred to the importance of respecting history, political culture, traditions, greater openness and links between the national parliaments and European Parliament (inaugurated by the 'Assizes'). But while subsidiarity was commended, the communiqué contradicted this with the proviso that the existing balance of power among the institutions should not be altered.

Subsidiarity, openness and transparency collide in unforeseen ways. In the context of enlargement, they should mean that the number of official languages, for example, expands with the number of states. But efficiency and effectiveness would be detrimentally affected unless the institutions reformed internal working practices, limited their size (as enlargement proceeded) and restricted the number of working languages. Already with nine official languages, there is a permutation of 72 possible pairs for translation purposes; another four produces a combination of 156; and an EC/Union with 21 languages would produce 420 pairs.

The crucial issue is the openness of policy-making and the legislative process. (Contrary to some governments' assertions, the Commission is comparatively open; the Council – which meets as one of the EC's legislative arms in secret – is not.) Transparency and democracy demand institutional reform; a change in inter-institutional power relations and the distribution of authority; sensible limitations on the size of each institution following enlargement; an expansion of the European Parliament's powers; and better information to the public about the EC/Union. The newly created Committee of the Regions will have a role to play in this even though its actual consultative role limits its ability to influence the content and outcome of policy. Instead, it must be a forum for debate and for articulating issues of cross-regional concern.

The 1990s: towards a Europe of the Regions?

The 1990s have been earmarked as a decade of regionalism. By this is meant the resurgence of the influence of sub-national levels of government. 'Regional authorities' do not constitute a uniform type. Rather, there is great variety among the EC's Member States both in terms of their size, financial resources, political recruitment and administrative personnel and in terms of their responsibilities, capacity to govern territorially defined areas, and relationship to and relative autonomy from national government. The regional (Land) government of Nordrhein-Westfalen, for example, covers a population of over 15 million whereas many of the EC's smaller states, such as the Republic of Ireland, have a population of less than 6 million.

The issue of 'regionalism' begs many questions. There is no agreed, uniform definition of what constitutes a region. Loose definitions abound. The Commission's official definition of a region is derived from economic performance indicators and not from politico-cultural identities and territorial politics. The term 'region' or 'border area' is, in EC parlance, virtually synonymous with relative economic deprivation. The degree of relative poverty and peripherality determines a region's ranking among those eligible for EC regional financial aid: the bulk goes to Objective One regions whose per capita GDP is less than 75% of the EC average. Objective One regions in the UK may soon comprise the Highlands and Islands, Northern Ireland and Merseyside. The EC has almost 10,000 km of land frontier, 60% of which is accounted for by borders between the Member States. Border regions account for 15% of the EC's land area and 10% of its population.

Regions are not homogeneous. They vary greatly in terms

of population density, wealth and economic development. Most border regions are eligible for economic development assistance from Community Structural Support Frameworks under structural funds. The Commission has created additional programmes to stimulate cross-border cooperation and development because, under the removal of the physical, fiscal and technical barriers to trade and mobility within the Single Market, internal borders must be eliminated and the common external frontier strengthened.

In July 1990 the Commission launched the special programme known as INTERREG to promote transfrontier cooperation in economic development. It is unique among EC programmes in that the budget has been allocated not by individual Member States but by border. This has helped establish and reinforce cross-border partnerships between national, regional and local authorities. Regional and local authorities have played an important part in designing INTERREG Operational Programmes, in implementing them, and in working with the Commission. The Commission is represented on the Monitoring Committees which oversee their progress. These programmes are to be completed by the end of 1993. INTERREG is a multifund programme with contributions from the European Regional Development Fund, the European Social Fund and the European Agricultural Guidance and Guarantee Fund with an additional slice from the ERDF for areas not normally eligible. Supporting actions have been launched to provide technical assistance in cooperation with the Association of European Border regions, known as the Observatory on cross-border cooperation.

An economic programme *par excellence*, INTERREG has a distinct political objective. It has serious political ramifications for the idea and the realisation of a European Union in which regional actors become increasingly relevant and instrumental players. This has been appreciated only belatedly. The possibility of setting up a Community legal framework for cross-border programmes has been mooted recently. The Commission has empowered the regions. Maastricht goes further still.

Taking a political view of the regions from a continental perspective, additional – often political – issues become salient. These relate to the questions of transfrontier cooperation among regional and local authorities and their interaction with the Commission (neither want it mediated by national government); the implications of networking among local and regional authorities both for European Union and for the transfer of administrative and socio-economic knowhow to Central and Eastern Europe; the value of the RECITE network in promoting information exchange and functional cooperation (as, for example, in the case of the Atlantic Arc Network, concerned with maritime cabotage; the ERNACT project to increase IT use; and the *Quartiers en Crise* project on the problems of social exclusion, socio-economic marginalisation and integrated strategies for promoting politico-economic revitalisation). Delors sees all these as instrumental in faciliating the uniting of peoples and the realisation of European Union.

The political face to the concept of region has been tackled outside the EC as well. The Council of Europe defines regional authority as a 'territorial authority situated immediately below the national level and administered by an elected council'. That definition immediately conflates the issue of democratic legitimacy and popular representation with the idea of a territorially defined administrative unit. But it says nothing about spatial matters, nor about policy competence. Nor does it say anything about sub-regional divisions. Too often it is assumed that regional governments exist and are one and the same thing as local councils. Even in Member States with well-defined systems of devolved government, such as the federally organised German Republic, smaller administrative units co-exist with larger ones. In the highly centralised United Kingdom, not only is the concept of a region contested, but broadly conceived regional lines embrace many small (and competitive) and by-and-large relatively powerless local councils. These contentious issues highlight the view that the regions ought to have a voice in policy-making which is heard as the legitimate expression of local interests. This would be the logical counterpart to the existing subsidiarity in action of the range of economic development programmes already under way.

The EC's structural funds have become a means of redefining the relationship between 'regions' and the EC. The Commission puts a premium on the concept of 'partnership' in the new regional policy. There is a proliferating network of offices and regional representations vying for Commission attention and favour. Some are more effective than others but even regions from within the same state can find themselves competing with one another for financial aid. The move to promoting economic and social cohesion under Maastricht implies recognition of regional diversity and heterogeneity that mirrors not only the simplistic economic indicators of the past but also politico-cultural attributes.

The Committee of the Regions

The Committee of the Regions is to be an independent consultative body entrusted with articulating the interests of local and regional authorities. The Committee of the Regions has been seen by most member governments as embracing elected representatives from regional councils, although the British seem minded initially in favour of the government selecting and appointing such members according to its own criteria. This led to the suspicion that it conceived of the Committee as a Quango at best, and as an irrelevance at worst.

Comprising 189 members, the Committee of the Regions shares an organisational structure with the Economic and Social Committee but has a separate existence. The Council and Commission are obliged to consult it where the Treaty so prescribes, although it may also issue an opinion on its own initiative in cases where it deems action appropriate. Neither the Council nor the Commission is obliged to respond. The Commission retains its primary role as the initiator of legislation and, theoretically, could ignore the Committee's views. Given the Council's dismissive treatment of the European Parliament when its 'advisory and supervisory' powers were far more limited than they are today, and given the very limited influence of the ESC, the capability of the new Committee to influence the course of events must not be exaggerated.

Unlike the ESC, however, its members will be politicians used to voicing their views and to behaving politically. It will not be beyond their ingenuity to fashion a role for the Committee. However, they need to be realistic. Those who initially had advocated it assuming the role at supranational level of a Senate or a Bundesrat were quickly disabused: the Council of Ministers more closely approximates the Bundesrat, and regional interests can also be articulated by Members of the European Parliament (MEPs) whose powers continue to grow.

In short, it cannot be credibly argued that regional concerns have not been or are not articulated within the existing institutions of the EC: only that they have not been given concrete expression and constitutional legitimacy by being codified and officially institutionalised until now. However, it would be erroneous to infer from this an absence of provision for regional needs. Quite the reverse is true.

It is perhaps the growing competition for slices of the EC's structural funds by local authorities which highlights an intrinsic difficulty with the realisation of regional aspirations. These are narrowly conceived of as the aspiration for political representation at EC level by elected public bodies representing sub-national levels of government. They have been responsible for securing such funding for projects from the EC. But glaring discrepancies in the extent of centralisation and decentralisation within states produce anomalies in the bidding for such monies. In some states, national government intervenes directly or indirectly to pre-select projects otherwise eligible for structural fund aid. This is certainly broadly true in the Republic of Ireland and in the UK where the issue of additionality has been so controversial and abused as to endanger local regions' acquisition of promised funding. The controversy over additionality certainly spurred local authorities' interest in direct links with the Commission and in effective, regional representation independent of national government.

Economics versus politics

There can be little doubt that the availability of EC financial assistance for economic development led local authorities to seek a share of it. For too long the EC was seen as a bottomless 'pot of gold' and the political objectives behind its programmes designed to encourage integration through programmes of economic development and cohesion were frequently ignored either deliberately or inadvertently. The realisation of the Four Freedoms and the removal of internal barriers impels a reassessment not only of the issue of centre versus periphery, regional economic development and social and economic cohesion programmes but of the implications, at the grass roots, of the Single Market. However, in the UK few public authorities have undertaken a thorough review of their actual needs in the Single Market. Yet this is essential if an authority or a region is to have any influence on policy. The Audit Commission estimated in 1992 that only 30% of local authorities had undertaken a policy review of this nature and, of those, only 13% had produced a strategy document. Moreover, intense competition among authorities within as well as between Member States has led to them outbidding each other, even to the extent of setting up special Euro-offices in Brussels. They neglected the possibility of working together. That is why some of the Commission's programmes (like INTERREG) are so potent when seen in a political light. Functional cooperation is essential, and Maastricht acknowledges the political implications of this by creating the Committee of the Regions. However, the Committee alone will not be sufficient to transform the European Union into a Europe of the Regions. Rather, advancing the concept of a Europe of the Regions is a necessary step to creating a solid basis on which to build the European Union.

The politics of a Europe of the Regions

The idea of a Europe of the Regions is not politically neutral. Many questions may be asked. Is the Europe of the Regions a devious strategy to bring in federalism by the back door (though I don't see it as the spectre of the British tabloid press); to emasculate the nation state; to make national government wither away for want of tasks; to check Brussels Eurocracy; to make the people think that Europe is somehow closer to them after the Single Market hype; and to underpin the Committee of the Regions? Or does the concept of a Europe of the Regions flag up the federal reality of the removal of internal borders? Does it provide a signal as to future funding? It does both. Many Maastricht provisions underline this potential: the trans-European networks stress transport, infrastructure and communication as a key to moving ideas, information, goods and persons around the EC more quickly.

In many respects, the notion of a Europe of the Regions (seen not as a quest for separatism, secession and the achievement of micro-state status but as the logical outcome of a deepening of European integration) is the least politically charged way of signposting the future. Functional regionalism, building on the EC's array of over 40 cross-border projects and programmes to promote cohesion, make a reality out of the principle of subsidiarity. The goal is the creation of an appropriate, decentralised and democratic system to take European Union beyond the rhetoric.

Beyond the rhetoric

European Union may be in its infancy as far as its citizens are concerned. But it does exist. We may not be conscious of it or aware of how an ideal is being realised on a gradual basis. Much of the rest of Europe and the international community sees the EC as far more integrated and united than it is. It is not designed to be uniform and homogeneous. Instead, it is to be a rich source of diversity, difference and tolerance. It continues to be seen as a model for peaceful, constructive cooperation and development. In Europe, we need this arguably more now than at any time in the past decade. The EC and the new Treaty have many weaknesses and many faults. The next IGCs in the mid-1990s on the eve of enlargement will have many issues to address: *unicité* will be but one. Creating a functioning, democratic, open and tolerant European Union is a task for all of us.

As Robert Schuman said: 'Europe will not be built in a day; nor as part of some overall design. It will be built through practical achievements that first create a sense of common purpose.' That sense of common purpose exists. A decade ago, Altiero Spinelli recognised that, thanks to the political imagination of Jean Monnet and to the awareness he created among statesmen, European unification, through the consensus of free peoples, emerged from the realms of dreams and became reality. As he put it: 'the European Community . . . is a first step towards a true and complete political union'. It behoves us to take the next steps.

Juliet Lodge's lecture was sponsored by the City of Edinburgh District Council and delivered at the City Chambers, Edinburgh, on 2 November 1992.

The lecture was chaired by Councillor Mark Lazarowicz and a response was given by Sandy Finlayson, WS.

DAVID EDWARD

4   *Nations, states, people and commerce*

IT IS A GREAT HONOUR TO HAVE BEEN ASKED TO DELIVER
this, the first Napier Memorial Lecture since Napier University
was granted that title, and to do so as part of the series of
Lothian European Lectures leading up to the European Summit
in December 1992.

It was rather surprising, coming back to Edinburgh from
Luxembourg, to see the genuine enthusiasm with which the
city threw itself into the preparations for the Summit. It is
really not the Edinburgh way to be overly enthusiastic about
anything. Not so long ago anything to do with Europe would
have been greeted with a yawn of disdain if not active hostility,
as indeed anything to do with Europe is now greeted further
south. But in this, as in so many other matters, the north and
the south seem to move in opposite directions.

Of course opponents remain here too and I noticed a letter in
The Scotsman when the Lothian European Lecture programme
was announced, complaining that the choice of lecturers showed
a 'striking imbalance', undermining the value of the series as
a contribution to a 'democratic debate about the Maastricht
Treaty'. I have to confess to being on the pro-Europe side of
the debate and therefore part of the imbalance. But it does not
seem to me that the complaint of most people is that the two
sides are not heard. As far away as Luxembourg we can hear
the din of battle between closed minds. The main complaint is
rather that people do not understand what the debate is about.
They do not understand the issues and they do not know how
they could decide which way to vote if they were ever called

upon to do so. So I hope that I can contribute in a small way to the debate by attempting to clarify what it is about.

I begin with what Professor William Paterson described in the first of these lectures as the 'bonfire of certainties' in 1989.[1] About that time, a group of members of the European Parliament went on a visit to Berlin. They were greeted by an officer from the British Military Mission, and they asked him what he expected to happen. He replied, 'One thing is quite certain: the wall will remain for the foreseeable future.' By midnight that night, the Wall was down.

The consequences of that event are, I think, at least threefold. The first and most obvious, though it was not obvious at the time, is that the fall of the Wall revealed the total moral and economic bankruptcy of the system that lay behind it. It has been a progressive revelation. It did not come all at once and the fact that the revelation was progressive may explain the euphoric attitude of West Germany towards reunification. As things have become clearer, we have become aware of the decaying industries, the appalling problem of pollution and, in a more detailed and deeper way, the ingrained acceptance of totalitarian practices and the lack of any sense of initiative among the people of many countries of the former Eastern bloc. This may be easier to overcome in countries such as Poland where the totalitarian system was something to react against. It has not been easy to overcome, and will not be easy to overcome, in countries such as the former German Democratic Republic where totalitarianism was accepted and had become a way of life.

A second consequence of the Wall coming down was that it brought into the open problems which had always been there but had been latent. The most obvious is what has been described as the 'restarting' of the Yugoslavian civil war which had simply been put into abeyance by Tito. Elsewhere, we have seen the emergence of ethnic tensions about which we in the West really knew nothing at all, and it has been estimated that there are now at least 40 potential flashpoints for ethnic conflict in Europe. The same authority estimated that there are 2,000 in the whole world.

Apart from that, there is, I think, a new and perhaps more sinister trend emerging. In the spring of 1989 and 1990 there was an enthusiastic embracing of Western values and methods, especially the values and methods of the free market and of democracy. But, if we look at what is happening in the elections in Romania and Lithuania and if we look at Mr Yeltsin's problems with the Congress of Peoples' Deputies, we see a yearning for the old certainties, both economic and political. The potential for a totalitarian backlash exists, with or without an intervening period of anarchy. Perhaps that is the most dangerous aspect of it all, because it is potentially nuclear anarchy. I have met a businessman who has been offered a cargo of enriched uranium.

Thirdly, as well as the consequences for the East, there have been consequences for the West because the bonfire of certainties has hit us as well. I leave aside the bonfire of military certainties which Professor Paterson spoke about, and the certainties inherent in the Yalta settlement at the end of the last war. The fall of the Wall gave rise in the West as well as in the East to a euphoria that led to people talking about a new world order based on free markets and democratic institutions. That euphoria has gradually given way to a realisation of the scale of the problem with which we are faced and which, at least until very recently, politicians were unwilling to admit. It is perhaps significant and encouraging, in a curious sort of way, that Chancellor Kohl is now prepared to recognise the scale of the problem by using words to the effect of 'the party's over'.

The fundamental problem with which we are faced in the West is whether the conventional Western certainties are adequate to cope with the scale of the problem. The scale of the problem can, I think, be judged by looking at what has been the effect of reunification on the economy of Germany. Remember that the German Democratic Republic was both relatively advanced and relatively small in terms of population. Its population was approximately the same as that of Czechoslovakia, three-quarters of that of Romania, less than half that of Poland, a tenth of that of Russia and a twentieth of that of the former USSR. If you consider that the incorporation of the relatively advanced and relatively small German Democratic Republic into the Federal Republic of Germany has caused a major economic crisis for the Federal Republic, then perhaps you will see the scale of the problem elsewhere.

Please do not be misled by stories of fast cars and fast food in Moscow and Warsaw. I was at the opening of the new university at Frankfurt on the Oder, a city which was devastated at the end of the last war. There you can still go through the streets and see the bullet holes in the stucco on the houses – such houses as remain: most of the rest of the city has all the charm of Easterhouse.[2] On the other side of the Oder is the other half of old Frankfurt which is now in Poland. You cross a bridge on which, every ten yards, there are people selling cigarettes for hard currency. At the ceremony for laying the foundation stone for the Polish College at the University of Frankfurt, the only place capable of offering hospitality to a relatively large group was the restaurant of a hotel for long-distance truck drivers. That is the reality of Polish life outside the big cities, and Frankfurt on the Oder with all its problems is nothing to what lies on the other side of that river.

If the free market is to offer a solution to these problems, then these countries must be allowed to trade with the West and the reality is that the West is arguing about whether we should admit cargoes of Polish strawberries.

A further example of the problem is this. A free market presupposes a working and enforceable law of contract. That presupposes a working legal system. That presupposes trained judges and lawyers. That presupposes law schools, and that presupposes books. I was talking about European Community Law with the Professor of International Law at the University of Wroclaw. He said they took a great interest in it. I asked

'Do you teach it?' His reply was 'We cannot teach it because we have no books.'

The problem of providing the intellectual infrastructure necessary to support the institutions of the Western democratic society is far greater than any of the problems of propaganda during the Cold War.

Most of all, we are faced with the difficulty of providing stable political structures. If change is not to be chaotic, there must be political institutions that are effective. As Professor Paterson pointed out, the available political institutions are those of the nation state: the building block of the international world order. Essentially the institutions in question are the institutions of a unitary state because experience in Czechoslovakia, in Russia, and most of all in Yugoslavia, has shown the difficulty of establishing acceptable federal institutions in the former communist countries. The result is that we are left with a proliferation of nation states, most of them small and economically not self-sufficient, many of then economically inefficient, and many of them, because they have sizable minority populations, potentially unstable.

We should realise that we have been here before. The old order has collapsed before – notably, in Europe, after the First World War. The Europe of kingdoms and empires before that war gave way, in obedience to the doctrine of self-determination, to the Europe of nation states, and that Europe of nation states lasted for rather less than 20 years. One of the main pretexts for the destruction of that Europe was the claim, on the part of Hitler, to protect national minorities within the frontiers of other states.

Let me at this point enter a disclaimer. I am not an apostle of some new world order in which the nation state will wither away. I accept that the nation state is the basic building block of international society. But the nation state has drawbacks and these drawbacks are inherent in its very nature.

If we look for a legal definition of a state, we can find it in the Montevideo Convention on the Rights and Duties of States.

Article 1 of that Convention defined the criteria of statehood. They are four:

- a permanent population;
- a defined territory;
- government; and
- capacity to enter into relations with other states.

These criteria are explained by Professor Brownlie, Professor of International Law at Oxford, in this way: the first, 'permanent population', means that there is a stable community; the second, 'defined territory', means that there is a stable community in control of a certain area; the third, 'government', means that the community supports a legal order in that area; and the fourth, 'legal capacity', means that this government and this community must be independent.[3] 'Sovereignty' – that greatly overused word – used in this context, 'is legal shorthand for legal personality of a certain kind, namely the legal personality of statehood'.[4] The two go together.

This means that the theory of the nation state is based on the hypothesis that there are identifiable nations living within definable territories, and that these nations can and should be able to choose their own form of government and to choose those who will govern them. At this point the theory of the nation state links with the theory of democracy, the theory of democracy being that the choice of those who are to govern shall be the choice of the majority. These are accepted as self-evident truths in most of the West.

Unfortunately the logic of the approach can have other effects and I found a very interesting illustration of that logic in a recent book by Patricia Meehan, *The Unnecessary War*. She quotes the Final Report presented to the Foreign Secretary, Lord Halifax, by Sir Nevile Henderson, the last UK Ambassador to the Third Reich:

It would be idle to deny the great achievements of the man who restored to the German nation its self-respect and its disciplined orderliness. The tyrannical methods which were employed within Germany itself to obtain this result were detestable but were Germany's own concern. Many of Herr Hitler's social reforms, in spite of their complete disregard of personal liberty, of thought, word and deed, were on highly advanced democratic lines . . . typical examples of a benevolent dictatorship.[5]

These are the words of a British Diplomat in 1939. He went on to say that, so long as national socialism remained an article for internal consumption, the government of Germany was the affair of the German people. 'Or', Meehan adds, 'as the Prince of Wales put it more pithily to the Prince of Hess – It's nobody's damned business what Germany does to Germany'. This reflects an attitude that goes very deep in British official thinking. You have only to look back at what was being said at the beginning of the break-up of Yugoslavia about the desirability of recognising Slovenia, Croatia and Bosnia.

The attitude is comprehensible. The reason for it is a lack of awareness of frontiers and their significance. It comes from living on an island and, particularly, from living in the southern part of that island. It is an attitude not shared by those to whom land frontiers are real and important. You can see that very clearly if you live where I now live in Luxembourg, where there are three frontiers and you can very easily take a Sunday afternoon drive and pass through four countries. It is also very easy to see in Ireland, although we tend to forget it.

The crux of the problem, so it seems to me, is that the legal criterion of 'a community living within a defined territory' necessarily implies the drawing of frontiers, and the drawing of frontiers necessarily implies an element of arbitrariness as regards the division of communities. The problem is to define the unit you are going to look at, and it is illustrated in Ireland. If you look at the island of Ireland, then the majority is the Catholic population of the whole island. If you look at Northern Ireland, then the majority is the Protestant population of Ulster.

How and where do you define the frontier by reference to the 'community'?

This is a relatively recent problem because the notion of a frontier as a fixed line of demarcation between two equal entities called states is relatively recent. The Roman frontier, the limes, was the 'limit' of the claim to rule: it marked out the limit of the Empire within which the Romans claimed to rule. In medieval times the notion was more that of 'marches', the Scottish Marches, the Welsh Marches and at the other side of Europe the Mark of Brandenburg – an area between claimed territories rather than a line separating them.

So this idea of frontiers is relatively new, and it is inherent in the legal concept of a state. History shows that it is the essential shortcoming of the nation state as the building block of an international order. The problem lies not just in drawing the frontier but in the consequences that flow from it. Because the third criterion of statehood is 'government', the theory that the community in control of a defined area is entitled to produce a government for that area, when taken together with the theory of democracy and majority rule, involves the permanent disadvantaging of the minority within that territory.

Of course, democracy is the least bad form of government and the nation state is the least bad building block. But both call for mechanisms to compensate for their defects, and a major preoccupation of the politicians of Western Europe after the Second World War was the search for mechanisms to compensate for the shortcomings of democracy in the nation state.

One approach, the approach promoted by the United Kingdom, was that of 'intergovernmentalism'. It led to the setting up of the Council of Europe which still exists and still does valuable work. Intergovernmentalism implies a willing cooperation between nation states but it also requires unanimity for action and we still hear echoes of that favoured method today. A surprising product of this approach, and I mention it because it would be unfair not to mention it, is the European Convention on Human Rights and the Court and Commission of Human

Rights in Strasbourg. These institutions were not intended by Britain to have the effect they have had. The idea of those who wrote the European Convention on Human Rights – principally an official in the Home Office – was that they were writing down the liberties of the British people as guaranteed by the Common Law. The intended targets were Hitler and Milosevic, rather than the Home Office, but that is not quite how it has turned out!

The opposite pole of thinking was the thinking which came to be epitomised by the phrase 'United States of Europe'. That indeed was an aim promoted by Winston Churchill as a goal for continental Europe, although not for Britain. The aim was nothing less than a superstate. The aim failed then and has consistently failed ever since, but it is very important to distinguish that aim, the creation of a superstate, from the aim which is customarily called in other countries federalism.

The third approach was the economic approach, crystallised in the European Coal and Steel Community and subsequently in the European Economic Community and EURATOM. The choice of coal and steel, as the beginning, was significant strategically and geographically. It was important strategically because in those days it was possible for Robert Schuman, Foreign Minister of France, to refer to coal and steel as 'the basic elements of industrial production'. It was important geographically because a major, and perhaps the major, zone of production of coal and steel lay in the area of the rivers which divide Alsace/Lorraine from Germany, and the Saarland from France. If we look at European history continuously over the period from Louis XIV right through to 1945, we will see that, for various reasons, conflict concentrated particularly on control of those areas. The aim of the Coal and Steel Community was quite simply to make a further war between France and Germany materially impossible by removing the basic elements of industrial production from the control of either of them and placing them under the control of a supranational authority. But the consequence, for the reason I have just mentioned, was also to defuse frontier problems because, by taking out of contention access to coal and steel, it became less important who owned Alsace/Lorraine and who owned the Saarland.

The special and new feature of the Community which was set up to achieve this was its institutional structure, because as Jean Monnet, the person who imagined it and got it put into effect, said, 'Nothing is possible without men; nothing is lasting without institutions'.[6] They set up four institutions: the High Authority (now the Commission) to control the production and distribution of coal and steel acting under the supervision of an Assembly (now called the European Parliament) representing the peoples, a Council of Ministers representing governments and a Court. This thinking was followed through in the EEC Treaty, the treaty which we know as the Treaty of Rome. Although it is quite different in scope and significantly different in institutional structure, it remains based on four institutions: the three political institutions – the Commission, the Council of Ministers and the Parliament; and one judicial institution – the Court. The peculiarities, compared with any other system, are that the Assembly or Parliament was initially only supervisory or consultative rather than legislative, the Council of Ministers being the effective legislature, and the institution of a new political animal, known as the Commission, an independent political body with sole power of initiative. A third peculiarity of the system from the British point of view was the establishment of a court with the widely expressed remit of 'ensuring that the law is observed'.[7]

The EEC Treaty is a long and carefully drafted document containing a precise prescription for economic integration, and it is important to emphasise that it is not just a prescription for a free trade area. Such a prescription was tried and has continued to exist in EFTA (the European Free Trade Association). As far as the EFTA states are now concerned, or most of them at least, such a free trade area is insufficient, as is shown by the new treaty between them and the Community creating the European Economic Area.

The EEC Treaty goes much further than setting up a free trade area because it attempts comprehensively to address issues which free trade agreements generally avoid. Let me illustrate some of them:

- hidden non-tariff barriers;
- barriers to trade resulting from legal differences;
- trade in agricultural products, normally excluded from free trade agreement because it has, until very recently with the Cairns Group, been almost universally the case that governments have subsidised their agricultural industry;
- free movement of wage and salary earners;
- free movement of the self-employed including profes-sionals, an area which has hardly been addressed in the United States or in Canada, which are much more deeply integrated units;
- free movement of the families of the self-employed;
- free movement of services, including transport;
- free movement of capital.

Another point I should mention in relation to the EEC Treaty was the remarkable inclusion, remarkable because it was included in 1957, of the rule against any discrimination between men and women in respect of remuneration. But the reason for that was quite simple and it illustrates the kind of problem that can arise: the French had already introduced that rule and they did not want to be faced with unfair competition from states which still allowed women to be paid less than men for the same work.

The Treaty was a complete programme for a market without internal frontiers in goods, skills, services and assets and it was designed to be in place by the end of 1969. The purpose was overtly more than to create a free trade area. On the contrary, it was expressly a political purpose, the political purpose being political integration through progressive economic integration or, as it was put in the preamble, the achievement of 'an ever closer union among the peoples of Europe'. The method used was the pooling of sovereignty, the exercise of joint sovereignty, for defined if limited purposes. To that extent what they set up was already a constitution, albeit an inchoate constitution.

That the Treaty is a constitution is demonstrated, I think, by two significant developments in the 1960s before the UK became a member. One was, at the beginning of the 1960s, the decision of the Court of Justice (the Court on which I now sit) that the law created by the treaties and the rights that derived from them could be asserted by individuals and companies before their own courts and that the national courts had an obligation to apply that law in preference to their own law.[8] The second development was what was known as the Luxembourg Compromise. This was the consequence of General De Gaulle's dissatisfaction with the Community system. He withdrew the French representative from the Council of Ministers and insisted that in future, if any Member State considered that a matter affected its own essential interests, any decision must be taken by unanimity. The point of significance of the Luxembourg Compromise is that it was an attempt to escape from the logic of the 'constitution', namely that some decisions could and should be taken by majority vote.

What kind of political structure did the treaties create? It is *sui generis*, but it seeks to reconcile and to harness the conflicting interests of nations or peoples, of states, of commerce and industry, and of individuals – hence the somewhat enigmatic title of this lecture.

The idea of reconciling and harnessing divergent interests through a constitution is not a new idea. More than 100 years ago in 1885, James Bryce, who was at that time Professor of Civil Law at Oxford but later became British Ambassador in Washington, and who was responsible for, among other things, major work on the Australian Constitution and was a great expert on federalism, wrote an essay called 'The Action of Centripetal and Centrifugal Forces on Political Constitutions'.[9]

He identified two forces, 'interest' and 'sympathy' which work in two ways:

- interest – the interest of the trader in having a large market but also the interest of the trader in protection from competition;

- sympathy – the natural bonds between people which produce collaboration between them but can also produce hostility: religion, race, language and so on.

He said that every constitution has three main objects: first of all, to provide the framework of government; second, to provide due security for the rights of the citizen; and, third, to strengthen the cohesiveness of the country. As to the last, he said:

It may do this in two ways. One is by setting the various centripetal forces to work. The other is by preventing all or some of the centrifugal forces from working.

He went on to say:

The most generally available of these centripetal tendencies is trade – that interchange of commodities which benefits all the producers by giving them a market, all the consumers by giving them the means of getting what they want, all the middlemen by supplying them with occupation. A Constitution can render no greater service to the unity as well as to the material progress of a nation than by enabling the freest interchange of products to go on within its limits.

He also saw law and religion as uniting influences. Then he turned to the centrifugal tendencies:

History tells us that the chief among them are race feeling, resentment for past injuries and grievances in respect of real or supposed ill-treatment in matters of industry, or of trade, or of education, or of language or of religion, where these grievances press on a part only of the population.

Having discussed how the centripetal forces are to be set to work, he turned to counteracting the centrifugal forces. He enumerated the means as being, first of all, by force; second, by providing constitutional securities against oppression; third, 'by means of varying general institutions or laws in such a way as to provide for special interests or feelings' and he gives the example of Scotland within the United Kingdom; fourth, by devolution of power to local legislatures; and finally by excluding certain matters from the competence of central government, and here he gives the example of religion in Switzerland and in the United States.

I believe that if we study the European Community system we will find that, as an inchoate constitution, it is already highly sophisticated in these respects. It does promote freedom of trade, it does provide ways of meeting grievances, and it does so by harnessing the law and the legal system to outlaw sex discrimination, discrimination on grounds of nationality and, for example, exclusion from the professions. If you ask 'Is the internal market working?', my answer, as a judge of the European Court, would be, 'Yes of course it is working because there are 700 cases waiting to be judged, and more than half of them come from national courts which are dealing with precisely the problems that have arisen in individual cases because of the rules of the market.' The EC system does respond to special interests or feelings, for example in the matter of language and also in the matter of abortion in Ireland and environmental concern in Denmark, and the powers of the centre are limited.

The constitution is there, but it is what Bryce also called a 'flexible constitution'.[10] He distinguished between flexible constitutions and rigid constitutions, taking the British constitution as the primary example of a flexible constitution. The Community constitution is a flexible constitution, but it responds to his concerns by balancing the interests of European integration, represented by the Commission which is, as it were, the motor, against those of the Member States, represented by the Council of Ministers, which is the governor on the motor. It balances those interests against those of the peoples represented by the Parliament, ideally elected in the future by a similar method of direct election throughout the Community, all working within a defined legal framework as interpreted by the Court of Justice.

I believe, further, that the current problems with which the Community is faced have actually demonstrated, not the weakness, but the strength of that institutional structure because it has proved to be strong enough to continue in spite of the enormous problems that have had to be faced.

If that is the position so far, what is the argument now about? It is not about sovereignty. If sovereignty is about statehood, then the statehood of the Member States is not an issue. If sovereignty is about powers, then powers are already shared. If sovereignty is about practical independence, then no state in Western or Eastern Europe can claim to have it. As far as sovereignty is concerned, the best quotation I can give you is again from Bryce:

> The controversies which the Doctrine of Sovereignty has provoked have been so numerous and so tedious that a reader – even the most patient reader – may feel alarmed at being invited to enter once again that dusty desert of abstractions through which successive generations of political philosophers have thought it necessary to lead their disciples.[11]

So I leave sovereignty. Is the argument about federalism? I don't think it is because the system is already significantly federal. It is federal because certain competences, certain powers, have already been transferred from the Member States to the Community and what the Community does has a direct effect on the citizen, and the citizen can enforce his rights, deriving from the Community, before his own courts. Nor do I think it is about subsidiarity which is really the counterpart of federalism. All of these are words which depend for their value on how we define them.

The real question which the Maastricht debate raises and puts before us is about power. Who is to exercise it, and how is it to be controlled? Who do we want to exercise power in relation to what? And what checks and balances do we require?

In that context a vote against Maastricht is not a neutral vote because it is a vote in favour of the status quo, and the status quo is one in which legislation which affects us is evolved by the Commission, a Commission which is not directly elected and not directly accountable except in a very specific and limited way. It is a status quo in which legislation produced by the Commission is brought into force by the Council of Ministers, representing the governments of the Member States, with only the most rudimentary democratic control through the European Parliament or through national parliaments. As my predecessor in the Chair of European Institutions at the University of Edinburgh said: 'Governments and governmental bodies have as many reasons for conniving amongst themselves as they have for opposing each other.'

If we want to vote against Maastricht, then we are voting for a status quo in which economic and fiscal decisions affecting us are taken by the Bundesbank. If we are voting against Maastricht, we are voting for a status quo in which decisions affecting the control of terrorism, drugs and immigration are taken by ill-defined processes of intergovernmental negotiation without even any certainty that they will produce an effective result at the end of the day. We are voting for a status quo in which, if we or our children are interested in going to work in another country, then in most of them we will not be allowed to vote unless we change our nationality.

The Maastricht Treaty tries, however imperfectly, to respond to these concerns, If it is not ratified, the flexible constitution which already exists will, I believe, continue to develop. It will go on, but the underlying issues and concerns will remain: and because they remain, they will make it more difficult to respond to the problems revealed or created by the fall of the Wall.

Maastricht is above all a political commitment – a political commitment, not to ditch the nation state, but to compensate more adequately and more effectively for its weaknesses and its shortcomings. It is said in some circles that we should be concentrating on the enlargement of the Community – widening, as it is put, rather than deepening: in the words of Baroness Thatcher, widening 'on the basis of a co-operation between independent sovereign countries loosely linked in a free trade area'. She should know better. That is not an answer to the problems of Eastern Europe any more than it was an answer to the problems of Western Europe 40 years ago, and our own history and experience tell us that that is so.

Let me end where I began by saying something about a University, in this case the new University in Frankfurt on the Oder. 60% of the students who went there in 1992 are German, 40% are Polish. You have only to be there to be aware that the tensions between those two peoples are not dead. But the fact is that these students want to study together and are prepared to be taught partly in German and partly in Polish. There were nearly 100 applications for the Chair of Philosophy, from all over the world, from people who said they wanted to go there to teach because this new University is symbolic of a new hope.

Neither these students nor others of their generation will forgive us if, through our selfishness, we deny them that hope.

David Edward's Lecture was given as *The John Napier Memorial Lecture* and delivered at St Margaret's Hall, Napier University, on 3 November 1992.

The lecture was chaired by Professor W.A. Turmeau, Principal and Vice-Chancellor, Napier University, and a response was given by A.H. Bridge, Chairman of the Court, Napier University.

5   *Imperialism and after: Europe, the US and the rest of us*

I WANT TO BEGIN WITH AN INDISPUTABLE FACT, NAMELY, that during the nineteenth century, unprecedented power – compared with which the powers of Rome, Spain, Baghdad or Constantinople in their day were far less formidable – was concentrated in Britain and France and later in other Western countries especially the United States. The nineteenth century climaxed 'the rise of the West', and Western power allowed the imperial metropolitan centres at the end of that century to acquire and accumulate territory and subjects on a truly astonishing scale. Consider that in 1800 Western powers claimed 55% but actually held approximately 35% of the Earth's surface, and that by 1878 the proportion was 67%, a rate of increase of 83,000 square miles per year. By 1914, the annual rate of European acquisition, or Western acquisition including the United States, had risen to an astonishing 240,000 square miles, and the West held a grand total of roughly 85% of the Earth as colonies, protectorates, dependencies, dominions and commonwealths.[1] No other associated set of colonies in history was as large, none so totally dominated, none so unequal in power to the Western metropolis. As a result, says William McNeill in *The Pursuit of Power*, 'the world was united into a single interacting whole as never before'.[2]

In Europe itself at the end of the nineteenth century, scarcely a corner of life was untouched by the facts of empire; the economies were hungry for overseas markets, raw materials, cheap labour, and sometimes hugely profitable land. Defence

and foreign policy establishments were more and more committed to the maintenance of vast tracts of distant territory
and large numbers of subjugated peoples. When the Western
powers were not in close, sometimes ruthless, competition with
each other for more colonies, they were hard at work settling,
surveying, studying and, of course, ruling the territories under
their jurisdictions.

As Richard Van Alstyne makes clear in his book *The Rising
American Empire*, from the very beginning of the Republic, in
the eighteenth century, the American experience was founded
upon the idea of 'an *imperium* – a dominion state or sovereignity
that would expand in population and territory, and increase in
strength and power.'[3] There were claims for North American
territory to be made and fought over (with astonishing success).
There were native peoples – I speak of course of the native
peoples of North America – to be dominated, variously exter-
minated, variously dislodged. Then, as the Republic increased
in age and hemispheric power, there were distant lands to
be designated vital to American interest, to be intervened in
and fought over, for example the Philippines, the Caribbean,
Central America, the Barbary Coast, parts of Europe and the
Middle East, Vietnam and Korea.

Curiously though, so influential has been the discourse insisting on American 'specialness', altruism, and opportunity, that
'imperialism' as a word or ideology has turned up only recently
and rarely in accounts of US culture, politics and history. But
the connection between imperial politics and culture is astonishingly direct. American attitudes to American 'greatness',
to hierarchies of race, to the perils of *other* revolutions – the
American revolution being considered unique and somehow
unrepeatable anywhere else in the world – have remained
constant, have dictated, have obscured, the realities of empire,
while apologists for overseas American interests have insisted
on American innocence, doing good, fighting for freedom. Graham Greene's character Pyle, in his novel *The Quiet American*,
embodies this cultural attitude with merciless accuracy.

Yet for citizens of nineteenth-century Britain and France, empire was a major topic of unembarrassed cultural attention. British India and French North Africa alone played inestimable roles in the imagination, economy, political life and social fabric of British and French society. If we mention names such as Delacroix, Edmund Burke, Ruskin, Carlyle, James and John Stuart Mill, Kipling, Balzac, Nerval, Flaubert, or Conrad, we shall be mapping only a tiny corner of a much larger reality than even their immense collective talents cover. There were scholars, administrators, travellers, traders, parliamentarians, merchants, novelists, theorists, speculators, adventurers, visionaries, poets, and every variety of outcast and misfit in the outlying possessions of these two imperial powers, each of whom contributed to the formation of a colonial mentality existing at the heart of metropolitan life.

As I use the term, 'imperialism' means the practice, the theory, and the attitudes of a dominating metropolitan centre ruling a distant territory; 'colonialism', which is almost always a consequence of imperialism, is the implanting of settlements on distant territory. As Michael Doyle puts it:

> Empire is a relationship, formal or informal, in which one state controls the effective political sovereignity of another political society. It can be achieved by force, by political collaboration, by economic, social, or cultural dependence. Imperialism is simply the process or policy of establishing or maintaining an Empire.[4]

In our time, direct colonialism has largely ended; imperialism, as I will be talking about it, lingers where it often has lingered, in a kind of general cultural sphere as well as in specific political, ideological, economic and social practices.

Neither imperialism nor colonialism is a simple act of accumulation and acquisition. Both are supported, perhaps even impelled, by impressive cultural formations that include notions that certain territories and people require and beseech domination, as well as forms of knowledge affiliated with domination: the vocabulary of classic nineteenth-century imperial culture is plentiful with words and concepts like 'inferior' or 'subject races', the notion of 'subordinate peoples', 'dependency', 'expansion', 'authority'. Out of the imperial experiences, notions about culture were clarified, reinforced, criticised, or rejected. As for the curious but perhaps allowable idea propagated a century ago by J.R. Sealey that some of Europe's overseas empires were originally acquired by accident, this does not by any stretch of the imagination account for their inconsistency, persistence, and systematised acquisition and administration, let alone their augmented rule and sheer presence. As David Landes has said in *The Unbound Prometheus*, 'the decision of certain European powers to establish "plantations", that is to treat their colonies as continuous enterprises, was, whatever one may think of the morality, a momentous innovation.'[5]

The primacy of the British and French empires by no means obscures the quite remarkable modern expansion of Spain, Portugal, the Netherlands, Belgium, Germany, Italy and, in a different way, Russia and the United States. Japan, of course, is another case. Russia, however, acquired its imperial territories almost exclusively by adjacence. Unlike Britain and France, which jumped hundreds of miles beyond their own borders to other continents, Russia moved to swallow whatever land or peoples stood next to its borders, which in the process kept moving further and further east and south. But in the English and French cases, the sheer distance of attractive territories summoned the projection of far flung interests, and that is what I am focusing on here, partly because I am interested in examining the set of cultural forms and structures of feeling which it produces, and partly because overseas domination is the world I grew up in and still live in. The Russian and American superpower status, enjoyed for a little less than half a century, derives from quite different histories and from different imperial trajectories. There are several varieties of domination, and responses to it, but the 'Western' one, along with the resistance it provoked, is in part the subject of my lecture.

In the expansion of the great Western empires, profit and hope of further profit were obviously tremendously important, as the attractions of spice, sugar, slaves, rubber, cotton, opium, tin, gold, silver, and later oil amply testify over centuries. But so also was inertia, the investment in already-going enterprises and tradition, and the market or institutional forces that kept the enterprises going. But I believe there is more than that to imperialism and colonialism. There was a commitment to them over and above profit, a commitment in constant circulation and recirculation, which, on the one hand, allowed sometimes decent men and women to accept the notion that distant territories and their native peoples *should* be subjugated, and, on the other, replenished metropolitan energies so that these decent people could think of the *imperium* as a protracted, almost metaphysical, obligation to rule subordinate, inferior, or less advanced peoples. We must not forget that there was very little domestic resistance or organised opposition to these empires in metropolitan centres until well into the twentieth century; that is, to the idea of empires, although these empires were very frequently established and maintained under adverse and even disadvantageous conditions. Not only were immense hardships endured by the colonisers and the adventurers, but there was always the tremendously risky physical disparity between a relatively small number of Europeans at a very great distance from home and the much larger number of natives on their own home territory. In India, for instance, by the 1930s 'a mere 4,000 British civil servants assisted by 60,000 soldiers and 90,000 civilians (businessmen and clergy for the most part), had billeted themselves upon a country of 300 million persons'.[6] The will, self-confidence, even arrogance necessary to maintain such a state of affairs can only be guessed at. But, as one can see in the texts of novels like *A Passage to India* and *Kim*, and certainly in *Heart of Darkness*, these attitudes are at least as significant as the number of people in the army or civil service, or the millions of pounds England derived from India.

For the enterprise of empire depends upon the *idea* of *having an empire*, as Conrad so powerfully seems to have realised. I want to include a quotation from *Heart of Darkness* which I think perfectly catches it. He says:

> the conquest of the earth, which mostly means the taking it away from those who have a different complexion and slightly flatter noses than ourselves, is not a pretty thing when you look into it too much. What redeems it is the idea only. An idea at the back of it; not a sentimental pretence, but an idea; and an unselfish belief in the idea – something you can set up and bow down before and offer a sacrifice to . . .[7]

All kinds of preparations for having an empire are made for that process within a culture. Then, in turn, imperialism acquires a kind of coherence, a set of experiences, and a presence of ruler and ruled alike, within the culture. 'Modern imperialism', I quote now from V.G. Kiernan, 'has been an accretion of elements, not all of equal weight, that can be traced back through every epoch of history. Perhaps its ultimate causes, with those of war, are to be found less in tangible material wants than in the uneasy tensions of societies distorted by class division, with their reflection in distorted ideas in men's minds.'[8]

One acute indication of how crucially the tensions, inequalities and injustices of the home or metropolitan society were refracted and elaborated in the imperial culture is given by the conservative historian of empire, D.K. Fieldhouse: 'The basis of imperial authority was the mental attitude of the colonist. His acceptance of subordination – whether through a positive sense of common interest with a parent state, or through inability to conceive of any alternative – made empire durable.'[9] Fieldhouse was discussing white colonists in the Americas, but his general point goes beyond that, I think:

the durability of empire was sustained on both sides, that of the rulers and that of the distant ruled, and in turn each had a set of interpretations of their common history with its own perspective, historical sense, emotions and traditions. What an Algerian intellectual today remembers of his country's colonial past, which had been dominated by France from 1830 to 1962, focuses severely on such events as France's military attacks on villages and the torture of prisoners during the war of liberation, on the exultation over independence in 1962. For the Algerian intellectual's French counterpart, who may have taken part in Algerian affairs or whose family lived in Algeria (like Albert Camus for example), there is chagrin at having 'lost' Algeria, a more positive attitude towards the French colonising mission, referred to as the 'mission civilatrice', with its schools, nicely planned cities, pleasant life. Perhaps there is even a sense among French men and French women looking back at the history of the French occupation or the domination of Algeria, that the 'troublemakers' and communists disturbed the idyllic relationship between 'us' and 'them'.

To a very great degree, the era of high nineteenth-century imperialism is now over. France and Britain gave up their most splendid possessions after the Second World War, and lesser powers also divested themselves of their far-flung dominions – the Dutch, the Spanish and so on. Yet, although that era of high imperalism clearly had an identity all its own, the meaning of the imperial past is not totally contained within it, but has entered the reality of hundreds of millions of people, where its existence as shared memory and as a highly conflictual texture of culture, ideology, memory and policy still exercises tremendous force. Frantz Fanon in *The Wretched of the Earth* says, 'We should flatly refuse the situation to which the Western countries wish to condemn us. Colonialism and imperialism have not paid their score when they withdraw their flags and their police forces from our territories. For centuries, the [foreign] capitalists have behaved in the under developed world like nothing more than criminals.'[10] A proper understanding of imperialism, therefore, must in my opinion take stock also of the nostalgia for empire in the metropolitan centres as well as the anger and resentment it provokes in those who were ruled, and we must also try to look carefully and integrally at the culture that nurtured the sentiment, the rationale and, above all, the imagination of empire. I think we need to try to grasp the hegemony of the imperial ideology which, by the end of the nineteenth century, had become completely embedded in the affairs of cultures whose less regrettable features we still celebrate.

Thus, imperialism did not quickly, suddenly, cleanly, neatly end. It did not suddenly become 'past', once decolonisation had set in motion the dismantling of the classical empires. A legacy of connection still binds countries such as Algeria and India to France and Britain respectively. A vast new population of Muslims, Africans, and West Indians from former colonial territories now resides, as we all know, in metropolitan Western Europe; even Italy, Germany and Scandinavia today must deal with these dislocations, which are to a large degree the result of imperialism and decolonisation, as well as expanding European population. The end of the Cold War and of the Soviet Union has also definitively changed the world map. The triumph of the United States as the last superpower suggests that a new set of force lines will structure the world, and they were already beginning to be apparent in the 1960s and 1970s.

In a preface to the 1970 second edition of his book *After Imperialism*, Michael Barratt-Brown argues that 'imperialism is still without question the most powerful force in the economic, political and military relations by which the less economically developed lands are subjected to the more economically developed. We may still look forward to its ending.'[11] It is ironic that descriptions of the new form of imperialism regularly employ idioms of gigantism and apocalypse that could not as easily have been applied to the classical empires during their heyday. Some of these descriptions have an extraordinarily dispiriting inevitability, a kind of galloping, engulfing, impersonal, and deterministic quality. Accumulation on a world scale; the world capitalist system; the development of underdevelopment; imperialism and dependency, or the structure of dependence, poverty and imperialism: the repertory is well known in economics, political science, history, and sociology, and it has been identified less with the New World Order that George Bush proclaimed than with members of a controversial Left school of thought. Nevertheless, the cultural implications of such phrases and concepts are discernible – despite their oft-debated and far from settled nature – and, alas, they are undeniably depressing to even the most untutored eye.

What are the salient features of the representation of the old imperial inequities, the persistence, in Arno Mayer's telling phrase, of the old regime?[12] One, certainly, is the immense economic rift between poor and rich states, whose basically quite simple topography was drawn in the starkest terms by the so-called Brandt Report entitled *North–South: A Programme for Survival* published in 1980.[13] Its conclusions are couched in the language of crisis and emergency: the poorest nations of the Southern Hemisphere must have their 'priority needs' addressed, hunger must be abolished (hollow words when we think of Somalia, for example, or the whole of the eastern part of Africa), commodity earnings strengthened; manufacturing in the Northern Hemisphere should permit genuine growth in Southern manufacturing centres, transnational corporations should be 'restricted' in their practices, the global monetary system should be reformed, development finance should be changed to eliminate what one writer has called the 'debt trap'.[14] The crux of the matter is, as the report's phrase has it, 'power sharing', that is giving the Southern countries a more equitable share in 'power and decision-making within monetary and financial institutions'.

It is difficult to disagree with the report's diagnosis, which is made more credible by its balanced tone and its silent picture of the rapacity, greed and immorality of the North, or even to disagree with its recommendations. But how will the changes come about? The post-war classifications of all the nations into three 'worlds', the First World, the Second and the Third, coined by a French journalist in the 1950s, has largely now been abandoned.[15] The late Willy Brandt and his colleagues implicitly concede that the United Nations, an admirable organisation in principle, has not been adequate to the innumerable regional and global conflicts that occur with increasing frequency. With the exception of the work of small groups (for example the World Order Models Project) global thinking tends to reproduce the superpower, Cold War, regional, ideological, or ethnic contests of old, even more dangerous in the nuclear and the post-nuclear era, as the horrors of Yugoslavia attest. The powerful are likely to become more powerful and richer, the weak less powerful and poorer; the gap between the two overrides the former distinctions between socialist and capitalist regimes that, in Europe at least, have become less significant.

Noam Chomsky concluded that during the 1980s

the 'North–South conflict' will not subside, and new forms of domination will have to be devised to ensure that privileged segments of Western industrial society maintain substantial control over global resources, human and material, and benefit disproportionately from this control. Thus, it comes as no surprise that the reconsitution of ideology in the United States finds echoes throughout the industrial world. . . . But it is an absolute requirement for the Western system of ideology that a vast gulf be established between the civilised West, with its traditional commitment to human dignity, liberty, and self-determination [meant sarcastically of course], and the barbaric brutality of those who for some reason – perhaps defectives genes – fail to appreciate the depth of this historic commitment, so well revealed by America's Asian wars, for example.[16]

Chomsky's move from the North–South dilemma to American, and Western, dominance is, I think, basically correct, although the decrease in American economic power; the urban,

economic, and cultural crisis in the United States; the ascendancy of Pacific Rim states; and the confusions of a multipolar
world have muted the stridency of the Reagan and Bush period.
First, it underlines the continuity of the ideological need to
consolidate and justify domination in cultural terms that has
been the case in the West since the nineteenth century, and
even earlier. Second, it accurately picks up the theme based
on repeated projections and theorisations of American power,
sounded in often very insecure and therefore overstated ways,
that we live today in a period of American ascendancy.

Studies during the past decade of major personalities of the
mid twentieth century in America illustrate what I mean.
Ronald Steel's book entitled *Walter Lippmann and the American
Century,* published in 1981, represents the mind-set of that
ascendancy as inscribed in the career of the most famous
of American journalists, the first pundit, Walter Lippmann,
the father or grandfather of so many of the columnists we
read today. He had the most prestige and power of all the
columnists and pundits of this century. The extraordinary
thing about Lippmann's career as it emerges from Steel's book
is not that Lippmann was correct or especially perspicacious
with regard to his reporting of the news or his predictions
about world events (he was not; he was always wrong);
but, rather, that from an insider's position (the term is his),
he articulated American global dominance without demurral,
except for Vietnam. He saw his role as a pundit to be that of
helping his compatriots to make 'an adjustment to reality'; the
reality of unrivalled American power in the world, which he
made more acceptable by stressing its moralism, realism and
altruism with 'a remarkable skill for not straying too far from
the thrust of public opinion'.[17]

A similar view is found in the influential thinking of George
Kennan who was the author of containment policy in the period
immediately after the Second World War, which guided US
foreign policy for much of the Cold War period. Kennan
believed his country to be the guardian of Western civilisation.

For Kennan, such a destiny in the non-European world implied no effort to be expended on making the United States popular (he called it 'rotarian idealism'), but it rather depended on what he called 'straight power concepts', and since no formerly colonised people or state had the wherewithal to challenge the US militarily or economically he cautioned restraint – this was in the 1950s. Yet in a memo written in 1948 for the Policy Planning staff, he approved of recolonising Africa and also, in something he wrote in 1971, he approved of apartheid in South Africa, but not of its abuses, although he disapproved of the American intervention in Vietnam, and generally of a 'purely American kind of informal imperial system'.[18] There was no doubt in his mind that Europe and America were uniquely positioned to lead the world, a view that caused him to regard his own country as a sort of 'adolescent', growing into the role once played by the British Empire.

Other forces shaped post-war US foreign policy besides people like Lippmann and Kennan. Both were rather lonely men, alienated from the mass society they lived in, who hated jingoism and the cruder forms of aggressive American behaviour. They knew that isolationism, interventionism, anti-colonialism, and free trade imperialism were related to the domestic characteristics of American political life, described by Richard Hofstadter as 'anti-intellectual' and 'paranoid'. These produced the inconsistencies, advances, and retreats of US foreign policy after the Second World War. Yet the idea of American leadership and exceptionalism is never absent; no matter what the US does, these authorities often do not want it to be an imperial power like the others it followed, preferring instead the notion of 'world responsibility' as a rationale for what it does. Earlier rationales for US imperial doctrine – the Monroe Doctrine, Manifest Destiny and so on – lead to the concept of 'world responsibility', which exactly corresponds to the growth in the United States' global interests after the Second World War and to the conception of its enormous power as formulated by the foreign policy and intellectual élite.

In a persuasively clear account of what damage these attitudes have done, Richard Barnet notes that a United States military intervention in the Third World had occured every year between 1945 and 1967 (when he stopped counting). Since 1967, the United States has been impressively active, most notably during the Gulf War of 1991, when 650,000 troops were dispatched 6,000 miles to turn back an Iraqi invasion of a US ally, and a principal oil supplier. Such interventions, Barnet says in his book *The Roots of War*, have 'all the elements of a powerful imperial creed . . .: a sense of mission, historical necessity, and evangelical fervour'. He continues:

> The imperial creed rests on a theory of law-making. According to the strident globalists, like [Lyndon Baines] Johnson and the muted globalists, like Nixon, the goal of US foreign policy is to bring about a world increasingly subject to the rule of law. But it is the United States which must 'organise the peace', to use Secretary of State Rusk's words. The United States imposes the 'international interest' by setting the ground rules for economic development and military deployment across the planet. Thus the United States sets rules for Soviet behaviour in Cuba, Brazilian behaviour in Brazil, Vietnamese behaviour in Vietnam. Cold War policy is expressed by a series of directives on such extra territorial matters as whether Britain may trade with Cuba or whether the government of British Guyana may have a Marxist dentist to run it. Cicero's definition of the early Roman Empire was remarkably similar. It was the domain over which Rome enjoyed the legal right to enforce the law. Today America's self-appointed writ runs throughout the world, including the Soviet Union and China, over whose territory the US government [in the 1950s, 1960s and 1970s] has asserted the right to fly military aircraft. The United States, uniquely blessed with surpassing riches and an exceptional history, stands above the international system, not within it. Supreme among nations, she stands ready to be the bearer of the Law.[19]

Although these words were published in 1972, they even *more* accurately describe the US during the invasion of Panama and the Gulf War, a country which continues to try to dictate its views about law and peace all over the world. The amazing thing about this is not that it is attempted, but that it is done with so much consensus and near unanimity in a public sphere constructed as a kind of cultural space expressly to represent and explain it. In periods of great internal crisis (for example, a year or so after the Gulf War), this sort of moralistic triumphalism is suspended, put aside, and during the 1992 election very little was said about the Gulf War. It just didn't seem to be relevant. Yet, while there is a foreign crisis, the media play an extraordinary role in 'manufacturing consent', as Chomsky calls it, in making the average American feel that it is up to 'us' to right the wrongs of the world, and the devil with contradictions and inconsistencies. The Gulf intervention was preceded by a string of interventions (Panama, Grenada, Libya), all of them widely discussed, most of them approved, or at least undeterred, as belonging to 'us' by right. As Kiernan in his book on American imperialism puts it, 'America loved to think that whatever it wanted was just what the human race wanted.'[20]

To complete this rather bleak picture, let me add a few summary observations about the formerly colonised Third World. Obviously, we cannot discuss the non-Western world as disjunct from developments in the West. The ravages of colonial wars, the protracted conflicts between insurgent nationalism and anomalist imperialist control, the disputatious new fundamentalist and nativist movements nourished by despair and anger, the extension of the world system over the developing world – these circumstances are directly connected to actualities in the West. On the one hand, as Eqbal Ahmad says in the best account that we have of the situation in the Third World after decolonisation, the peasant and pre-capitalist classes that predominated during the era of classical colonialism have dispersed in the new states into new, often abruptly urbanised and restless classes tied to the absorptive economic and political power of the metropolitan West. In countries such as Pakistan and Egypt, for instance, the contentious fundamentalists are led not by peasant or working-class intellectuals but by Western-educated engineers, doctors and lawyers. Ruling minorities emerge with the new deformations in the new structures of power.[21] These pathologies, and the disenchantment with authority that they have caused, run the gamut from the neo-fascist, in a state such as Iraq, to the dynastic–oligarchic, with only a few states retaining a functioning parliamentary and democratic system.

For all its apparent power, this new overall pattern of domination which I have been trying to describe, which developed during an era of mass societies commanded at the top by a powerfully centralising culture and a complex incorporative so-called world economy, is, I think, very unstable. As the remarkable French urban sociologist Paul Virilio has said, it is a polity based on speed, instant communication, distant reach, constant emergency, insecurity induced by mounting crises, such as Yugoslavia, the Gulf, the Falklands, some of which lead to war. In such circumstances, the rapid occupation of real as well as public space, sometimes called colonisation, becomes the central militaristic prerogative of the modern state, as the United States showed when it dispatched a huge army to the Arabian Gulf, and commandeered the media, and the country of Saudi Arabia, to help carry out the operation. As against that, Virilio suggests that the modernist project of liberating language/speech has a parallel in the liberation of critical spaces – hospitals, universities (one thinks of the rebellions of the 1960s), theatres, factories, churches, empty buildings; in both, the fundamental transgressive act is to inhabit the normally uninhabited.[22] As examples, Virilio cites the cases of people whose current status in the West is the consequence either of decolonisation (migrant workers, refugees, the so-called *Gastarbeiter* in Germany) or of major demographic and political shifts, which produce the large numbers of African populations in Britain for example, immigrants, urban squatters, students, popular insurrections

and so on. These transgressive occupations of space constitute, he says, a real alternative to the authority of the
state, which is busily occupying, in some instances, territory
abroad.

If the 1960s are now remembered as a decade of European
and American mass demonstrations (for example the university
anti-war uprisings), the 1980s must surely be the decade of mass
uprisings outside the Western metropolis. I am developing a
little the thought of Virilio and applying it to the non-Western
world; if we think of the demonstrations that took place
in countries such as Iran, the Philippines, Argentina, Korea,
Pakistan, Algeria, China, South Africa, virtually all of Eastern
Europe, as well as the Israeli-occupied territories of Palestine,
during the last 10 or 15 years, these are some of the most
impressive crowd-activated sites, each of them crammed with
largely unarmed civilian populations, well past the point of
enduring the imposed deprivations, tyranny, and inflexibility
of governments that had ruled them for far too long. Most
memorable are, on the one hand, the resourcefulness and the
startling symbolism of the protests themselves (the stone-
throwing Palestinian youths, for example, or the swaying
and dancing South African groups, or the wall-traversing East
Germans) and, on the other hand, the offensive brutality or
collapse and, in many instances, ignominious departure of some
despotic governments.

Allowing for great differences in ideology, these mass protests have all challenged something very basic to every art
and theory of government, including empire, the principle
of confinement. To be governed, people must be counted,
taxed, educated, and of course ruled in regulated places (house,
school, hospital, worksite), whose ultimate extension is represented, at its most simple and severe, by the prison or
the mental hospital, as Michel Foucault argued 20 years ago.
True, there was a carnivalesque aspect to the milling crowds
in Gaza or in Wenceslas and Tiananmen squares, but the
consequences of sustained mass unconfinement and unsettled

existence were only a little less dramatic (and dispiriting) in the 1980s than before. The unresolved plight of the Palestinians speaks directly of an undomesticated cause and a rebellious people paying a very heavy price for their resistance. And there are other examples: refugees and 'boat people', those unresting and vulnerable itinerants; the starving populations of the southern hemisphere; the destitute but insistent homeless who, like so many Bartlebys (in Melville's story of Bartleby the Scrivener) shadow the Christmas shoppers in Western cities; the undocumented immigrants and exploited 'guest workers' who provide cheap and usually seasonal labour. Between the extremes of discontented, challenging, urban mobs and the floods of semi-forgotten and uncared-for people, the world's secular and religious authorities have sought new, or renewed, modes of governance.

None has seemed so easily available, so conveniently attractive, as appeals to tradition, national or religious identity, or patriotism, as in 'France for the French'. Think of people like Le Penn in France, think of the anti-semitic people in Rostock. This is a resurgence of tradition and, I think, of ideas of national identity and the purity of the nation. It is interesting that it is sometimes replicated not only in mobs on the streets, like these fascists that I refer to, but also in the case of governments, who appeal to tradition, and important and responsible political parties, as in the case of France and elsewhere. Because these appeals are amplified and disseminated by a perfected media system addressing mass cultures, they have been strikingly, not to say frighteningly, effective. When in the spring of 1986 the Reagan administration decided to deal 'terrorism' a blow, the raid on Libya was timed to occur exactly as prime-time national evening news began. 'America strikes back' was the headline on the news, although of course America hadn't been attacked by Libya, but it sounded as if it had. This claim was answered resoundingly throughout the Muslim world with appeals to 'Islam', which in turn provoked an avalanche of images, writings and postures in the 'West', underscoring the value of 'our' Judeo-Christian (Western, liberal, democratic) heritage and the nefariousness, evil, cruelty and immaturity of theirs (Islamic, Third World, non-white, etc.).

From the details of daily life to the immense range of global forces (including what has been called 'the death of nature') all these, therefore, in the New World importune the troubled soul, and there is little to mitigate their power or the crises they create. The two general areas of agreement that have emerged nearly everywhere are that personal freedoms should be safeguarded, and that the Earth's environment should be defended against further decline. Democracy and ecology, each providing a local context and plenty of concrete combat zones, are set against a cosmic backdrop. Whether in the struggle of nationalities or in the problems of deforestation and global warming, the interactions between individual identity (embodied in minor activities such as smoking, or using aerosol cans) and the general framework are tremendously direct, and the time-honoured conventions of art, history and philosophy do not seem well suited to them. Much of what was for four decades so exciting about Western modernism and its aftermath in, for example, the elaborate interpretative strategies of critical theory, or the self-consciousness of literary or musical forms, such as those of Eliot, Joyce and Stravinsky, seems almost quaintly abstract, desperately Eurocentric today. More reliable, in forms of art, are the reports from the front line, where struggles are being fought between domestic tyrants and idealist oppositions, hybrid combinations of realism and fantasy, cartographic and archaeological descriptions, explorations in mixed forms (essay, video or film, photograph, memoir, story or aphorism) of unhoused, exilic experiences.

The major task, then, is to match the new economic and socio-political dislocations and configurations of our time with the startling realities of human interdependence on a world scale, despite the fact that there is, as I say, in the North–South conflict a persistence of a kind of imperial world order. If the Japanese, East European, Islamic and Western instances express anything in common, it is that a new critical consciousness is needed, and this can be achieved only by revised attitudes to education and culture. Merely to urge our students to insist on their own identity, history, tradition, and uniqueness may initially get them to name their basic requirements for democracy and for the right to an assured, decently humane existence. But we need to go on to situate these in a geography of other identities, peoples, cultures. We then need to study how, despite their differences, they have always overlapped with each other through unhierarchical influence, crossing, incorporation, recollection, deliberate forgetfulness, and, of course, conflict.

We are nowhere near the 'end of history', as Fukuyama has called it, but we are still far from free of monopolising attitudes towards history. These have not been much good in the past, despite the rallying cries of the politics of separatist identity, multiculturalism, and minority discourse; and the quicker we teach ourselves to find alternatives, the better and the safer. The fact is, we are mixed in with each other in ways that most national systems of education have not dreamed of. To match knowledge in the arts and sciences with these integrative realities is, I believe, the intellectual and cultural challenge of moment, if there is to be an 'after-imperialism'.

The steady critique of nationalism, for example, which derives from the various theorists of liberation, should not be forgotten, for we must not condemn ourselves to repeat the imperial experience. How, in the redefined and yet very close contemporary relationship between culture and imperialism, a relationship that enables disquieting forms of domination, can we sustain the liberating energies released by the great decolonising resistance movements and the mass uprisings of the 1980s? Can these energies elude the homogenising processes of modern life? Can they hold in abeyance the interventions of the new imperial centrality?

'All things counter, original, spare, strange' says Gerard Manley Hopkins in 'Pied Beauty'. The question is, *where*? And where, too, we might ask, is there a place for that astonishingly harmonious vision of time intersecting with the timeless that occurs at the end of T.S. Eliot's poem 'Little Gidding', a moment that Eliot saw as words in

> An easy commerce of the old and new,
> The common word exact without vulgarity,
> The formal word precise but not pedantic,
> The complete consort dancing together.

The notion of Paul Virilio, the urbanologist I mentioned earlier, is counter-habitation. We must all try to live, he says, as migrants do, in habitually uninhabited but nevertheless public spaces, a metaphor for him of a kind of endless restlessness, not accepting a single identity. A similar notion occurs in *Mille Plateaux*, volume 2 of *Anti-Oedipus: Capitalism and Schizophrenia* by Gilles Deleuze and Félix Guatarri. A great deal of this immensely rich book is not easily accessible, but I have found it mysteriously suggestive. The chapter entitled 'A Treatise on nomadology', about being a nomad, sub-titled 'The war machine', builds on the work of Virilio by extending his ideas on movement and space to a highly eccentric study of an itinerant war machine. This quite original treatise contains a metaphor about a disciplined kind of intellectual mobility in an age of institutionalisation, regimentation and co-optation. The war machine can be assimilated, Deleuze and Guatarri say, to the military powers of the state. But since it is fundamentally a separate entity, it need not be, any more than the spirit's nomadic wanderings need always be, put at the service of institutions. The war machine's source of strength is not only its nomadic freedom but also its metallurgical art, by which materials are forged, fashioned they say, 'beyond separate forms; [this metallurgy, like music] stresses the continuing development of form itself, and beyond individually differing materials it stresses the continuing variation within matter itself'.[23] Precision, concreteness, continuity, form: all these have the attributes of a nomadic practice whose power, Virilio says, is not aggressive but transgressive.[24]

We can perceive this truth on the political map of the contemporary world. For surely it is one of the unhappiest characteristics of our age to have produced more refugees, migrants, displaced persons, and exiles than ever before in history, most of them as a corollary to and, ironically enough, as after-thoughts of, great post-colonial and imperial conflicts. As the struggles for independence produced new states and new boundaries, it also produced homeless wanderers, nomads, vagrants, people unassimilated to the emerging structures of institutional power, rejected by the established order for their intransigence and obdurate rebelliousness. In so far as these people exist between the old and the new, between the old empire and the new state, their condition articulates the tensions, irresolutions, and contradictions in the overlapping territories shown on the cultural map of empire.

There is, however, a great difference between the optimistic mobility, the intellectual liveliness and 'the logic of daring', on the one hand, and the massive dislocations, waste, misery and horrors endured in our century's migrations and mutilated lives on the other hand. Yet it is no exaggeration to say that liberation, as an intellectual mission, born in the resistance and opposition to the confinements and ravages of imperialism, has now shifted from the settled, established, and domesticated dynamics of culture to its unhoused, decentred, and exilic energies, energies whose incarnation today is the migrant, and whose consciousness is that of the intellectual and artist in exile, the political figure between domains, between forms, between homes and between languages. From this perspective all things are indeed 'counter, original, spare, strange'. From this perspective also one can see, as Eliot said, 'the complete consort dancing together'. While it would be the rankest dishonesty to say that the bravura performances of the intellectual exile and the miseries of the displaced person or refugee are the same thing – they are not – it is possible, I think, to regard the intellectual today as first distilling, and then articulating, the predicaments that disfigure modernity: mass deportation, imprisonment, population transfer, collective dispossession and forced immigrations. In other words, I think it important to look at that experience and use that experience as a model for getting beyond the mind-set of imperialism.

'The past life of *émigrés* is, as we know, annulled', says Theodor Adorno in *Minima Moralia*, which is subtitled 'Reflections from a Damaged Life'. Why? 'Because anything that is not reified, that cannot be counted and measured, ceases to exist',[25] or, as he says later, is consigned to mere 'background'. Although the disabling aspects of the fate of *émigrés* are manifest, its virtues or possibilities are worth exploring. Thus the *émigré* consciousness – 'a mind of winter' in the phrase of the great American poet Wallace Stevens – discovers in its marginality that 'a gaze averted from the beaten track, a hatred of brutality, a search for fresh concepts not yet encompassed by the general pattern, is the last hope for thought'.[26] Adorno's 'general pattern' is what, in another place, he calls the 'administered world', or, insofar as the irresistible dominants in culture are concerned, 'the consciousness industry'. He says we live in an imperial administered world, ruled by the consciousness industry, dominated of course by the media. There is, then, not just the negative advantage of refuge in the *émigré*'s eccentricity. There is also the positive benefit of challenging the system, describing it in language unavailable to those it has already subdued. We could say that this is a very small thing to do, although a few pages later Adorno expands the possibility of freedom from the system by prescribing a form of expression whose opacity, obscurity and deviousness move away from the dominant system, enacting in its 'inadequacy' a measure of liberation.

Most people would say, reading Adorno, that it is just too private, too special, too philosophical. Yet we can rediscover this form of liberation not only in the obdurately subjective, even negative, tortured philosophical phrases of Adorno, in his private, hermetic language, but also in the public accents of an Islamic intellectual like Ali Shariati, a prime force in the early days of the Iranian Revolution, when his attack on what he called 'the true, straight path, this smooth and sacred highway', which he calls organised orthodoxy, contrasted with the deviations of what he called constant migration:

> man, this dialectical phenomenon, is compelled to be always in motion . . . Man, then, can never attain a final resting place and take up residence in God . . . How disgraceful, then, are all fixed standards. Who can ever fix a standard? Man is a choice, a struggle, a constant becoming [and one has to note the exclusively masculine language]. Man [one can say man and woman] are infinite migration, migration within the self, from clay to God. Man [and woman] are migrants within [their] own souls.[27]

Here we have a genuine potential for an emergent non-coercive culture being presented, which in its awareness of the difficulties and the concrete steps that have to be taken – exactness without vulgarity, precision but not pedantry – shares the sense of a beginning which occurs in all genuinely radical efforts to start again:[28] for example, the tentative authorisation of feminine experience in Virginia Woolf's *A Room of One's Own*, or the fabulous re-ordination of time and character that gave rise to the divided generations in Salman Rushdie's *Midnight's Children*, or the remarkable universalising of the African-American experience as it emerges in such brilliant detail in Toni Morrison's novels *Tar Baby* and *Beloved*. The push, or tension, comes from the surrounding environment – the imperialist power that would otherwise compel you to disappear or to accept some miniature version of yourself as a doctrine to be passed out on a course syllabus. These are not new master discourses, strong new narratives, but, as in John Berger's programme, another way of telling. When photographs or texts are used merely to establish identity and presence, to give us merely representative images of *the* Woman or *the* Indian or *the* Briton, they enter what Berger calls 'a control system'. With their innately ambiguous, hence negative and anti-narrativist waywardness *not* denied, however, these photographs permit a new subjectivity to emerge. He describes here the pictures of their family carried by migrants, which become symbolic of what he calls 'fragile images, often carried next to the heart, or placed by the side of the bed, used to refer to that which historical time has no right to destroy'.[29]

From another perspective, the exilic, the marginal, subjective and migratory energies of modern life, which the liberationist struggles have deployed when these energies are too toughly resilient to disappear, have also emerged in what Immanuel Wallerstein calls 'anti-systemic movements'. Remember that the main feature of imperial expansion, historically, was accumulation, a process that accelerated during the twentieth century. Wallerstein's argument is that at bottom capital accumulation and territorial accumulation is irrational; its additive, acquisitive gains continue unchecked, even though its costs – in maintaining the process, in paying for wars to protect it, in 'buying off' and co-opting 'intermediate cadres', in living in an atmosphere of permanent crisis – are exorbitant, and not worth the gains. Thus, Wallerstein says, 'the very superstructure [of state power, and the national cultures that support the idea of state power] that was put in place to maximise the free flow of the factors of production in the world economy is the nursery of national movements that mobilise against the inequalities inherent in the world system'.[30] Those people compelled by the system to play subordinate, or imprisoning, roles within it emerge, therefore, as conscious antagonists, disrupting the system, proposing claims, advancing arguments that dispute the totalitarian compulsions of the world market. Not everything can be bought off.

To conclude, all these hybrid counter-energies at work in many fields, individuals and moments provide – in my opinion – an alternative community or culture made up of many anti-systemic hints and practices for collective human existence that is not based on coercion or the domination of empire. They fuelled the uprisings of the 1980s, which I mentioned earlier. The authoritative, compelling image of empire, which crept into and overtook so many procedures of intellectual mastery that are central in modern culture, finds its opposite in the renewable, almost sporty discontinuities of intellectual and secular impurities: mixed genres, unexpected combinations of tradition and novelty, political experiences based on communities of effort and interpretation (in the broadest sense of the word) rather than classes or corporations of possession, appropriation, and power.

I find myself returning again and again to a hauntingly beautiful passage by Hugo of St Victor, a twelfth-century monk from Saxony. He says (also speaking only in masculine terms):

> It is therefore a source of great virtue for the practised mind to learn, bit by bit, first to change about in visible and transitory things, so that afterwards it may be able to leave them behind altogether. The person who finds his homeland sweet is still a tender beginner; he to whom every soil is as his native one is already strong; but he is perfect to whom the entire world is as a foreign place. The tender soul has fixed his love on one spot in the world; the strong person has extended his love to all places; the perfect man has extinguished his.[31]

Erich Auerbach, the great German scholar who spent the years of the Second World War as an exile in Turkey, cites this passage as a model for anyone – man *and* woman – wishing to transcend the restraints of imperial or national or provincial limits. Only through this attitude can a historian, for example, begin to grasp human experience, and its written records, in all their diversity and particularity. Otherwise, one would remain committed more to the exclusions and reactions of prejudice than to the negative freedom of real knowledge. But note that Hugo twice makes it clear that the 'strong' or 'perfect' person achieves independence and detachment by *working through* attachments, not by rejecting them. Exile is predicated on the existence of, love for, and a real bond between, the human being and things. In Eliot's phrase, reality cannot be deprived of the 'other echoes [that] inhabit the garden'. It is more rewarding – and more difficult – to think concretely and sympathetically about others than only about 'us'. But this also means not trying to rule others, not trying to classify them or put them in hierarchies, above all not trying constantly to reiterate how 'our' culture or country is number one (or not number one, for that matter). For the intellectual today there is quite enough of value to do without that sort of pure patriotism and nationalism.

Edward Said's lecture formed part of the *Lux Europae* Education, Outreach and Events Programme, funded by Lothian Regional Council. It was delivered at the Playfair Library, the University of Edinburgh, on 4 November 1992.

The lecture was chaired by Professor Jill Forbes, Professor of French at the University of Strathclyde, Glasgow, and a response was given by Professor Yasir Suleiman, Professor of Islamic Studies, the University of Edinburgh.

PETER PALUMBO

6   *Vision of a new Europe*

IN HIS PREFACE TO *Literature and Dogma*, MATTHEW ARNOLD made two comments about culture. 'Culture', he said, 'is acquainting ourselves with the best that has been known and said in the world and thus with the history of the human spirit', and later, 'Culture is the passion for sweetness and light and (what is more) the passion for making them prevail.' These lofty sentiments may appear far removed from the current turbulence and lack of cultural focus that afflict late twentieth-century civilisation. But there is every reason to concentrate upon those things which, whatever the dizzying changes, remain as the fundamental immutable principles which the human spirit will always seek out in times of uncertainty.

It is a commonplace that during turbulence, in which it is difficult to see very far ahead, there is an instinctive search for the reassuring, the constant. In this search, the arts provide what Matthew Arnold described as 'sweetness and light'. It is significant that the Arts Council of Great Britain itself was born of just such a sensation. During the last war, when Western civilisation was under threat and there was in Britain a heightened awareness of the frailty of life, an enterprise designed to bring a little comfort became an enormous success. Maynard Keynes and others promoted the Council for the Encouragement of Music and the Arts (CEMA), whose object was, by means of the visual and performing arts, to raise the spirits, and spread cultural cheer.

Many musicians and others banded together and gave performances in unlikely, and often dangerous, locations, which brought for the first time to many the mysterious balm that only the arts can produce. So successful was the enterprise that the Arts Council was set up by Royal Charter after the war to build upon the hugely successful work of CEMA. To introduce the new body, Maynard Keynes went on the air and, in a radio broadcast in 1946, described both the artist and the purpose of the Arts Council in these terms:

> The artist walks where the breath of the spirit blows him. He cannot be told his direction; he does not know it himself. But he leads the rest of us into fresh pastures and teaches us to love and to enjoy what we often begin by rejecting, enlarging our sensibility and purifying our instincts.

and this:

> The purpose of the Arts Council of Great Britain is to create an environment, to breathe a spirit, to cultivate an opinion, to offer a stimulus to such purpose that the artist and the public can each sustain and live on the other in that union which has occasionally existed in the past at the great ages of a communal civilised life.

I know of no better description of the originality and importance of the artist, nor of the expectations or impact of the arts upon the civilised community.

In our own times the need for certainty and reassurance is just as great. The high hopes that flowed from the destruction of the Berlin Wall and the defeat of communism have given way to profound anxiety about the shape of the societies that are emerging from the chaos of the socialist vacuum. The uncovering of ancient animosities, the fierce tribal struggles for power and territory, the passionate reassertion of local and national identity, threaten the stability of Europe. It is little wonder that in these troubled times the arts should be the great illumination. I have always maintained that the artist is the most important individual in society, for the good and simple reason that, at its best, art is the highest achievement of the human spirit.

It is inescapable that the response to the arts is akin to religious impulse and that the two are inextricably entwined in the roots of European culture. In the Christian tradition, the references to light, and the frequency of the images of light as a means of communicating the infinite, are contained in some of the most wonderful phrases in the English language, such as this verse from Psalm 36: 'For with thee is the well of life: and in thy light shall we see light.'

That catches the sense of wonder that art can evoke; the effect sought after by the artist in his or her own way; the mysterious depth of creativity.

Whatever may be the complexities of the new political scene and the differences there may be upon how Europe should be developed, there can be no doubt at all about the importance of artists. The arts appeal across barriers of race, colour, creed, ideology and geographical circumstance. As ambassadors, the arts are infinitely more effective than the most skilled diplomat, because they do not have to plead a case or conduct negotiations. They speak for themselves. Just as, in the war, people from all backgrounds, educated or not in the arts, can hear the resonance of the infinite that the artist purveys.

It is true we are now in the period of profound scepticism abut what it is to be European, but on one subject there is no scepticism. That is that artists in every medium express the reality of our shared culture which can be understood, and enjoyed, without wounding debate.

The creation of a European City of Culture has had a great beneficial effect. Glasgow was that City in 1990. The concentration of effort and will, the stimulus that the enterprise created, gave a great boost to the Scottish artists who found themselves the recipients of the contemporary patronage that the European Commission could bestow. I am not sure that those who dreamed up the City of Culture had imagined what their brainchild could spawn. How could they fully appreciate the fertile imagination and drive of the Scots, particularly when Brussels gold was raining down upon them.

The happy by-product of that year as City of Culture is a thriving tourist industry – and I bear in mind that for each visitor to the Burrell Collection, something like an average of £36 per head is generated in the ancillary activities of travelling, eating, hotels and the buying of souvenirs and catalogues.

It seemed to the Arts Council that the Glasgow initiative must be built upon. We accordingly initiated the 'Arts 2000' project. A city, town or region is nominated each year, between now and the millennium, to celebrate a particular art form. Birmingham is the City of Music this year, and has triumphantly inaugurated the project. The by-product of the celebration of the art form in question, as in Glasgow in 1990, is the concentration that it produces upon the place concerned and the generation of local pride. Glasgow and Birmingham attract people from all parts of this country, and all parts of Europe and new life and vitality are generated wherever a particular medium is celebrated.

It is clear to me that there is a great hunger for things spiritual in every degree. In every part of Britain there are exhibitions, concerts, literature festivals, poetry festivals, music, dance and drama festivals. There is much more concern for the maintenance of our culture than at any time I can remember.

In much the same way, the enterprise of *Lux Europae* must be built upon. In times of stringency, a great festival of this kind is precisely the way to generate sweetness, through light. But it would be an enormous waste of creativity if the investment was not to produce by-products, such as Arts 2000. I can hear the whispered criticism that careful, artistic creations of light and lighting material are essentially ephemeral, and how can we justify such extravagance at a time of economic uncertainty? That is not, for us, the question. The only question that must be asked of any artistic creation is the impact of its creative excellence, even if it has only the brief life of an image upon the sand drawn by Picasso to be washed away by the next tide. For one moment the authentic print of artistic genius was there, visible, unique; the talent that produced it could, and did, produce similar images in a permanent medium.

I hope that the talent of the artists who have contributed to the success of *Lux Europae* will be encouraged and publicised in every possible way, so that they may illuminate other places, and leave a vivid imprint there.

At last the arts are accepted as nationally crucial and are fully upon the political agenda. Government funding to the Arts Council is, in the present year, almost £221 million. The fact is that the arts are an enormously successful national business, quite apart from their being vital to national cultural identity. The total money expended by central and local government on the arts, libraries, museums and galleries in Britain is approximately £1 bn a year, which is 0.25% of total public expenditure. The total business of the arts, that is to say all those enterprises in which the arts are practised and performed, and all ancillary businesses and agencies which are directly concerned with an artistic enterprise, mass £13 bn in turnover in one year. Of this, £6 bn directly contributes to the balance of payments, compared, for example, with £4 bn from the motor industry.

The British Government earns from the arts, through tourism, taxation, VAT, a *great* deal more than it spends directly on encouraging the arts. Statistics are not necessarily always illuminating, but for the purposes of this lecture they shine with great intensity. If the arts, by their inspirational quality, illuminate in the spiritual sense, they certainly shine extremely brightly in the firmament of our national economy.

It would be folly to restrict the amount expended on the arts in this way because, even on the simplest level of value for money, the argument is compelling. I know that there is much discussion about the way the figures are made up, but however you put them together the total effect is inescapable. The arts are described as an industry, but an industry with a warmly beating heart whose life blood to extend that image is the abundant talent which is the generating factor upon which the whole structure depends.

To restrict development of the arts and their success and their impact upon national life, at this time of all times, would be foolish and purblind. I profoundly hope that vision and good sense will overcome the call of the short-term expedient.

It is no coincidence that there is now a Cabinet Minister with responsibility for the arts and a Department of State to promote the arts. They are no longer simply the optional, or recreational, choice of the privileged or educated; they are seen as a vital resource to be available for everyone. There is currently in Britain an intense debate about how the arts should be managed; what the strategy for them should be; how the resources should be deployed; whether they should be deployed centrally or locally. The debate is also concentrating upon the role of the great national companies.

It is not seen as simply vain-glorious to have a Royal National Opera and Ballet House, but essential to Britain's cultural standing, to maintain and exploit the quality of its own national talent in these matters. Similarly, the Royal National Theatre, the Royal Shakespeare Company, the English National Opera, all contribute enormously to the quality of national, cultural life. The debate is now not whether such flagships should be maintained, but how best they are to be maintained.

This is a debate not wholly appreciated by some of Britain's European neighbours, because for them the arts are the endorsement of national pride. The British are more reticent, more cautious. But there is now a marvellous opportunity to brighten the mood by making sure that great national companies can not only survive, but thrive, attracting new audiences, and taking their products abroad, as Britain welcomes productions from other countries. *Lux Europae* should illumine the landscape of shared artistic experience. The more we play to, sing to, dance to, each other, the more we will cross-pollinate the true seeds of a shared European experience. The distrust and cynicism which bedevils the political debate could be dispelled, or at any rate alleviated, in the surge and flow of the arts across Europe. In Scotland, of course, the point need hardly be made, because Scots have always been international in outlook, and adventurous.

It is devoutly to be hoped that the President of the European Commission is not faced, as Voltaire once was, by an angry English crowd of xenophobes bent upon hanging him, until he charmed away their wrath by saying 'Men of England! You wish to kill me because I am a Frenchman. Am I not punished enough in not being born an Englishman?' If our cultural links are strong, the unity of purpose which often eludes politicians could be found in the mutual enjoyment of those things of the spirit that the arts so readily nourish.

Similarly, in Europe, we must jointly consider how we can shape and influence the natural and built environment of which we have become so very conscious. What should we preserve? What should we build? How do we construct the monuments in this generation to represent the quality of our culture in the next? In architecture, above all, the most obtrusive, noticeable and assertive of the arts, it is vital that the talent available, in Britain or elsewhere, be encouraged. It is vital that we strike an intelligent balance between preserving the best that we have inherited, and making room for the creation of the best in our own generation. A society which decides that the time has come to undertake no more building is a society which has run out of creative energy. In our society today there is abundant artistic talent which we must cherish; if we do so, we will give our children and grandchildren a culture fit to inherit.

The buildings I hope we can create will, in their own authentic way, catch something of the excitement that our brilliant modern technological skills can create. Will we create buildings to excite and move; to ravish the eye and catch the breath and generate that sensation of pure excitement that is felt at, say, Chartres or Durham? Will a modern army of foot soldiers, probably tourists, fall down in astonishment before any buildings we create as did Napoleon's foot soldiers at the great Temple of Karnak in 1798 at the height of the Egyptian Campaign?

They were ordinary, uneducated, men but faced by the wonder of the place and its extraordinary images, they rejoiced with music and applause. That is what architecture can do; that is what the arts at their best can do.

Wherever and whenever they achieve such quality, a new element is added to the international language of the arts. This can only be achieved by encouraging all our artists, by allowing them to fail, and giving them the opportunities that *Lux Europae* offered with the help of the European Commission, Lothian Regional Council, the Scottish Arts Council, the City of Edinburgh District Council, Lothian and Edinburgh Enterprise Ltd – contemporary patrons all. The notion of staging a sculpture Biennale in Edinburgh was translated into *Lux Europae*, a temporary exhibition designed to illuminate the winter gloom in Edinburgh, and to celebrate the build-up to the Edinburgh EC Summit: here was expediency cunningly adopted by artistic enterprise.

This is what modern patronage should be about. In Britain, we need to extend our patronage by all means. In our plurally funded English arts world we must allow the government's input, whether from central or local government, to be supplemented by the private sector, be it personal or commercial. Every encouragement is needed, both fiscal and by government example, to give substance to the new enthusiasm for the arts. Britain needs the support of all its European partners in exploiting the distinct appeal of the arts, and truly treating the artist as the most important individual in our midst.

What a prospect for the millennium, if we placed our disparate talents at the disposal of all those throughout Europe who hunger and thirst for spiritual comfort. Nowhere is this more important than in those parts of Europe that are struggling to come to terms with the new post-communist reality. Notions of freedom of choice, human dignity, respect for person are the raw material of artistic creativity; they can articulate a response to anarchy, and temper its terrible capacity to recreate, out of chaos, replicas of older, and more terrible, repressive regimes. Where the artist is free to express talent, there must exist the tolerance that is the enemy of totalitarianism, of whatever stamp or hue.

The arts are a vital means of creating anything approximating to a civilised society. *Lux Europae* should not be simply an attractive, exhilarating show of light and sweetness – but a beacon which can shine elsewhere. That is my vision for the new European perspective in the arts: a group of nation states, united by common civilised standards, diverse in the expression of artistic talent, tolerant of that diversity, permitting the artist freedom, freedom of choice, freedom of expression, and freedom to fail and try again. Then, we can endorse Matthew Arnold's plea that there should be passion for sweetness and light, passion to make them prevail. Passion for a true European culture can realise the call of Goethe, that great artist of the Enlightenment, and make his alleged last words, 'more light', a living reality.

Lord Palumbo's lecture formed part of the *Lux Europae* Education, Outreach and Events Programme, funded by Lothian Regional Council. It was delivered at the Fruitmarket Gallery, Edinburgh, on 11 November 1992. *Lux Europae*, an official event of the European Arts Festival, was an exhibition of light works by artists from the Twelve Member States of the European Community staged in Edinburgh from 22 October 1992 to 5 January 1993.

The lecture was chaired by Sheena MacDonald, broadcaster, and a response was given by the Hon. Lord Prosser, Chairman, Royal Fine Art Commission for Scotland.

JOHN SIMPSON

7   *Politics and the new Europe*

I WENT OUT YESTERDAY AND BOUGHT THE *Times Atlas of the World*. I thought I owed it to myself. It cost me £85 and is a heavy and entirely new volume. It has on it a little label describing it as 'The New Nations Edition' which I thought was a rather nice idea: every time there is a new nation, you bring out a new atlas. The first time that the *Times Atlas of the World* was introduced to the world was in 1922 when there were many new nations. They could have very adequately put 'New Nations Edition' on the cover then, because new nations had been churned out with the frequency and sometimes with the awkwardness of new dolls from a doll-making factory, an extraordinary time of 'the making of nations'.

It was Thomas Hardy, the great poet of the pre First World War period, who wrote in 1914 a poem entitled 'In the Time of "The Breaking of Nations"'. The period from 1919 onwards was, however, a time of the making of nations and Lord Northcliffe, the originator of Lord Copper and all sorts of other horror stories, said 'A world remade must be a world remapped.' It was suitable that a man may see in the changing world the chance to make a quick buck, but nevertheless he was the proprietor of *The Times* (fortunately not for very long) and he launched the Atlas 1922 edition with some satisfaction.

I looked at that edition side by side with my brand new 1992 edition and also looked at the 1978 edition. That was not a time of either the making or breaking of nations, but the time of just simply assuming that nations were going to stay exactly as they were for the indefinite future. The 1978

edition listed 165 countries including such old 'time pieces' as
Rhodesia, the Central African Empire, the Territory of the Afars
and Issars, which I have always wanted, but never managed, to
get to, and other names which have, alas, gone the way of the
Kingdom of the Two Sicilies, as well as other places that we
know from the past which had, of course, also gone from the
Times Atlas of 1922. Iran was still a monarchy; Spain had just
become one not long before; Ethopia had recently (in 1978)
ceased to be a monarchy; Afghanistan had too, under rather
different circumstances. China's population was 852 million
and the USSR, as it then was, covered an area of 8.6 million
square miles with a population of 280 million people.

The definitive account given in the 1992 *Times Atlas of the
World* has changed most of that. There are 21 more countries
than in 1978, which is not a bad rate of production. China's
population is now 1,088 million, 200 million more than it was
in 1978. The Russian Federation by contrast covers 2 million
square miles less than it did in 1978 and has a population of
112 million people fewer. Of course there have been a number
of amalgamations: Germany, Yemen, Vietnam very probably,
possibly Korea quite soon. Of course, it's no coincidence
that each one of these countries – Germany, Yemen, Korea,
Vietnam – each thinking about or actually moving together
and combining, is a country with a Marxist–Leninist past of
some kind. My central point is that the period since 1989 has
been the period in which one of the great pillars of our world
has simply disappeared. It has crumbled away so fast that some
of us have almost forgotten what it was like under the old
system. We have become so used to a constant changing scene
of new leaders, new policies, new attitudes, new alliances that
we have almost forgotten in this spate of change what life was
like a matter of only a few years ago.

That was a world which used to make us somewhat afraid.
'Mutually assured destruction' was the name of that particular
type of extremely disturbing game, the notion that something
only had to go slightly wrong and the entire world would suffer

the consequences, not as it suffered the consequences in 1914 or 1939 but in a very different and much more frightening way.

My childhood, in the 1950s and early 1960s, was spent under the shadow of the planning and the careful forethought of people like Dr Herman Kahn (the Dr Strangelove of nuclear planning), a figure I don't suppose anybody much remembers now. The notion existed that there were stages which each superpower would follow which would lead slowly towards the policy of mutually assured destruction, which we all remembered by its acronym, MAD. No single piece could move on the entire world board without affecting in some small, or sometimes large, way the pattern of relationships between two super-powers, essentially between two men and their advisers. If the USSR switched from Somalia to Ethopia as it did in the late 1970s and decided that one was more of a people's republic than the other, then the tremors were felt in Washington. If Portugal gave up its African colonies, then the world saw some more 'People's Democracies' and the American President of the day was regarded as having 'lost' those pieces.

The world essentially had two players sitting opposite each other and the changes, the decisions, of relatively few people could alter one's entire perception of the world. In 1978 and 1979 Jimmy Carter 'lost' Iran, as was often said in Washington at the time; he had already 'lost' Angola, he nearly 'lost' Zaire (perhaps not a bad loss) and he had altogether 'lost' Afghanistan on Boxing Day 1979. The US seemed critically weakened by those obscure places in the *Times Atlas*, places you had to look up for yourself to discover where they were. It paralleled what became known as 'The Great Game' in the nineteenth century, when Britain and Russia faced each other across Central Asia, capturing or taking over or whatever you might choose to call it, obscure desert cities that nobody had seriously heard of outside the pages of a poetry book: Bukhara, Samarkand, Khiva, Merv. These places would be regarded as altering the balance of power in the world. It was the same during the 1950s, the 1960s in particular and the 1970s, countries starting to move from one side of the ledger to the other side of the ledger.

This old balance of power was extremely delicate or seemed to us to be extremely delicate. One of the things I want to argue throughout this lecture is that the dangers that we perceive are often not the dangers which actually come upon us. I think that is an important thing to bear in mind at a time when there seem to be so many dangers surrounding us. The danger which came to absolutely nothing, at any stage, and which we endured for 30 years, was the danger on the one hand of mutually assured destruction and the on other hand that, if there was not going to be nuclear war, perhaps the West's interest might be chipped away. We might be losing 'the world' bit by bit. Well, we didn't really lose the world and we didn't suffer the kind of fate that our fears might have led us to believe.

As time went on and the awfulness of Stalin faded a little bit in Eastern Europe, though Hungary in 1956 amd Czechoslovakia in 1968 kept the memory going, it became fashionable – particularly on the left – to see the United States and the Soviet Union, the two players at the chess board, as being in some way mirror images of each other, both rather large, unpleasant bruisers, each of them capable of doing quite unpleasant things to small countries which were close by to them and which came within their sphere of influence. The two of them kept each other going, they needed each other.

I felt this very strongly at times in my more leftward days and it's only now, I think, that one can see that really it was partly, but not seriously, like that. In the long run, that pattern that we had come to expect – that there were only two players in the game, that only two could play – was a pattern which was temporary and not permanent. As we know from past ages, empires do not last. There is a passage in Francis Bacon who, although he didn't really see any empires collapse in his time, wrote in 'On the Vicissitude of Things':

For great empires while they stand do enervate and destroy the forces of the natives which they have subdued resting upon their own prospective forces, and then when they [the empires] fail also all goes to ruin and they become a prey. So it was in the decay of the Roman Empire and likewise in the Empire of Almayne [presumably Germany after Charles the Great], every bird taking a feather.

This is a great phrase or concept describing exactly what we have now started to see. But the important thing is that, although Francis Bacon didn't have any particularly modern examples to consult writing in the 1590s or the early part of the seventeenth century, he did appreciate that basic rule which we forgot in the 1950s, 1960s and 1970s, which is that empires are essentially mortal; the structure of them cannot withstand long periods of time. An individual nation state can survive because its members have something greater in common but an empire of the kind that we saw in Soviet terms and indeed in American terms in its Western European aspect, those empires had nothing to hold them together except simply the political desires at the centre of the empire. When those political desires change or the economic circumstances change, then the empires start to dissolve, and every bird takes a feather. What we are seeing now is a lot of feathers and a lot of birds.

For the once powerful and independent countries of Europe, which had been so damaged in two world wars, near absolute obedience was required on both sides of the dividing line. Hungary wanted to break with the Warsaw Pact in 1956 and that forced Khrushchev – as he saw it – to invade. The same thing happened in 1968 in Czechoslovakia which wanted to leave the Warsaw Pact, or seemed to be about to in spite of its assurances, and so Brezhnev felt he had no alternative but to invade. On the western side of the line things were never, of course, anywhere near so ferocious. Nevertheless when France, for instance, pulled out of the integrated military structure of NATO it shook the entire structure. It was a very difficult step for the Americans to have to put up with and probably only a

de Gaulle could have done it. West Germany's *Ostpolitik* in the
1970s worried the Americans – and not only the Americans –
very greatly because it seemed like a leaking away of value and
virtue from the West. Too much closeness in the middle was
perhaps a little bit too reminiscent of the troops at Christmas
1914 playing football in no man's land. It wasn't a good idea;
you had to keep the lines clear, it was felt, otherwise the players
might start to lose the game.

It is important to remember how powerful this structure
was only the day before yesterday. My first view of the Berlin
Wall, actually seeing the Wall at night for the first time, was
something I shall never forget. I approached it carrying two
enormous suitcases, sweating, nervous, watching the search
lights playing on that strange patch of no man's land in between
the two sections of Wall, knowing that there were automatic
guns there, for which Eric Honneker is now on trial, knowing
that people were watching and there was a very large camera
which very noticeably, intentionally noticeably, photographed
you as you came towards it; people then checked your face
against known files to see if you were a character that they
wanted to let in. You were treated extremely unpleasantly
and, having entered one side of the Friedrichstrasse in West
Berlin, you came out into a different society, about 25 yards
further on, along the same street. This was a different world
where there was a system of government that was supported
by a police state, a system where it was every citizen's duty to
inform on every other citizen who wasn't doing his job right,
a system where you could not go to university, for instance,
if your cousin or uncle had done or said something wrong.

A very different economic system operated too. Just crossing
those few yards from one end of the Friedrichstrasse to another
was like going back to the late 1940s, to a society which was grey
and grim, where there wasn't very much electricity. It always
seemed to me afterwards that all the electricity seemed to be
drawn out of East Berlin in order to fire up those enormous
arc lights that shone along the wall, just to make sure that

nobody crossed them or, if they did so, it was in bright light so that they could be shot at will.

It really was a very powerful system indeed. If anybody had suggested to me when I crossed the Wall first in 1979 that nothing more than a brief touch would break through that extraordinarily thin crust I don't think I would have believed them. I don't think that anybody really would have believed this was possible except perhaps the most extreme form of right-wing supporter in the West, because it seemed to people like me, who felt we knew what Eastern Europe was, that although it was clear people didn't support the regime strongly in any sense they weren't prepared to do anything about it. We saw those brief upsurges in East Germany in 1953, in Hungary in 1956 and Czechoslovakia in 1968; we saw them as being what we longed to see throughout the whole Eastern bloc but knew nobody would dare to execute in any kind of coordinated way. We saw them as people either being goaded beyond endurance, in Hungary and Germany, or else in Czechoslovakia doing it out a naive belief that Marxism–Leninism could be given a human face.

This gave people like me in particular the feeling that, although it was a society we didn't like, it was a society that we had to live with, that we had to accept. We could criticise it, of course, and it was right to criticise it but it wasn't right constantly to question the basis of it. I look back to that period, the late 1970s and the early 1980s, with a certain amount of shame because I don't think that we really kept the torch burning as we should have done, as we would have liked to have done, given the way things were. I think a lot of us felt we were doing the right thing because, by regarding Eastern bloc countries and the Soviet Union as being the correct and acceptable and worthwhile interlocutors for any kind of peace negotiations between East and West, we had to take them seriously; we couldn't constantly question the basis on which Soviet troops were in Eastern Europe. We couldn't question the basis on which long-established mercantile societies could have been turned overnight in the 1940s into Marxist–Leninist states where the ordinary commercial relations of people ceased to have the same values as they had had in those societies for 1,000 years. I think one has nowadays to look back on the world of the day before yesterday in a way which is self-critical because I think in a sense the wrong people were defending the right issues. The people who defended them tended to be the far right, not even the centre right, and they were doing it in a way which, with hindsight, was not acceptable; and, on a broader level, we should have supported the sense that what had happened in Eastern Europe was an illegal assumption.

This shows how the passage of time can change our approach to these things. As late as 1956, most people in the West would have regarded what had happened in Eastern Europe as unacceptable – Hungary really reinforced that very powerfully in that year. But it was in the 1960s and 1970s, when things weren't changing very much in Eastern Europe but we felt nevertheless that they were becoming more acceptable to us, that we sat down and believed that what they were doing was acceptable. I feel quite strongly about this nowadays and I look back at what I used to write then with some doubt and some self-questioning.

So how did it all come to an end? In about February 1990 I went back to Berlin to see a man called Guenthor Schabowski who was a very important member of the East German politbureau during the last stages of the East German state. He lived in a rather small, nicely furnished flat, overlooking the Berlin Wall. I really took to Guenthor Schabowski, a man who wanted to change things and didn't simply want to accept the old system as it was, believing that it was possible to give Marxism–Leninism a human face. As part of that, in the latter stages of the crisis that had come upon East Germany, the crisis in which people were leaving in vast quantities and the pressure was growing for others to be able to leave, he and his colleagues decided to make it possible for people simply to cross the Wall without the necessary visa requirements that they had always had. At 7 o'clock on the night of 9 November 1989 Guenthor Schabowski had gone into a press conference at which he was going to announce the latest decisions of the politbureau. At first it was plain that the man was under some pressure, under some stress. There was a vast congress of about 400 or 500 journalists, he was sweating heavily, his hands were shaking a little bit, it was all going out live on East German television and being watched in the West as well. He went through a number of extraordinarily dreary decisions that had been taken, decisions about the new philosophy of the party, about the new forthcoming congress of the party; then there was a pause and everyone felt a little bit embarrassed and shifted in their seats. He seemed to be messing around with his papers and he said 'I have got one other thing to tell you.' Everybody went quiet and he said 'Today the decision was made to make it possible for all citizens to leave the country through the official border crossing posts. This order is to take effect at once – *unverzueglich.*' It had an extraordinary impact, people standing up, shouting out questions. Somehow the way that it was announced seemed to be as extraordinarily exciting, as dramatic, as the fact that he was announcing it. Afterwards, quite serious people in East Germany would say that somebody whom nobody knew had handed him a piece of paper at the last moment; he had read this out though he didn't know what the piece of paper contained and nobody had ever seen the person before. I spoke to somebody, a communist of many years standing, who said it was 'the finger of God' that opened the Wall that night. I said 'But you don't believe in God', and he said 'I believe that the Wall was opened by the finger of God that night, whatever else I believe.'

So I went to see Schabowski three months after these events to find out what it was that had happened that night, the night that had opened not only the Berlin Wall but also the various societies in Eastern Europe, had opened up Czechoslovakia, had opened up Romania in a rather different and more violent way, and had indeed encouraged the Hungarians and the Poles and everybody else to continue along the line that they were already following. And, of course, you will be astounded to know the manner of the announcement was all a terrible mistake; he had lost the papers, he couldn't think what he had done with them, they had been on the top when he came into the room, he was nervous, he had stuck them at the back, he knew they would be somewhere and he waited until the end to reveal this news: sad end of miracle. Indeed, it's not regarded by most Germans now as being very much of a miracle at all; you won't find them talking about the finger of God now, but at the time they were, if you recall, extremely buoyed up.

It struck me as being a very suitable way for such a strange set of experiences to be foisted on the human race, that we should see people lifting themselves up by their own efforts and making themselves free. I would particularly like that to be true in Czechoslovakia because Czechoslovakia is a country for which I have a great love, and always have had during the dark, depressing days, as well as during the good days. I was there at the time when Alexander Dubček came out and the crowds welcomed him for the first time since 1969. I wouldn't like anyone to forget that The Song of Comenius was sung, the old official anthem of the Czech nation which says 'May disputes and envy fade, may the governing of your affairs come back to you, at last, my nation.' To hear those words sung on a night when a very frail Alexander Dubček was standing there in front of a crowd of possibly 1 million people was some thing that not many of us will forget. At a time when Alexander Dubček is only newly in his grave, it is a good time to think about that as well.

But I have to say to you that a Parliamentary Commission, not very much reported on in the West, found that in fact the great freedom of Czechoslovakia seems to have been planned for them by the KGB and by their own much loved Internal Security Organisation, the STB. It all seems to have been carefully worked out in something like September, possibly August, of 1989 that the best thing for the Soviet Union would be for Czechoslovakia to have a new government which was not the old hard-line, tough-guy characters who had little sympathy with Mikhail Gorbachev but somebody more acceptable, both to the Soviet Union and to the Czechoslovak people – let it not be said that secret police are always the most anti-democractic elements in any society; they are often not. So the plan was worked out by a gentleman called General Alois Lorens, head of the STB, who worked this out in conjunction with his KGB opposite number and the KGB Deputy Chairman, Viktor Grushkov, who came and had dinner with him on the night of 17 November. That night, in an extraordinary plot which I don't think has ever been properly reported, the KGB's candidate (as it were) for the new government of the country was identified and the process by which the Czechoslovak system started to collapse was got under way.

It was done in an extraordinary manner. A lieutenant in the STB led a group of demonstrators down into a blind alley where they could only be attacked by the security police. They were beaten up by the security police and then this lieutenant himself, Lieutenant Zivčak, fell to the ground pretending to be dead. One of his colleagues put a blanket over his head, he was taken away in full sight of everybody to an unmarked ambulance and driven off and the word put round that he was dead. As word went out people were horrified. 17 November was an extremely important date in Czech history, the 50th Anniversary of the shooting of a Czech student when the Germans entered Prague in 1939. For the Czech Government and its agents to have killed a student who was protesting and demanding a more open society brought people out in great anger on to the streets, not violent anger but peaceable and very determined anger. Even when it became clear that the man had not died, that he had pretended to be somebody who in fact was clearly alive and went on television to prove it, it was too late. As the KGB and the STB had worked out in advance, tempers were raised, the crowds grew, it became impossible to hold them back and it didn't work out quite the way that the KGB would have liked. Neither the system nor the crowds in the street were prepared to settle for somebody who was merely half way to being a democrat. They weren't prepared to settle for somebody who simply wanted Marxism–Leninism with a human face; they wanted the real thing and they got the real thing.

If you think I might be making this up, I have to say that I have read the Parliamentary Commission's report into the whole incident in which they not only interviewed the lieutenant from the STB who pretended to be dead but also they questioned the General who planned the whole episode. Not a bad little coup really, except it didn't work from their point of view. Now I wonder, when I look at what happened next door in Romania, whether that might also have been a little bit planned. It was awfully useful that it should have worked precisely as the KGB in Moscow would have liked, since an ex-communist came into power in Romania and all sorts of strange things happened there, but there has been no Parliamentary Commission to investigate this and I don't suppose that there will be any such thing while President Iliescu is in power.

Finally, of course, the wave of demand for freedom reached Moscow itself. There again I was fortunate enough to be outside the Russian Parliament, although you won't find many people now saying they weren't outside the Russian Parliament. On a Tuesday night, the second day of the three days of this absurd coup, I remember that there were only about 120 people defending the Russian Parliament; a well-armed platoon could have done for them and chased them off. But that is not in the nature of revolutions.

I have been fortunate enough to see one or two of them and they succeed because the old system has lost its way to such an extent that it is not prepared to defend itself. We saw this in Iran. We have seen this in a number of other places, where genuine popular revolt can snap through that very thin line of defence which the old system is prepared to put up. There was no armed platoon which was prepared to go and clear out the White House. So, fortunately, we are not left with the reality of the thing, we are not left with the notion that the KGB organised what I regard as one of the noblest processes I have ever witnessed, which was the revolution in Czechoslovakia. We don't recall that there were only 120 people who were prepared to stand up and be counted on a wet, rainy August night in Moscow; but we do accept that a lot of people wanted it to be and therefore it was. We need to have these myths of our own importance and significance in affairs; we need to have that sense that our own actions as free men and women can change things.

What I would like to turn to now is the effect of those myths on the way that we exist, that sense that at least we, the free peoples of the world, were able to break through the old system which had two chess players facing one another across the table. Of course the world is a very dangerous and nasty place at the moment. There is no questioning that. Some times it could almost be the 1930s, with slumps or potential slumps, with crowds of Germans out on the streets, storming the streets, storming buildings, breaking windows, throwing things at their lawful President. We could see Russia in turmoil with the weaponry going to God knows who. We see the European Community, which after all was created to take advantage of the moment when the superpowers ceased to be the superpowers, in turmoil, and, given Europe's history in this devastating century, one might be tempted to think that another cycle of disaster was about to begin.

A lot of very well-informed people think that is happening but I don't agree. I don't think we are back in the 1930s; even the economic circumstances are not at all similar. What is happening in what used to be Yugoslavia is an appalling affront to all of us and certainly to the people who run European foreign policy, but there is no Austria waiting to snap up Bosnia as it did in 1908. There is no likelihood of a war in which, for instance, countries will move in and regard the warring factions as their potential allies in a nasty little conflict as perhaps we could say was the case in Abyssinia in the 1930s, or indeed in Spain, where countries were gearing themselves up to get involved and prepare themselves for a wider war. This is not taking place. If Yugoslavia had blown up when Tito died in 1980 it might indeed have caused us to move down that terrifying road to mutually assured destruction. It simply hasn't been like that. It's been a little war, vicious and evil, but carried out within the confines of the old Yugoslavia.

Although the European Community is clearly in bad shape, its very future isn't in question. It's merely the speed and direction of its future that is in question. One problem has been that economic and monetary union always seems to come up at the wrong time in the international cycle. It came up in 1972 and people committed themselves then to it. By 1980, it fell at the very first hurdle, which was the oil crisis of the 1970s and now, no doubt, we will not get economic and monetary union in exactly the way that the Maastricht Treaty envisaged. But it has to be said that this is a British problem; it is not necessarily a French problem, not necessarily a German problem now; it is a question of Britain's relationship to this new Europe. The difficulty will be Britain's if it doesn't go along with the system but the system will move along in a slow sort of way. The system will move along in such a way as to ensure the relative prosperity of the people of Western Europe and, the more I think about it, the more I am convinced that it is that sense of relative prosperity which is the important thing because it gives people a sense that their lives are becoming better. It was precisely for those reasons, precisely for the very basic and ordinary reason that they weren't getting the kind of things that they wanted and not for any very elevated reason, that people in Czechoslovakia, and indeed even in Romania, came out onto the streets. It even brought the Russians onto the streets because they felt that life was not being run as they wanted it to be and they wanted a better existence.

New nations can indeed mean greater nationalism, but the

second point I want to argue is that, when nationalism comes to the fore, as it is at the moment ('every bird taking a feather' in Bacon's phrase), this is not necessarily the kind of nationalism that most of us were brought up to disapprove of, to dislike; that is the nationalism of the 1930s. In the 1930s, the nationalistic instinct in people was seized upon and used as an engine to drive through the old and inadequate structures which were created mostly by Woodrow Wilson and his colleagues after the First World War. It was the result of the Treaty of Versailles and the other peace treaties that followed. So here again, I think, what we are talking about is not a process of Hitlerian intensity, even when people are smashing windows and demanding that refugees should go home or be returned to their homes. We are not seeing a return to the 1930s in the terms that most of us have always been afraid of. It is a different sense; it's an unruliness, a vat of liquid boiling away, but it is not, I would suggest, a process which is going to go further and threaten the new structures of Europe. The dangers are different, the dangers are much more regional, much nastier in many ways than anything we have seen in the last 30 or 40 years, but they are not dangers which are going to spill over into other countries. I don't mean to say that civil war is a 'nicer' form of war than other wars, but it is certainly much less dangerous if other countries do not get involved. With the disappearance of one superpower and the increasing withdrawal of another superpower, it is no longer the kind of chess game I was talking about earlier, the kind of game where if a town in Yugoslavia falls one way it can seem to weaken the West, if it falls another way it can seem to weaken the East.

We are living in a different world now: a world where there are so many centres it is difficult to point to let alone name many of them. There is no doubting the sense of awareness of the national instincts, that after all was what one of the more noble aspects of Marxism and Leninism set out to prevent. It was extremely noble for Tito to have tried to weld together the people of Yugoslavia into Yugoslavs, yet there is nobody now who regards themselves as being a Yugoslav; a few months of violent upsurge has persuaded people that they are Bosnians or Serbs, or they are Muslims or Christians, or they are whatever particular badge of a particular tribe it happens to be safe to assume, because we are talking about tribalism, rather than nationalism. We are talking about the kind of thing that people from Northern Ireland know, where it is safe to have one type of accent or to worship in one particular type of way, or to have one particular type of surname, and it's not safe to have another if you live in a certain area.

A savage, vicious little process has opened up and the departure from the world stage of the old, in some ways reassuring, powers who nevertheless could kill each other if things went wrong, has meant that these kinds of savageries are able to emerge, not as world threatening but as local, regional savageries. It's not nice, but it isn't necessarily going to threaten the lives of anybody outside that area.

Nationalism this century has been an ugly feature in many ways. I believe that what we are seeing now is the froth on the surface of the creation of the new states. The time of the making of nations can be a dangerous time but it doesn't have to be a long-term danger. I think it can be a temporary danger. The end of the empires in Europe should mean opportunity, not simply for the nasty little demagogues but for the statesmen, and it is as well for us not to panic. The barbarians are not at the gate; the danger is not that we are going to be invaded, not that our standards of living are going to be taken down by outsiders but that our standards of living will decay from the inside and the kind of stresses which we always see at times of economic decay will come up in that sense.

There are of course thousands and thousands of other dangers. I was in Central Asia for a few weeks and I was looking round some of the old former Soviet military bases there. The weaponry is in an absolutely appalling condition: rockets rusting, covered with cobwebs, machinery incapable of being used, the guards unarmed, not even having the petrol to be able to drive from one part of their compound to another; the place is simply open for terrorists to take it over. If it was true in that one case I am certain it is true in all sorts of other cases. Nevertheless there is nobody to take these bases over as things stand. It is states that take over that kind of weaponry, not individuals, but only individuals are around at the moment to take advantage of that.

So what lessons can we, should we, learn? Marxism–Leninism regarded itself as a system for regenerating the human condition and we saw what happened to it. It became a system for keeping in power rather large, elderly men in grey suits and wide ties. It became a system which simply reinforced itself, rather than creating the kind of societies which the people that served those governments wanted. We are now seeing not just the break-up of Stalin's order but also of Woodrow Wilson's, the end of the peace treaties that followed the First World War. We see this in Czechoslovakia and Romania, in a host of other countries, not least of which is Yugoslavia. It's sad in some ways, but it cannot be stopped. If people want these things (and I am sorry to sound sentimental about this) they cannot be stopped permanently from getting them.

I remember very clearly thinking the first time I want to Romania in 1989, about six months before the revolution broke out, this is a country where the very instinct for independent thought, the very instinct to desire freedom, has gone; this is a nation of slaves. Within six months, those people that I thought were slaves were coming out on to the streets and, no matter who may have sponsored the revolution they supported, they supported it in some cases with their lives. When the chips were down, they showed that that was what they wanted. You cannot block people off permanently from wanting that essential notion that they have the ability to run their own lives. 'No peace without freedom' was a great Quaker slogan during the 1960s and 1970s and I think it as true today as it was then.

Governments must learn from what has happened to Marxism–Leninism, learn that we simply cannot stop people doing things the way they want to do them in the long run. In the short run, and in Russia it lasted for 75 years, they were stopped from doing things the way they wanted to do them but the narrow, thin little layer which is all the system was by 1989, didn't stop people from remembering the past and knowing, somewhere within them, what it was they wanted.

It applies also in the United Kingdom. I think the other lesson that we must learn is that if people want to be independent, in whatever way they choose to be independent, they cannot be stopped permanently from doing it. And as a way of ending, I would just simply like to remind you of the hymn that was sung in Wenceslas Square on the night that Alexander Dubček went out and saw the people again for the first time in 30 years: 'May disputes and envy fade, may the governing of your affairs come back to you, at last, my nation.'

John Simpson's lecture was sponsored by Lothian Regional Council and the National Museums of Scotland and delivered at the Royal Museum of Scotland on 12 November 1992.

The lecture was chaired by Sheena MacDonald, broadcaster, and a response was given by Professor Philip Schlesinger, Department of Film and Media Studies, University of Stirling.

ADRIAN BIRD

8   Understanding the human genome: Scottish science in Europe

THIS LECTURE HAS TWO AIMS – FIRSTLY TO GIVE SOME IDEA of what the genome project is, highlighting the excitement and some of the misgivings which it engenders, and also to show how Scotland, Europe and the world are approaching the enormous logistical problems which the project poses.

First we need to make clear what the genome actually is: it is all the genes that an organism has. This is not very enlightening unless we know what genes are – the genes are the sets of instructions for building the organisms concerned. Genes do not do the building themselves. They just sit there holding their information in a stable way until the organism reads them and carries out the coded instructions. This part of the process, the reading of the genetic instructions, is analogous to a tape recorder reading a tape to produce audible music, or a computer reading software to carry out some calculation or other. The crucial difference is that the genome 'tape' carries the instructions for assembling complete copies of itself. It is as if we could make a computer that, all alone, would get together the materials, make the keyboard and wiring, plug itself in, and start work – making yet more copies. Man-made devices cannot do this, but human beings can, and so can mice, dogs, dandelions and germs. That is the essential characteristic of living things – they make copies of themselves, or, as biologists tend to say, they self-replicate.

The genes, then, carry all the information for making new copies, but what does the information in genes actually specify?

The simple answer is – proteins. Organisms look like they do and behave like they do because of the proteins which they contain. Hair is protein, skin is protein (bone is not protein, but it can only be made by proteins). Muscles, nerves, the lens of the eye and blood are all made of or assembled by proteins. In fact, everything living is made of or by proteins. The connection between proteins and genes is pleasingly simple. Each gene specifies one protein. That is, each time a gene is decoded, the result is a brand new molecule of protein. Which new protein it is depends on which gene is read.

Now we are almost in a position to appreciate the significance of the genome project. The processes of life depend utterly on proteins, so if we could describe all of the proteins in an organism, we would have a list of vital parts. Simple, you may say. Just isolate all of the proteins from an organism and describe their structure. Unfortunately there are insurmountable problems with this approach. Without going into the details, suffice it to say that it would be impossible. Not only would it take for ever, but it probably would not give us all the proteins anyway. There is a much easier way. Instead of describing the structure of the proteins themselves, we can read the coded instructions for the genes as written in the genome. By reading *all* of the genome, we automatically read all the structures of *all* the proteins.

So how many genes are we dealing with? (We could equally well say how many proteins are there? – it's the same question.) Well in man, to choose an organism at random, there are estimated to be 100,000 genes/proteins. And of these 100,000 genes how many do we know about? The answer is a paltry 4,000 – a small percentage. What is more (or, rather, less) although we have names for all of the 4,000, the *function* of many of them, that is, where they fit in the scheme of life molecules, is still completely mysterious. Most are little more than names. No wonder we understand so little about how living things work – we know hardly any of the parts that they are made from. The important message is this: biologists, despite the impression they sometimes give, are still pretty ignorant. The genome project is not about dotting the i's and crossing the t's to put the finishing touches to our vision of life at a level of molecules. In a very real sense, we are at the beginning.

I said earlier that reading the genes was a much easier way to obtain a human parts-list than the alternative of looking at proteins directly. 'Easiness' is a relative thing, however. To give you an impression of what is involved, let me describe the genome. If you were to look at human cells in a microscope, you would see the genome in the form of sausage-shaped objects called 'chromosomes'. They are just vehicles for carrying the genes on and, as far as we are concerned here, of little interest. Where is the DNA we have heard so much about? Well, by abusing the chromosomes, and then looking with the electron microscope which allows us to look more closely, it becomes possible to see the ghost of one X-shaped chromosome, with a fog of stringy material around it. The string is the DNA spilling out of the chromosome, and there is an awful lot of it there. In fact, the statistics are staggering. Each human cell contains nearly 3 metres of DNA. If the DNA in all the cells of your body were to be laid end to end it would stretch 100 times the distance from here to the sun!

Fortunately, each cell has the same genome, so if we are to read all the genes, we only need to think about the 3 metres. Nevertheless, this is still a daunting task. The string-like DNA which spills out of the exploded chromosome, like some real string, is made of two spiral structures wound round each other. This is the famous double helix discovered by Watson and Crick in the early 1950s. Each rung in the twisted ladder of the double helix is a letter of the code. It is these letters that are read to make a protein, and it is these letters that the genome project aims to read. In the entire 3 metres of DNA that the genome contains, there are 3,000 million letters. When we read the genome, the result looks like the page of a book, but with several differences. There are only four letters and there is no punctuation. In the whole human genome there are one million tightly packed pages like the ones in this book. And out of those million pages we have read only a few thousand pages.

There is yet another complication (the last one that I am going to allude to). The genome is sometimes referred to as the 'Book of Man'. Obviously, no one is going to come home after a hard day's work and curl up for a good read of the Book of Man. It is a difficult read. Not just at the superficial level, but even for biologists equipped with computers. The problem is not that we don't understand how to decipher the code; that was cracked more than two decades ago. The problem is that most of the 3 metres of DNA does not appear to have anything to do with genes, and the genes themselves are split into small pieces and scattered over a quite long stretch of DNA. So out of a page of DNA, one stretch might code for part of a protein, and the rest of the same protein might be coded by another stretch further down the page, or even on a different page altogether. The DNA in between, and above and below the coding regions, seems to not code for anything at all. Hence its nickname 'junk DNA'. The problem this causes is that it becomes very difficult to find genes at all (not impossible, just difficult) and it means that most of the 3 billion letters that one reads will be junk.

I have talked about the genome project as though it is aimed at reading all of the DNA indiscriminately in order to get at all of the genes. That is certainly the ultimate goal. But in the meantime there are many questions which cannot wait for the whole genome to be sequenced. I refer of course to the hunt for genes responsible for genetic diseases in man. Sometimes genes get altered so that the protein which they code for does not work properly. The result can be disease, which, because it originates in the DNA code, runs in families. For example, haemophilia is caused by one of the clotting factors (a protein, of course) not working properly because the gene has an error in it. The result is that blood does not clot and bleeding does not easily stop. Here we know the nature of the faulty gene, but for an enormous number of genetic diseases we have no idea what has gone wrong. As a result most of these diseases are untreatable. The number of diseases in this category is large; it is estimated that one in every 20 people is affected by genetic or part-genetic disease by the age of 25. Suddenly, over the last couple of years, we are plunged into a phase where the faulty genes are being identified at an amazing speed. Almost every week brings a new breakthrough. The genetic diseases, once seen as mysterious acts of blind fate, carried from generation to generation 'in the blood', are being understood.

One success story among the many is cystic fibrosis. This is one of the most common genetic diseases of all among people of European ancestry. It causes a build-up of mucus in the lungs, and early death. It is a very unpleasant disease indeed. About 100,000 people worldwide have it, and one in every 20 Europeans is a carrier – that is, they got the mutated gene from one of their parents, but a normal working gene from their other parent, and, because the normal gene can compensate, they do not show any signs of the disease. Only if two carriers get together and have children, and only then if they both happen to pass their mutant genes to the child, does the disease show itself.

Up until three years ago, we had no idea about which gene caused cystic fibrosis. Then, following a massive effort from groups in several countries, two groups in the US and Canada announced that they had found the gene. This allows us to do several things that we could not even contemplate before.

- We can identify most foetuses that will get the disease before they are born.
- We can seriously consider the possibility of gene therapy strategies (that is, administer the correct gene so that the correct protein is made after all).
- We can attempt to devise rational ways of treating those who suffer from the disease with drugs. (I shall have more to say about this last approach later).

I have run a serious risk of submerging you in a quagmire

of scientific facts. The reason for taking this liberty is partly that I believe that everyone is going to need to know at least something about the explosion of knowledge about genetics. But there is another reason – I wanted to convey to you that the subject itself is quite easy to understand. The woeful ignorance of science among the public at large is due to the widespread misconception that only boffins and eggheads can understand it. At least in the case of basic genetics, this is not the case. So if you still did not understand it, I ask you to believe that it is because of the way I explained it, not because it is difficult to understand. The United States can teach Europe a lot in this respect. There, the genome project is something that nearly everyone knows a bit about. The Sunday supplements and weekly magazines there are not frightened to put science top of the bill. In Britain, journalists have been more pre-occupied with the Bloomsbury set, Lawrence of Arabia, or the real story behind the abdication of Edward VIII. It is changing, but slowly. Of all current science, none is more accessible, exciting and relevant than the study of genes.

This lecture is in the Lothian European series, so you could be forgiven for wondering where the European dimension has got to. It comes here, because I am now going to talk about where and by whom all of this work on the genome is being done. I have said that *we* can do this and *we* can do that. Who is *we*? To a working scientist like me, *we* is all the biologists in the world who choose to be involved. When scientific inquiry is relatively pure and basic (as it was when I started to do research in the late 1960s) national boundaries mean little. Competition is fierce, vitriolic even, but this has nothing to do with nations. The study of genomes, and particularly the human genome, has changed that. The new knowledge can be applied in medicine, agriculture, archaeology, forensics, even horse racing. Applications nearly always mean money; and money automatically attracts the attention of governments. The genome project has a political dimension.

First on the scene, perhaps predictably, were the Americans.

They announced a billion-dollar genome project initiative. After the moon, the genome. The two endeavours sound very different, but in fact they have a lot in common. Both cost an enormous amount of money, both involve discovering new territory, and both offer the prospect of economic exploitation. Since the genome promises to make far more money than the moon did, the world's other big economies were not about to leave it to the Americans. In 1992, the table of earmarked expenditure for genome-related research looks like this:

USA	$100 million
Japan	$25 million
France	$10 million
UK	$4 million
EC	$6 million

Australia, Canada, Denmark, Italy, Sweden, the Netherlands, Russia have smaller projects.

There are complications which make this table less meaningful than one would like. The biggest drawback is that money also comes from elsewhere. For example, in the UK the amount shown is only about one-fifth of what is spent by government on genetic research. The rest comes through established channels of research support. Then there are the charities, such as the Wellcome Trust in Britain, and the Muscular Dystrophy Association in France which may put in as much, if not more, than the government itself. Finally, it is appropriate to mention the EC. They are relatively new to the game but, in 1993, their funding will double. It remains to be seen what Britain's commitment will be. I think we can be fairly confident that it will not double.

The table refers only to national research programmes; there are other aspects of the project that are transnational. Each chromosome out of the 24 has its devoted followers who need to get together at meetings and exchange ideas and results. They also have to store their new information on computers in such a way that anyone can add data and have access to what is known. This so-called 'Genome Data Base' has been paid for up to now by the Americans (in the form of the Howard Hughes Medical Institute), but is moving towards funding of 40% by the US, 40% by Europe and 20% by Japan. The cost of meetings will also be shared internationally.

So how is the work itself being shared? At first the idea was to parcel out chromosomes to different countries or laboratories. The Italians made an early play for the X chromosome (that's the sex chromosome that women have two of and men one of), and the Japanese hitched their wagon to chromosome 21 (that's the one that causes Downes Syndrome if you have three instead of two). This 'chromosomes for countries' idea has, however, come to nothing. At present, laboratories in different countries work together, or drift apart apparently randomly. There is an awful lot of genome out there, so people need not tread on one another's toes. Even the institutions that are doing the work differ greatly in style. The most dramatic departure from standard practice has been by the French, who have set up a factory as part of their genome project, and employed non-scientists to operate the machines which read DNA and map landmarks on the chromosomes. This has paid off handsomely, and the French now lead the world in detailed mapping by their spectacular work on chromosome 21 (that was the one the Japanese announced as their national chromosome).

Another European breakthrough is the first-ever reading of all the DNA in a chromosome. The work was done in 35 European laboratories with money from the Biotechnology Action Programme from the Commission of the EC. This is not a human chromosome; it is a chromosome from baker's yeast. Irrelevant, one may think, to the human genome project, but here one would be mistaken. An extraordinary conclusion from genome studies is that many of the genes that humans have are almost identical to those of yeast. Indeed, one can take a yeast strain that has a crippling mutation in one of its genes, insert the equivalent gene from the human genome, and cure the yeast. Many genes are interchangeable. The fundamental similarity of all organisms once one gets down to the level of genes means that in some respects we can use yeasts, or indeed insects or bacteria, as models for man.

A statistical representation of articles on genetic mapping in the EC, and in the world as a whole, shows that Britain had the lion's share of publications in 1990. In genome research, Britain is a major force. It must be remembered that the structure of DNA was worked out in Britain, and this seminal discovery, arguably the most important of the twentieth century, was the start of the revolution in molecular biology. Britain, in spite of the worst efforts of successive governments right up to the present day, is a prime mover in genetics research. Successful science begets more successful science, and so far the cultural continuity of generations of teachers and their students has not been broken in Britain. It is a robust plant, but not an indestructible one, as those in power must recognise if Britain and the European Community are to reap the ultimate rewards of what started here.

Worldwide, the US is responsible for nearly half of all publications, with the EC taken as a whole not far behind, but figures like this have to be taken with a pinch of salt. They represent weight of papers published. Quality is not a parameter that can be measured that easily. Perhaps the most interesting aspect is that people are prepared to represent research in this nationalistic way. The scientific ideal, like the olympic ideal, is reduced to a medal table. This simply shows that the stakes are perceived to be high. Just how high is evident from recent behaviour of the US National Institute of Health (the American equivalent of the Medical Research Council). Having read a random selection of genes – not the whole genes I should point out, just tiny pieces of them – they have sought to patent the information. Not only were the genes only partly read, but those who read them had not the faintest idea about what their function was in human beings. Fortunately many people in the US and around the world have questioned the reasonableness of patenting the mere existence of something which all human beings have; not its use, just the fact that it is there. Legal wrangles are in full swing. The consensus view is that one should only be allowed to patent things that can be used (for example medically). If everyone is going to plant national flags in the little bit of the genome that they study, and spend time and money building barbed wire fences around it, then only one group of people is bound to benefit – the lawyers. And that would be a great shame.

So where does Scotland fit into the picture? With a population of only 6 million what can it contribute? The surprising answer is that Scotland, and Edinburgh in particular, has contributed out of all proportion to its size to the study of genetics. The first-ever isolation of a gene in pure form was carried out in Edinburgh – by Max Birnstiel in the late 1960s – and several of the techniques behind the molecular biology revolution were developed here. Most famous is probably the 'Southern Blot', a wonderfully simple and powerful way of seeing one particular bit of DNA among the vast excess of almost identical bits of DNA that are in the genome. Ed Southern invented the technique at Kings Buildings in 1975, and so useful has it been that the *Oxford English Dictionary* includes 'Southern Blot' in its latest edition. Today, Edinburgh's historical pre-eminence as Scotland's centre for genome research can no longer be assumed. Both Glasgow and Dundee Universities, particularly the latter, have become expanding centres of excellence in the modern genetical research. Scotland is one of Europe's foremost centres for genome research.

I would like to illustrate this by picking one piece of research of worldwide significance that Edinburgh biologists have recently completed. Earlier in the lecture I talked about cystic fibrosis, a genetic disease which particularly afflicts European populations. As I mentioned, the human gene which, when mutated, causes this disease was isolated in 1989 after a protracted search. One of the things we would now like to do is devise drug therapies that can alleviate the symptoms of the disease. Several laboratories around the world have therefore been trying to introduce the cystic fibrosis mutation into mice. By first looking for drugs that cure the disease in mice, many drugs can be tested in many different ways. First, one has to make the mutant mouse. The technology is spectacular. Cells are removed from an embryo and grown in a flat dish, where DNA is added to them. A few cells out of the millions in the dish take up the DNA and replace the normal gene with the mutant gene. These cells are then selected and re-inserted into a mouse embryo, where they become incorporated into the body of a new mouse, and Bob's your uncle. In the past few months, four different groups (one in Cambridge, one in Edinburgh and two in the US) have succeeded in causing the cystic fibrosis mutation in mice. Only one group, however, has mice which show the crucial symptom which causes death in children (that is, uncontrolled build-up of mucus in the lungs) and that was the group at the MRC Human Genetics Unit in Edinburgh under David Porteous.

So far I have referred only to the positive aspects of the genome project, its benefits for knowledge, medicine and bio-technology. Even among biologists there are differing opinions about its value. An eminent biologist who is unashamedly in favour is Nobel laureate Walter Gilbert.

. . . The existence of this informational resource and our ability to compare gene structures from human to other species will transform medicine and biology. In medicine one will identify genetic predispositions, not just to clear genetic dis-eases, but also to many common diseases. This will produce a medicine of diagnosis and prognosis based on individual variation and drugs tailored to the genetic makeup of the individual.

. . . The extensive knowledge of human genetics and the human genome will have philosophical and societal effects. It will affect our knowledge of our place in the universe and our relationship to other species.

Gilbert speculates that at the end of the next century we will wander into a drug store, leave a blood sample, and come back in half an hour to pick up the CD with our very own genome written on it. But not everyone is starry eyed about the implications of the genome project. At the opposite extreme are those who believe that it is all part of a sinister plot to create armies of subservient clones.

Attempts are being made to come to terms with the ethical implications of the new knowledge. What safeguards are needed to prevent misuse of genetic information? What should be done to protect confidentiality of personal genetic information? Could such information be available to employers? to insurance companies? Can genetic information be patented? Everyone is aware that these problems urgently need to be addressed. For example, the EC Commission on Future Initiatives will hear recommendations on all this from a new Working Group set up to study the ethical, legal and social aspects of the genome project.

You may ask, if the new information is so difficult to handle, why bother? I have pointed out a few of the medical benefits, and there are bound to be many more. But there is another somewhat philosophical aspect which I regard as crucial. I believe that, the more we can understand about what life is, and where we fit in to the scheme of things, the better. As I have tried to show, we have an enormous amount to learn. Much of biology resembles chemistry before Mendeleev devised the Periodic Table of the elements. Chemistry before Mendeleev was not very different from alchemy. Afterwards it became a rational science. Biology before we know all the genes still has the character of nature study. We sally forth in our pith helmets, butterfly nets at the ready, cataloguing the wonders of living things. Knowing all the components that it takes to make a living thing will move biology into a new era: the era when we finally understand what makes things live. Much of this will happen in Europe, and the more that happens in Scotland, the better.

Adrian Bird's lecture was sponsored by the University of Edinburgh and delivered at the George Square Theatre, the University of Edinburgh, on 17 November 1992.

Professor Emeritus Sir Alastair Currie, President of the Royal Society of Edinburgh, presided.

JOHN SMITH

9   *Europe and the world: preparing for the twenty-first century*

IT IS NOW THREE YEARS SINCE THE PEOPLE OF BERLIN TORE down the concrete wall that had divided their city for nearly 30 years and which so powerfully symbolised the division of an entire continent. In 1989, the largely peaceful revolutions that swept throughout the former communist countries of Eastern Europe not merely liberated the peoples of Poland, Hungary, Czechoslovakia, Romania and East Germany, they changed all our lives. It was an extraordinary moment in European history, a triumph for democracy and the determination of ordinary people to assert their fundamental human rights. It was a moment of euphoria and inspiration for all Europeans.

The breaking of the Wall in 1989 and what has flowed from it, the reunification of Germany, the break-up of the former USSR, and the end of the Cold War are nothing less than a total transformation of Europe and of our world. All the parameters have changed: political, social, economic, military. And not surprisingly, today, we are still unable to fully comprehend or anticipate what these changes will mean for the future not just of Europe but of the entire world.

And I believe it is because of this sense of uncertainty that the public mood in many countries of Europe is much more subdued today. The euphoria and enthusiasm of 1989 has given way to anxiety and the fear that Europe may once again repeat the mistakes of the past with all the terrible consequences that we have seen in the first half of the twentieth century. The tragic reality of what is happening in former Yugoslavia has provided a grim reminder of a terrible European past. Like a recurring nightmare we are again witnessing violent persecution and the horrors of so-called ethnic cleansing.

It is perhaps not surprising that, to some, the stability and simplicity of the Cold War era is now being looked back on almost with nostalgia as some sort of golden age. A Europe divided between two superpowers was a Europe easy to understand and to manage, provided that everyone knew their place and which side to be on. The military stand-off between the East and the West was like a giant game of chess played out over Europe. The board was carefully marked out in black and white. The rules were mutually agreed. US Pershing missiles matched Soviet SS20s – and we all know that the Americans and the Russians produce great chess players. So we in the West could relax, and even at times enjoy the Cold War watching the latest Bond movie or reading a new le Carré novel. Occasionally, of course, the Cold War turned uncomfortably hot, but these events happily occurred outside Europe, in Korea, Vietnam and Afghanistan.

Today the chess board in Europe has gone. Thankfully, so too have many of the pieces – the massive nuclear arsenals that were always the most alarming and dangerous aspect of the relative stability of the Cold War era. But in place of chess, Europeans now find themselves in a kind of three-dimensional game of snakes and ladders. The focus has shifted away from problems of military strategy in a world dominated by the superpowers, to an infinitely more complex set of social, economic, environmental and political problems that involve a wide diversity of countries both in Europe and all around the world.

These are the new challenges facing Europe and the world as we prepare for the twenty-first century. And no matter how intractable, I believe it is infinitely preferable to confront these new problems rather than to tolerate the military stalemate of the Cold War, and I would like here to outline some of the major issues which I believe will shape our lives, and those of future generations, in the years beyond 2000.

A central dilemma we face today is how to reconcile the growing demand of people, of regions and of nations to self-determination with the fact that we live in an ever more interdependent world. It is the problem of safeguarding national sovereignty at a time when the ability to act both economically and politically increasingly transcends the power of any individual country. Whether we like it or not, the reality of the modern world is that matters of vital importance to our lives, such as our economic prosperity, our military security and the protection of our environment, all depend on international collaboration and agreement between and beyond the traditional nation state.

In Europe, in particular, we are ever more interdependent both economically and politically, but at the same time, as individual people, we remain deeply committed to our own national identities. And whilst we are determined to defend what we perceive to be in our national interest, we are also increasingly aware that to do so we must work in partnership with other nations.

I believe the European Community has been extraordinarily successful in achieving an agreement between independent nations to pool aspects of their sovereignty and to exploit the economic and political opportunities of interdependence. Of course, that success has been built over the last three decades upon shared prosperity. And it is that which has been absolutely vital in securing the democratic consent of people throughout the European Community.

Today, as we are poised on the edge of the Single Market and in the midst of the ratification process of the Maastricht Treaty, the problem of combining interdependence and self-determination could not be more obvious. The narrow rejection of the Maastricht Treaty in Denmark and its similarly narrow acceptance in France shows just how delicately these issues are balanced. Many people in Europe are anxious about the threat to sovereignty and sceptical about the potential economic benefits of further integration. If the public begin to believe that inter-dependence is a source of economic weakness and not strength – that it will diminish the opportunities for employment and prosperity – then the clamour for purely 'national' solutions, however misguided, will grow.

In far more dramatic form the same dilemma has come to the forefront in Eastern Europe. The collapse of communism has released a wave of nationalist feelings and ambitions both in the former USSR and elsewhere. In one sense, the Russian Revolution stopped history in its tracks. Totalitarian government froze over ethnic, regional and nationalist tensions which, with the thawing of the Cold War, have re-emerged almost precisely as they existed before – or worse – exacerbated by the experience of Soviet domination as one ethnic group was deliberately set against another.

In 1991, there were more than 160 border disputes in the former Soviet Union. We are all too well aware of the problems of Georgia, of Armenia and Azerbaijan, in Moldavia and Uzbekistan, and of the problems of minorities such as Slovaks in Hungary, Germans in Poland, Hungarians in Romania and other examples throughout Eastern Europe.

This tide of nationalism has coincided, of course, with the collapse of the former COMECON economies. Economic dislocation has caused a severe economic slump throughout Eastern Europe. Since 1989, the Bulgarian economy has shrunk by about 30%, that of the Poles and Czechs by about 20%. The Russian economy was reduced by about 14% in the first quarter of 1992 alone.

Under such economic conditions it is all too easy for the pain and hardship of ordinary people to ignite the fires of extreme nationalism, of unrest, persecution of minorities, and civil war. I am sure that we all agree that it would be ghastly if what has happened to Yugoslavia becomes not a grim reminder of old European history but a foretaste of things to come.

There is no question, I am certain, that Western Europe can ignore or remain unaffected by such developments in the

East. Whether driven by political unrest or attracted by the prosperity of the European Community, there is already a significant pressure for migration from East to West, pressure which has raised tensions and provoked political extremism and the reappearance of the far right in Western Europe. Whilst it may have been possible to hold back the threat of Soviet expansionism during the Cold War, I am far from certain that it would be as straightforward to stop rising levels of economic chaos and civil disorder in Eastern Europe from spreading across borders into the European Community.

If there is any doubt about the significance for us of the changes in Eastern Europe, just look at the way in which we have all been affected by German unification. The impact of the absorption of East Germany into West Germany has been immense. The economic shock of unification has been transferred directly through to the economy of Western Europe as a whole, with consequences for levels of growth, trade and employment throughout the Community. And, of course, it was the combination of higher German interest rates and the failure to agree a general realignment of the European Exchange Rate Mechanism, compounded by the weakness of Britain's domestic economy, which provoked the currency crisis that caused the devaluation of the pound sterling on 16 September 1992. In this way, we can see quite clearly how the events of 1989 have already had a profound affect on arrangements at the very heart of the European Community. The lesson of these events is that we in Europe must respond more imaginatively to the new political challenges which have arisen since the end of the Cold War. And that means that, whilst we continue to deal with important issues of the European Community's internal economic and political structure, we cannot afford to neglect vital questions about our role in a wider Europe and a wider world.

It is perhaps an accident of history that the blueprint for the next phase of internal change in the Community – the plans for Political and Economic and Monetary Union – were drawn

up just before the full extent of the changes since 1989 were
known. As a result, the Community has sometimes given the
impression that, like those hankering after the Cold War, it
would have preferred not to have to worry about Eastern
Europe just now.

And I believe it is unfortunate that discussion about the future
of Europe in the last few years has been so dominated by debate
about the Maastricht Treaty. After all, no one knows for certain
whether or not a single European currency will be agreed by the
end of this century. The Community will clearly be financially
and industrially more integrated, not least because of the impact
of the Single Market. That, in itself, will underpin the rationale
for EMU although, I suspect, on a timetable less ambitious than
that envisaged in the Maastricht Treaty.

In passing, I am reminded of a remark by the former President
of the Bundesbank, Karl Otto Pohl, who wondered if it was
significant that EMU was named after an Australian bird that
had no wings, couldn't fly but would not go backwards. But
whatever happens to EMU there are other urgent, and equally
important, concerns for the Community to consider.

My plea, therefore, is for the Community to put greater
emphasis on Europe's external role in a world that is transformed and continuing to change rapidly. I believe that this
is important not simply as a selfless act on the part of good
Europeans – as a kind of moral imperative to look kindly on
our neighbours, entirely honourable though that would be – I
believe Europe needs to look outward in its own best interests
and as the only sure way to achieve the peace and prosperity
which has been our very good fortune over the last forty years.

The external agenda that I believe should receive the concentrated attention of the European Community includes aid and
support for the reform process in Eastern Europe, new efforts
to overcome the crisis of debt and deepening poverty in the
Third World, greater European responsibility for management
of the world economy, and a deeper commitment to safeguard
the international environment.

The description I have already provided of the severe difficulties facing many of the emerging democracies in Eastern Europe raises the obvious question of whether we in the West are doing enough to help the process of reform. The answer, I am afraid, is almost certainly no.

There is growing unease that the scale of our response to the crisis in Eastern Europe is totally insufficient to secure the great advance for democracy that occurred after 1989. Release of credit and measures of debt relief have been very slowly disbursed and the International Monetary Fund has been given the decisive role in administering the reform process in Russia and throughout Eastern Europe. Whilst I do not dispute for one moment the legitimacy of a role for the IMF alongside the World Bank and the European Bank for Reconstruction and Development, I am not alone in questioning the wisdom of their policy advice which invariably proposes severe reductions in social expenditure, and austerity measures applied almost regardless of the political consequences.

The IMF suffers from two critical weaknesses: it lacks resources and it lacks political skill. The Fund's quota increase is still held up in the US Congress, just at the moment when more and more countries, particularly from Eastern Europe, have taken up membership – placing increased demands on its borrowing facilities. What the IMF needs is political leadership from the Group of Seven. Without it, I fear the IMF will fail to develop a reform programme in Eastern Europe that is both economically and politically feasible.

The contrast with the experience of the post-war reconstruction of Western Europe is striking. Consider the sheer scale of the Marshall Plan initiative launched by President Truman in 1948. Aid from the US amounted to a staggering $70 billion in today's prices. Political leaders on both sides of the Atlantic including the then Labour Foreign Secretary Ernest Bevin played a crucial role in mobilising the political will for an unprecedented act of statesmanship and generosity. Above all, they recognised that failure was unthinkable, and the Americans, in particular, appreciated that their own security depended on prompt and decisive assistance.

But where is the George C. Marshall of 1992? The best the West can offer are IMF officials bearing privatisation plans. It would be far better, I believe, for the Group of Seven leading industrial nations to appoint a leading statesman or woman to provide the political flair, leadership and judgement that is needed to galvanise our assistance to the East.

In fact, help on the scale of the Marshall Plan is probably far in excess of what is needed. Eastern Europe is not lacking in natural resources. To take one important example, Russia is an oil-rich country with the potential for substantial economic growth. The problem for most countries in Eastern Europe is severe economic dislocation and the collapse of the COMECON trading system within the former Soviet bloc. What they all need most of all is the ability to earn hard currency through international trade.

I have spoken of the great upheaval in Eastern Europe and of the massive consequences of this change for us in the West. But we must, at the same time, look farther afield, because similar problems also bedevil the developing world. The debt crisis is still shackling many countries in Latin America and in Africa. Both regions have endured a lost decade of falling per capita incomes and severe social decline. The hesitant and delayed efforts to reschedule and write down the debt burdens of the so-called middle-income countries of Latin America are, of course, welcome, but long overdue. And in comparison, Africa's debt burden, owed overwhelmingly to Western governments rather than to private banks, is still seriously neglected.

Our failure to come up with a concerted response to the debt crisis is not just a human tragedy for millions living in poverty, it has acted as a drag anchor on the world economy. For the poorest countries, prospects remain grim. There is still lack of agreement to implement fully official debt relief under the so-called Trinidad Terms which was first proposed in 1990.

And to make matters worse it looks likely that negotiations currently underway to replenish the World Bank's fund for very low interest loans will fail to secure any increase at all. This at a time when the World Bank forecasts for the year 2000 at best minimal, and more likely negative, levels of per capita income growth in Sub-Saharan Africa.

The rich countries, I believe, have a moral duty to provide a combination of debt relief and generous levels of official aid. But a commitment to aid alone is not enough. 'Trade is better than aid' is an old saying, but it is true nonetheless.

That is why it is absolutely vital to overcome the crisis that has hit the current round of international trade talks. The risks to the world economy are far too great to allow brinkmanship over the GATT to degenerate into a trade war. A compromise agreement between the European Community and the United States must be reached now, which will provide a solution to the enduring problem of agricultural protectionism. A trade war would not just be a disaster for us. It would deal a fatal blow to the emerging democracies of Eastern Europe and it would be a catastrophe for the debt-ridden Third World.

It is important to realise just how significant agriculture is to most developing countries. Agriculture accounts for about 40% of the economic output of the poorest countries, and provides work for over 70% of their people. Compare that with Europe, where agriculture accounts for less than 3% of output and employs less than 10% of the workforce.

It really would be absurd if – after all the staggering changes that have occurred since 1989 – the only institution that remains unchanged and immutable is the EC's Common Agricultural Policy. The CAP must be reformed and we must abandon protection of agriculture which makes our own food more expensive and impoverishes millions in the Third World.

Trade wars and recession threaten a downward spiral into a global slump and political disintegration. That was the awful lesson of the 1930s. In Europe we have, I believe, a special responsibility to prevent anything like that ever happening again.

Serving to remind us of our past mistakes is a favourite political cartoon of mine which, although published in 1932, contains a powerful message for us all today. The cartoon by David Low depicts a boat called the 'World Money Problem', sailing in very rough seas and leaking heavily. At one end of the boat the 'big three' leading economic powers sit on the bow with not even their feet wet. At the other end sit the smaller nations with their heads barely above water. One of the big three says to the other, 'That's a nasty leak – thank goodness it is not at our end of the boat.' The same characteristics of complacency and short-sightedness are still with us sixty years on. Today, the reality of the modern world is that we are all in the same boat – and the rough seas of recession are threatening to drag us all down.

Interdependence is a double-edged sword. We share the rewards of economic progress, but we also share the consequences of our mistakes. That is why we must insist that the only solution lies in international economic cooperation and action to ensure growth, employment and investment which remain the best guarantees of peace and prosperity for all people across the world.

The threat of worldwide recession is real. Britain, first into recession, remains seemingly stuck with no growth and rising unemployment. The United States has experienced a very weak recovery and now Germany is drifting from slow growth into recession itself. The economic slowdown is most acute in the European Community. Growth in the Community has fallen sharply and unemployment has risen dramatically. I cannot stress too strongly the urgency of the need for action to reverse this trend.

That is why the Labour Party has been insisting that, during the UK Presidency, recovery, growth and jobs be put at the top of the European agenda. We believe there is considerable scope for joint action at the Community level to tackle unemployment, to increase support for training and spending on European-wide projects for infrastructure and investment. On the initiative of the European Commission President Jaques Delors, it now seems possible that these issues will be discussed at the European Summit in Edinburgh. What is astonishing is that the British Government have not already used their period in the Presidency to push them to the forefront of European decision-making.

We must also put growth back on the agenda of the Group of Seven leading industrialised nations. We will certainly find a willing partner now following the election of President-elect Bill Clinton. Similarly, the Japanese, also experiencing an unusual period of sharply reduced growth, would be, I believe, receptive to a strategy for growth. They have, in fact, already undertaken a significant boost to public investment to stimulate their own economy. The time is ripe for a Group of Seven Summit to consider a coordinated strategy for growth that replicates what I hope will be agreed for Europe at the Edinburgh EC Summit.

The emphasis I have placed here on growth may raise concern that protection of the environment must inevitably take a lower profile; that a growing world cannot be a green world. But I have long rejected the view of some in the environmental movement that growth and conservation are incompatible. In fact, I believe sustainable growth and rising prosperity are the essential pre-conditions for effective international action to protect our environment.

It is far more likely that industrial and agricultural systems that pollute and degrade our environment will remain unchecked and unreformed whilst the threat of recession hangs over so many countries in the world today. The necessary adjustments that we must all make to reduce greenhouse gases and to curb global warming will be far easier in an economic environment of development and rising prosperity. And that, of course, was the explicit understanding of 1992's Earth Summit in Rio de Janeiro. The Summit's full title was the United

Nations Conference on Environment and Development – with a significant emphasis on the 'D' for development as well as the 'E' for environment.

Many of the high expectations of the Rio Summit were unfulfilled. It was always over-ambitious to expect a single gathering of world leaders to provide solutions to the complex problems and threats to our environment today. Nevertheless, the Summit was an important breakthrough and there is a real opportunity for Europe to take a leading role in setting meaningful targets, both for environmental protection and for advancing development.

Above all, we must avoid the situation in which disagreement between the industrialised nations and developing countries causes a new international stalemate. It would be tragic if, having so recently overcome East–West tensions, we then stumble into a bitter new North–South divide. New patterns of international cooperation must be agreed and Europe should point the way forward.

It should be possible, I believe, to construct a 'green alliance' of countries from the North and the South that are committed to practical measures that encourage sustainable development and environmental protection, an alliance willing to lead by example, rather than wait for a consensus which can only be achieved at the lowest common denominator. Once again, I hope, the election of Bill Clinton and Al Gore, as his Vice-President, will ensure swifter progress in following up the agreements already made in Rio in June 1992.

The end of the Cold War gives us all tremendous and unprecedented opportunities: the chance, as a truly international community, to devote our economic and political resources to tackle the world's most serious underlying problems. That is the agenda which we in Europe should grasp with imagination, energy and leadership. For the choices we make today, here in Europe, will profoundly affect our future and the future of the world in the next century. The choice, I believe, is stark. We can turn our backs on these opportunities and treat them only as problems to be avoided. But I am certain that any attempt to lock our prosperity inside a Fortress Europe is bound to fail. We would be repeating the mistakes of the past which caused such havoc for so many people in our continent earlier this century.

Alternatively, we can seize the opportunities of a world transformed. It is within our grasp to close the gap between the North and the South and arrest the slide into poverty and despair that is still the fate of many millions of our fellow human beings. We have the opportunity to respond to the great challenges of the environment. And we have the responsibility to strengthen democracy, to defend human rights and extend social justice. That is the agenda of opportunity that faces us today – opportunities we simply cannot afford to miss.

That we have these opportunities is because of the courage and sheer determination of the people in Eastern Europe who destroyed the Wall in Berlin and brought the Cold War to an end. If we begin building a new Europe for the twenty-first century with the same determination and the same enthusiasm with which they inspired us all in the autumn of 1989, we will not fail.

John Smith's lecture was sponsored by Lothian Regional Council and delivered at the Playfair Library, the University of Edinburgh, on 20 November 1992.

The lecture was chaired by Kirsty Wark, broadcaster, and a vote of thanks was given by Councillor Eric Milligan, Convener, Lothian Regional Council.

DAVID MARTIN

10 *Beyond 1992 – a deeper and wider Europe?*

WE HAVE ARRIVED NOW AT A WATERSHED IN THE HISTORY of Europe; decisions taken in the next few years will have a profound impact on the development of Europe for at least a generation, possibly for longer. This is something I have believed for the last two years or so, and as each day passes it seems to me to become more and more obvious. When the great European project of this century was initiated by Winston Churchill, in his now famous speech at Zurich in 1946, the motive was the preservation of the peace which had just, at such appalling cost, been established. He aimed to reconcile France and Germany; to avoid the mistakes which had characterised earlier periods of peace; to give Germany its rightful role in the new Europe; and to stand up to the Soviet communists in order to secure the freedom and democracy of Europe west of that famous line 'between Stettin and Trieste'.

The aims were deeply political, but the means developed for the process of integration were economic: the tying together of the coal and steel industries of the continent of Western Europe, the decision to set up a customs union and a common agricultural policy. These economic means achieved the political aims intended: from being throughout the twentieth century a main source of instability and tension in Western Europe, the relationship between France and Germany has turned into the most important source of stability. Peace among Western European nations is now so secure that we have difficulty in explaining to young people how it can ever have been otherwise. The wars of the generation of my parents will, to my children, be as distant as the Battle of Waterloo. But if we look back in history, and this is becoming increasingly important in order to understand the future, we see that there were really over and over again two major problems that threatened the stability and peace of Europe.

The first was, obviously, the conflict between France and Germany. That issue has, I believe, been resolved once and for all. But the other has always been a question of the political order of Central and south-eastern Europe, of the security order of the Danubian lands and the surrounding areas, with their exceedingly complicated pattern of languages, nationalities and traditions. What we see happening now is this great, unresolved question being put once again onto the European agenda.

For a long time this issue was regulated by the dominance of the German, Russian, Austro-Hungarian and Ottoman empires. This failed to work. Then an effort was made at Versailles in 1919 to reorder the entire region by, among other things, the creation of new, multinational states. That did not provide sufficient stability to withstand the pressure of the 1930s. The entire region was then put under the occupation of the Soviet communist forces for half a century, which only aggravated the long-term problems of the region. For me, the problem of the security order of Central and south-east Europe during the decades ahead is the most pressing and critical of all the problems we have to address.

We have won the Cold War, but we have yet to secure a new peace that can make us confident of the stability and durability of our victory, and I do not need to elaborate at great length about the dangers that lie ahead. The break-up of Yugoslavia has resulted in a conflict more brutal and more horrible than anyone could have foreseen. In the winter of 1992–93 we are facing a catastrophe of starvation in Bosnia, in the very heart of Europe. No one could be blind to the danger of Serbian policies provoking an open conflict in Kossova that puts a torch to a large part of the southern Balkan region. In Russia, hyper-inflation is just around the corner, with all the social and political consequences with which we know hyper-inflation is always associated. Although a return to the past is no longer an option, we see a more assertive Russian nationalism on the rise. In Central Europe itself, the break-up of Czechoslovakia may bring the tragedy of the economic, political, monetary and social disintegration that we are seeing throughout the former Soviet empire right to the doorsteps of Vienna and Berlin.

I recently re-read J.M. Keynes' *The Economic Consequences of the Peace* (which I first read as a student here at Heriot-Watt University) which Keynes wrote in 1919 after taking part in the Peace Conference at Versailles. He wrote that 'on the continent of Europe, the foundations are trembling and no-one can fail to hear the approaching thunder'. In a thoughtful article in the *Herald Tribune* recently, the Foreign Minister of Hungary, Mr Jeszenszky, describes the mood one increasingly encounters in the other half of Europe, commenting that 'close to 500 million people live in this region, and yes, when people hear such phrases as "a new architecture of European security" they no longer listen with curiosity, but with an increasingly bitter smile. They may not yet shudder, but they know that they have no bunkers in which to hide.'

It is becoming increasingly easy to see how things can go badly wrong in the 1990s, and we must all be aware of the fact that if things do, in fact, go badly wrong in one part of Europe, that is going to have severe repercussions in all parts of Europe. During the decades of the Cold War, it was obvious that in the long run we could not live in a Europe that was only half free, and now it should be equally clear that we cannot live in a Europe that is half stable, secure and prosperous and half unstable, conflict-ridden and increasingly economically desperate.

During the past decades, economic integration has established peace among the nations of Western Europe as well as contributing substantially to the most impressive economic development of its member countries. Now, it will have to go back to fundamental political purpose and be the force that eventually brings stability and prosperity to all of Europe. There simply is no other institution, or mechanism, or way in which this can be done. Either it is done by the emerging European Union, or it is not done at all. If it is not done at all, I have great difficulty in seeing how we can ensure the long-term security and prosperity of the nations of Western Europe.

The Community is now going through a difficult period. Never has good, strong visionary leadership been more necessary in Western Europe and I am afraid it has to be said that never has it been more lacking than at the present time. People around Europe see their economies suffering from recession and increasing unemployment at the same time that the carnage just goes on and on around Sarajevo. This is not what their politicians had led them to believe. Just a few years ago, we were told about the wonders and the economic prospects that would be opened up by the 1992 programme, and the wonderful opportunities and prospects that would be opened up by the fall of the Berlin Wall. No wonder there is in practically all the Member States of the Community a feeling of popular confusion, concern and perhaps even resentment at the great European plans and dreams of just a few years ago. But not only should we not be surprised at this, I believe that we should welcome it. We should have been worried if such was not the reaction; if the schemes and dreams of yesterday had not been met by questioning today, we should have been asking ourselves what have we been doing all of this time? Who have we been informing about our plans for Europe?

Fortunately, that is not what we have seen. We are instead in the middle of a great debate about the vital European issues, and I believe if that debate is handled correctly it could give our joint endeavours strength in the years ahead. But to do that, we have to make clear what the Community is really about, and that is the creation of peace and prosperity for the future prospects of the whole of Europe.

Today, to many of our citizens, it looks as if the Community is about ratification for ratification's sake, finance for finance's sake or meeting for meetings's sake. They fail to see the relevance of what the Community is doing today. They do not see that the Community could be a bulwark against the increase in unemployment felt by so many of them, a defence against the uncertainties concerning the future security of Europe which are now becoming increasingly obvious. To make this clear, we have to assert that the Community has to move on. Because the challenges of the years ahead require a Community which does not stand still or, even worse, slides backwards, but a Community which moves forward in the vital areas of economic and monetary union, of political union, of an emerging common foreign and security policy, and indeed of enlargement.

With all the difficulties the Community and its Member States are facing at this time, there is a risk that the question of enlargement with the remaining members of EFTA, although much less controversial today than it was in 1991, will be dragged down into technicalities of the sort seen too often before in the history of the Community. Yet, to my mind, enlargement is of crucial importance and might even be the key to the realisation of some of the great tasks in the years ahead. It is imperative to the stability of all of Europe that the Community makes it abundantly clear that it is not a 'closed shop' but rather a Community open to all democracies of Europe, as envisaged in the Treaty of Rome. Only by making this clear, and thus opening up the prospects of eventually becoming part of the European Union, will it send a signal to the political forces in Central, Eastern and south-east Europe that the road to Europe is through cooperation. If the signal is not sent, it will play directly into the hands of those increasingly strong forces of aggressive nationalism and surviving communism that seek their future in the setting of nation against nation, and people against people. The speedy enlargement of the Community with the EFTA countries that have already applied or will apply in the near future will demonstrate that, in the long term, the Community is open to all democracies of Europe.

In my opinion, this enlargement could be completed in a very short period of time, if the political will is there – but the big question is 'if'. After all, most of the issues of substance have already been dealt with during the process of setting up the European Economic Area. The European Economic Area created a unified, West European market which accounts for something like 47% of world trade. It is a deal between the Twelve Member States of the European Community and the seven EFTA countries: Austria, Sweden, Finland, Switzerland, Norway, Iceland and Liechtenstein. It features free movement of goods from 1993; from 1993 EFTA will assume EC rules on company law, consumer protection, the environment, research and development and social policy. The EFTA countries will adopt European Community competition rules on anti-trust matters, the abuse of dominant position, public procurement, mergers and state aid. From 1993, individuals are free to live, work and offer services throughout the European Economic Area, with mutual recognition of professional qualifications. For the privilege of all these things the EFTA countries will pay 425 million ecus as a contribution to the European Community Structural Funds.

However, major differences do remain between the European Economic Area and full EC membership. There is no customs union between the Economic Community and the EFTA members, and border controls remain. The EFTA countries did not join the EC's Common Agricultural Policy and they retain their own farm policy. There is no common foreign and security policy and EFTA countries are not members of the European Monetary System, although many of them do shadow the deutschmark. The biggest difference is that the EFTA countries will not participate in EC decision-making, yet they will have to accept the outcome of any decisions taken inside the European Community that affect the European Economic Area agreement. Unsurprisingly, therefore, they are not particularly happy about the European Economic Area. A deal that started off as an alternative for many of the EFTA countries and, it has to be said, for many of the Member States of the European Community, has become a catalyst for membership.

Despite all the difficulties and all the problems the European Community is currently facing, perhaps the best advert for the European Community is the queue that is currently forming at its door. Five of the EFTA countries have either applied or are in the process of applying to join. Austria, Sweden and Finland have formally applied; the Swiss parliament has voted to do so, and Norway's ruling Labour Party has indicated that it will support Norway's application. In addition to the EFTA countries Malta, Cyprus and Turkey all have applications on the table. The so-called Europe Agreements between the European Community and the Visigrad countries – Hungary, Poland and the Czech and Slovak Republics – explicitly mention membership of the Community as a long-term objective, 'long-term' for the Visigrad countries being seen as the year 2000.

John Major has talked about a Community of 24 Member States. Not to be outdone, Jacques Delors has talked about a community of 35 Member States, and *The Economist* recently produced a very interesting map of a possible future Community of 39 Member States, with Czechoslovakia still as a unitary state.

The first enlargement will undoubtedly be by the EFTA countries and I have no doubt that they would considerably strengthen the existing Community. They would add firstly to the wealth of the Community. All the EFTA countries have a per capita GDP far greater than the European Community average. This would give the European Community budget a much needed boost, and it is estimated that Austria alone would make a net contribution to the Community coffers of 658 million ecus. All the EFTA countries have strong commitment to social democracy and undoubtedly would sign the Social Chapter of the Maastricht Treaty, from which Britain is in isolation. Despite some recent difficulties, they would all be far more able to meet the rigours of a single currency than at least six of the present Member States. Of all the problems that might be faced by the potential applicant countries, only two pose what might be seen as major difficulties for the European Community, but I believe both, in fact, can be easily overcome.

The first one is farm policy. To those who think of the Common Agricultural Policy as highly protectionist, and I include myself among them, it is perhaps surprising to learn that the EFTA farmers are even more cosseted and protected than the European Community farmers. However, in supporting the EC's stance in the GATT negotiations, the EFTA countries have indicated that they are prepared to adjust their farm policies to facilitate membership, certainly no easy option for a country like Finland where 40% of the voters are farmers.

The other potential difficulty for membership, which I believe will prove to be an illusion, is the fact that four of the five EFTA applicants were Cold War neutralists, and a number of them have neutrality written into their constitution. In a world that is no longer a bipolar world divided between two superpowers, I don't think that neutrality will prove a major obstacle to membership of the EC and the common foreign and security policy shouldn't, in fact, place an undue burden on any of these Member States. I believe they will find it easy to accept being part of a common foreign policy.

A long-term difficulty, of course, would be created if the Community becomes a defence Community. Many in the Community advocate it becoming exactly that. Perhaps I find the EFTA countries' neutrality easier to live with because, despite regarding myself as very pro-European, I do not believe that the EC should develop a defence function. If it needs a defence arm, it should continue to operate either through NATO or through the Western European Union.

In my view, the biggest obstacle to enlargement is not the applicant countries themselves, but the existing institutional structure of the Community which I wish to concentrate on now. In order to facilitate enlargement we must face the major challenge of reshaping the Community since the present institutional arrangements, even as modified by the Maastricht Treaty, are barely workable in a Community of twelve; they would collapse totally if they had to be applied to a Community of a size greater than that. Jacques Delors, the President of the European Commission speaking at the European Parliament in Strasbourg, talked about the 'political, intellectual and institutional shock' that an enlarged Community would create, and I think he is absolutely right to put it in those terms. It has been pointed out, for example, that in a Community of perhaps 30 countries, each country would hold the Presidency of the Council of Ministers once every 15 years. It wouldn't matter so much that the politicians would have changed over that time (although they would lose a bit of prestige), but what would matter is that the civil service would have changed in that period and – in Community jargon – the 'institutional awareness' would not exist within the national civil services to enable officials to handle the six-month Presidency. When any country takes the Presidency for the first time, its usually a fraught affair, although the country gets a lot of 'first time' support, but virtually every country would feel like a novice if there was a cycle which meant that you saw the chair only once every 15 years.

Similarly, with the European Commission after enlargement: if we kept the system where each of the big countries has two Commissioners and each small country has one Commissioner, there would be over 30 Commissioners. It's already argued that there are not enough posts of suitable status for 17 Commissioners and, in the course of Maastricht negotiations, there was serious discussion about reducing the existing number to 12: it seems certain there would not be enough jobs for 38.

Then there is the question of how many Euro MPs could the European Parliament cope with? Academics tell us that a Parliament that goes much beyond about 750 members becomes an inefficient institution because members don't get enough time to speak in debates, to ask questions and so on, meaning the parliamentary process starts to move into disrepute. Representation is also very uneven at present: one German member has something like a million electors, whereas one Luxembourg member has less than 100,000 voters with which to contend. Enlargement could well exacerbate that problem. Therefore, I believe that, not as an alternative to or in advance of, but in parallel with the enlargement process, the existing Twelve and the applicant states should sit down and collectively negotiate a constitution which would allow the EFTA countries to join in 1996 and give the European Community an institutional structure which could last it well into the next century.

There are, broadly speaking, three options. The first is to do nothing, and I have made clear my opinion that that would simply mean the Community going into the mire. There are two other serious options being canvassed. The first has been nicknamed the 'United Nations of Europe'. This concept is based on the UN model, with the Big Five Member States of the Community acting a bit like the Security Council. Each would have a veto on key policy areas, the other members would simply vote by majority. Each of the Big Five would chair the Community one year at a time with two smaller states as vice-chairs. The Commission would have one place reserved for each of the big countries while the small countries would agree to nominate in blocks. Thus, the Benelux countries for example – Belgium, Luxembourg and the Netherlands – would elect one Commissioner between them or, as an alternative, the smaller countries would get a Commissioner-ship on the basis of 'Buggins' Turn' in rotation. The concept of every Member State having an absolute right to a Commissioner would disappear.

Having put that concept before you, I want to state that I completely reject it. I don't think it's workable and it would not be acceptable to the existing small states, it would therefore be the likely subject of a veto. I prefer a far more wide-ranging set of changes whereby the nations and regions of the European Community share power as equals. The time has come, or will come when we address the next set of reforms, for the Commission to be drawn from the European Parliament, in much the same way as national executives emerge from national parliaments. This would firstly increase the accountability of Commissioners: they would be accountable directly to a parliament which had just appointed them and, through that, answerable to the electorate in a way that they are not currently. It would also mean that Commissioners could be appointed on the basis of ability, rather than nationality. A Commission emerging from the European Parliament would be more effective, more transparent, more democratic.

If it achieves those three objectives, the Commission should then have day-to-day responsibility for the management and running of the Community, with the Council one step further into the background. The Council of Ministers as presently structured is an anachronism in terms of normal democratic structures. There are very few examples in the world where the two functions of government are mixed, where the executive and the legislative are the same people meeting at the same time and taking decisions concurrently on two different planes. The time has come to separate those two functions. Even with a stronger Commission, there will still be major policy areas that will have to be referred to the Member States and decisions taken by national ministers. Realistically, those decisions will be taken in secret since there isn't a government in the world that makes its executive decisions in public and the European Community is probably the least suitable model to lead the field in that way.

On the other hand, there is hardly a legislature in the world that makes its decisions behind closed doors, yet the Council of Ministers currently passes binding laws in complete secret. That has to end and the Community decision-making structure has to be opened up to public scrutiny. I would like the Council of Ministers to pass legislation in public, but I go further: having opened up the Council, I don't see why passing Community law should remain any longer the prerogative of the Council as we currently know it, the exclusive prerogative of Ministers of the Member States.

I would like this function to be taken over by a kind of 'European Senate' – the best term I can find for this – in which countries like Luxembourg, Malta, Cyprus would have one seat, but countries like Germany, France, the United Kingdom might have perhaps 10. That being the case, once we move to that structure, there's no good reason why the representation could then not be drawn from the sub-Member State level of government; from the German Länder or the Spanish autonomous regions or, in the United Kingdom's case from Scotland, Wales, Northern Ireland and the regions of England. This gives us a chance to solve what I see as another growing problem in the European Community, which can be expressed as almost an inversion of the old slogan the 'Greens' used to have on their posters: 'think global, act local'. Increasingly, we see the need to act at a European level, but the population is thinking more at a regional level. A Senate of the type that I propose would give the German Länder, the Spanish regions, the Italian League and the submerged nations of the United Kingdom a direct voice in European affairs.

The embryonic structure for that already exists in the Maastricht Treaty which created a Committee of the Regions, made up of people from the different regional levels. It acknowledged that these people needed a direct voice in the European Community decision-making structure. At the moment, it is only a consultative assembly, but I believe it can grow from that consultative assembly into a much stronger institution and organisation. The Secretary of State for Scotland, Ian Lang, recently spoke about the need for the Committee of the Regions to be well served, and I agree with him there; he talked about bidding up the Scottish representation on that Committee, and I agree with him on that. But he was talking simply in numbers and there I disagree quite strongly, because if we have four, five or six members it doesn't matter if they're not representative. The key thing is that they should be representative, and they should be drawn directly from elected local politicians. Those local politicians, having been elected to that Committee of the

Regions, should not be there to represent Lothian Region, or Strathclyde or the Highlands and Islands; they should be there to represent Scotland. They should be provided with a secretariat to introduce a Scottish voice into European affairs. We already have local representation; each of the areas I have mentioned already has a Euro MP giving local representation. What we don't have is a collective Scottish voice at the European level. The Committee of the Regions has the potential to fulfil that function, and if Mr Lang really is talking about 'beefing up' Scottish representation at the European level, he shouldn't just talk about numbers, but he should make sure that this is constituted by directly elected politicians who are adequately resourced.

Another potential change which would help this process of a move towards a senate is the case being argued by the German Länder with the support of their Government that Article 146 of the Treaty should be amended to allow from time to time representatives of the lender rather than Government Ministers to cast votes at the Council of Ministers. If a peculiarly regional issue is being discussed at the Council, then regional representatives should have a voice in the present institutions and organisations.

Thirdly, and perhaps of growing importance in the future: as we move towards monetary union, and the Single Market has what I am afraid will be some negative effects on the peripheral regions of the Community, and as the Community puts increasing emphasis on its regional policy, it will look for vehicles to deliver that policy. Bruce Millan, as Regional Commissioner, has already acted to strengthen the regional role in Brussels. That can only gather pace when we get economic and monetary union. As we try to counter the impact of the 'golden triangle', or whatever we call the 'banana shape' emerging in Europe, we are going to look for local agencies. I believe the omission of a Scottish parliament in that structure will be one that the United Kingdom will come to regret as areas and regions that already have their own parliamentary structure will be able to take advantage of the new policies growing out of Brussels.

Some of this might sound marginally, but I hope not too, far fetched. Some of it, I freely admit, is for the future. But for my conclusion, I want to return to my introduction: we are living in unique times; we are living in an extraordinary moment of opportunity. I am sorry to say that I haven't seen from the leadership of the Community much sense of vision about where we might be going. I thought the low point was reached at the time of the Birmingham Summit when John Major called together leaders of twelve countries, some of the most politically and economically important in the world. This was a moment when one in ten Europeans was unemployed; when a civil war was raging in Yugoslavia; when the GATT talks were about to collapse with the threat of world trade wars, and a whole number of other issues were pressing. John Major called the leaders of the Twelve together not to discuss any of these vital issues, but to discuss subsidiarity.

Anyone who knows me is aware that I am as keen on subsidiarity as the next person, but if we get bogged down in relatively unimportant issues rather than tackling the major issues, the Community is not going to serve the people it was designed and built to serve. What we need from the Edinburgh Summit is real vision, to create the sort of Europe in which we all want to live in the next century.

David Martin's lecture was sponsored by Heriot-Watt University and delivered at the James Watt Centre, Heriot-Watt University, on 25 November 1992. Professor Alistair G.J. MacFarlane, Principal and Vice-Chancellor, Heriot-Watt University, presided.

A response was given by Dr David Boak.

GENNADY GERASIMOV

11   *Russia as an integral part of Europe*

YOUR INVITATION TO A RUSSIAN REPRESENTATIVE TO contribute to this series of lectures on European affairs is, in itself, proof of the fact that Russia belongs to Europe. In Portugal, where I serve as an Ambassador, we tend to look at Europe as a piece of land between Portugal and Russia. This is certainly wrong, as your invitation testifies, so here I prefer to define Europe as a chunk of territory between Edinburgh and Yekaterinburg, our city in the Urals, whose name sounds similar to the Russian pronunciation of Edinburgh.

Our Yekaterinburg, famous as the place where Mr Yeltsin made his political career, is also where Europe meets Asia and Russia is, of course, a little bit schizophrenic. We cannot agree with the observation of that great British writer Rudyard Kipling that 'East is East and West is West, and never the twain shall meet': they seem to be meeting satisfactorily in Russia and our newly adopted – and also old – national emblem is the double headed eagle, looking east and looking west with both heads (though some sceptics call this bird a 'Chernobyl mutant'). The double vision of our eagle was reflected in the recent itinerary of our President who visited Britain, then Hungary, then he turned east to visit Korea and plans next to visit China.

My concern here, however, is with Russia facing west. To understand it better I must start with the radical change that has taken place that stemmed from Perestroika. Before, the Soviet Union was an empire based on ideology rather than on national identity or territory. It was based on the messianic teaching of Marxism–Leninism. We thought that we knew all the answers and were so generous that we were ready to open other people's eyes to the real truth and to show them the way to their own happiness. This is rather like the story about the three boy scouts who helped an old lady to cross the street. When they reported this deed to their scout master he complimented them, saying how good it was to help an old lady but why had it taken three of them to help her? They answered, of course, that it was because she hadn't wanted to cross the street.

So we brought to our side of the street Poles, Bulgarians, Hungarians and others in Eastern Europe. Certainly I must add the communist ideology has its universal appeal and there are special cases – China, Cuba, Albania, Yugoslavia. But for us it was just another proof that we were riding the wave of the future. This messianic zeal explains Berlin in 1953, Budapest in 1956, Prague in 1968 and Afghanistan in 1979. This was the reflection of the so-called 'Brezhnev' doctrine: when socialism is in danger somewhere it is the duty of all socialist states to put things right.

Now we understand that we made the same mistake that Columbus made when he sailed west 500 years ago to find a way to India. He failed because he found something he hadn't expected to find. It was the same with us: we tried to sail to the bright communist future, and we ended up with empty shelves in the shops and general discontent. The system simply did not work and this could be seen easily by everybody who travelled abroad and compared different systems, or seen just by going to a cinema in Moscow where foreign films were shown. We wanted to change human nature, but we didn't read Adam Smith, that great Scot, which we do now. So our system simply didn't work.

To make a long story short, the system was undermined by Perestroika and, in my humble way, I hope I helped in this. The system collapsed in August 1991 and, by the end of that year, the Soviet Union had disappeared, which was not what we planned. But it had disappeared. This is the fact, and it was an agonising personal experience. As Ambassador to Portugal from March 1991, the Ambassador of a big superpower – the Union of Soviet Socialist Republics – I gradually started to lose first the Republics, then the socialist characteristics of these Republics, then their soviet peculiarities. Every morning, I had to have a role call until, at last, I had lost them all.

This was, if I may say so, the second stage of the so-called 'Sinatra doctrine' which replaced the Brezhnev doctrine. The Brezhnev doctrine, which I mentioned earlier, was abandoned when 'we discarded the plans to paint our planet red', as Yeltsin once put it. It was over and, remembering that popular song 'I did it my way', we gave our allies freedom to do it their own way. They lost no time in crossing the street back to their own side. The nations of Eastern Europe discarded the Warsaw Pact, socialism, and promises of eternal friendship. They also started to quarrel with each other and between themselves, but that is another story.

But the process didn't stop there. The Republics comprising the Soviet Union followed. Each one of them wanted to do it 'its own way' and each had its own historical, economic, psychological ambitions – an explosive mixture. The explosion itself happened in Minsk in December 1991; the Soviet Union was dead. People said 'long live the CIS' (Commonwealth of Independent States). Originally there was some hope that the Republics would adopt a common foreign policy and would have common embassies abroad, representing the Commonwealth as a new political, geographical entity. But national feelings, interpretations of national interests and a clash of political ambitions make the Commonwealth more of ideal than of substance and, at least for now, there is no central office, no telephone number and no stationery for this Commonwealth.

But even this was not the end of the process. The 'Sinatra doctrine' entered its third stage. Several parts of the Russian Federation itself decided to try to do it 'their own way'. All this may be a little difficult for you to understand, and taxing too, because it pushes you along the road of new geographical discoveries. Where, for instance, is Chechnya? And where are the borders of Tatarstan? Or, what is the difference between North Osetia and South Osetia? If you want to be *au courant* you must know all these things. This is something, as I mentioned, which we did not envisage. We followed the advice of that Irish writer, Oscar Wilde, who said once that a problem does not exist if it is not talked about. We didn't talk about our national problems and we thought that they were not there, but they were there, under the carpet. When we proclaimed our Glasnost and started to discuss our concerns, we discovered that we had a lot of skeletons in our closet and the most awful one was the skeleton of nationalism. I remember reading a book 20 years ago, whose author I have forgotten, but the title was *Nationalism as the Last Stage of Communism*, which, of course, hints at Lenin's work *Imperialism, the Higher Stage of Capitalism*. To give you just one example of the paradoxes we have: the chairman of our Parliament is Mr Khasbulatov who succeeded Yeltsin in this extremely important post. He was elected a Deputy to the Parliament in his native land of Chechnya, which later proclaimed its complete independence from Russia and withdrew its three Deputies from the Russian Parliament. So, Mr Khasbulatov is in Moscow without a mandate yet he is the chairman of the Parliament, an extremely important job, which once prompted Yeltsin to quip 'it's a long time since Khasbulatov visited his constituency'. This is just one example of the difficulties that have arisen.

In a year, we have completely changed the map, not only of Eastern Europe but also the map of the Soviet Union; and I do not envy those who prepare the next edition of the *Times Atlas of the World*. But this is the background which I think it is necessary to have in mind when we are talking about our new foreign policy for Russia. When former Soviet Republics went their own way, there was some talk in certain quarters about creating a special bureaucracy, a separate ministry, maybe a Commonwealth Ministry, to deal with these Republics, relations with them and the problems they created for us, for themselves and for the world. But it was decided, and I think rightly, to add these Republics and their problems to the Ministry of Foreign Affairs as it exists. It was also decided, this time I think wrongly, to leave the Ministry with the same budget. This has not been easy. We are cutting our staff in Portugal to send people to more important posts in Kiev, Tashkent, or wherever.

We have now three circles of foreign policy concerns. The first circle includes our neighbours, all those new independent states, but also Finland, Iran, Turkey, China and, arguably, the United States. Remember that Alaska is just three miles from Russia – the distance between the island of Little Diomede which is American and the island of Big Diomede which is Russian is just three miles, yet they have different dates and crossing from one to the other involves a change of day.

The aim of our foreign policy in this region is to secure friendly relations with everybody and to develop economic ties. This is not at all easy, but that is beyond my topic here. The name of the game is establishing, in our phrase, 'the belt of good neighbourhood, or good neighbours', and also of ensuring centralised control of nuclear weapons. This is most important. We also aim to guarantee the civil and human rights of Russians who lived in the former Soviet Union and who live now in different countries around us, who total around 30 million people. The third circle is the rest of the world. We do not want, naturally, to offend, or to neglect, anyone and recently, for instance, the ambassadors of the African countries in Moscow were called to the Foreign Ministry and reassured that we were not forgetting them, but there are priorities, and sometimes it is not easy to choose between them.

One of the problems is actually dictated by geography. I think it was Sigmund Freud who said once that 'autonomy is destiny'. I think geography is destiny – at least for us. We have this dual character and it is reflected in our history, in our national psychology and, of course, in our politics. The great divide between so called 'Westernisers' and so called 'Slavophiles' recently re-emerged, together with habitual bitter discussions on the subject of which road to take – the one to the west or the one to the east (meaning our old customs and traditions). The government, and the majority of our people, have no doubt as to which road to take. This is the same road taken by our Tsar, Peter the Great, who, as we say, 'opened the window to Europe'. Peter the Great wanted to modernise Russia, to bring it to Europe, and we want the same today. We want to join the family of European nations as an equal, normal member, not just as something special or a special case, but just as a normal member of the European nations. Although we have more than 100 nationalities in Russia, our cultural values are predominantly European, and although we have many religions in Russia, we talk mainly about Christian values. I don't want to repeat here the mistake one politician made recently in the United States – he defined the United States as a Christian country and he was rebuffed. We do have others – we have Muslims, of course, we have Jews – but we also have certain Russian traditions.

We are, perhaps, a little too fascinated with the consumer society of the West, but we do want for ourselves all the things in life that modern technology makes available. We have certain achievements of our own – for instance, we were the first in space. We have other achievements recognised universally, for instance in military-related matters, perhaps unfortunately. What we do need is organisation, management and a lot of help, and for help we are looking west.

But is the West looking east? We are in very bad shape: my society, I must admit, is now in a very deep crisis of many dimensions, economic, political, ecological. You could write very thick books about any aspect of the crisis which we now face. In the old days we had a joke, 'Is this communism already, or is it going to get worse?' Now people are asking 'Is this capitalism already, or is it going to get worse?'. The same idea may also be put this way: under socialism, people had money but no goods to buy; under capitalism, people now see the goods in the shops but have no money with which to buy them.

There is great disappointment in Russia because, as you
know, when society undergoes great change, people tend to
think that this big change will improve things overnight. It
doesn't happen overnight, and I would be a bad ambassador
not to emphasise the complaints which my President and my
Minister for Foreign Affairs are making all the time. We
appeal to the democratic allies in the West (in the phrase
of Mr Kozyrev, the Minister), for more participation, and
the most serious approach to what is happening in Russia.
The 'worst case' scenario leads to restoration of dictatorship,
although the form may be different from the previous one
which was, as I mentioned, internationalistic in outlook based
on Marxist ideology. This is not going to happen again, but
this time dictatorship may be based on nationalistic theories of
'Mother Russia'. It may be based on attempts to bring back
former Republics, not as a Soviet Union but as a Russian
empire. The consequences will be disastrous, not only to the
territories of the former Soviet Union.

President Yeltsin addressed our parliament recently, and he
quoted Pushkin, our most eminent poet who said 'God save
us from Russian revolt, cruel revolt, without mercy.' This is a
warning, coming from the President. There may exist a school
of thought that a weak Russia is good for the west, but this old
geopolitical approach ignores the interdependence of countries
in our nuclear age. M. Jacques Delors, says 'The European
Community is interested in cooperation with a stable state
that is developing on the basis of integration not on the
basis of fighting between small separate kingdoms.' This is
what Robert Strauss, who has just retired from his post as
American Ambassador to Russia, is saying. He says 'Russia
is weak, impoverished and unsettled, but we should have
no illusion that it will or should remain weak, or that a
weak Russia somehow serves Western interests.' And the last
quote, this time from the *Financial Times* editorial, 9 November
1992, 'Understandably distracted by the United States elections,
the debate over Maastricht, a looming US/EC trade war and

gathering recessionary clouds, the West has thus far failed to do enough to stiffen Mr Yeltsin's resolve. Mr Yeltsin needs help to stay the course.' I intentionally quote all these things to try to show that this is not just my point, but is something which is shared by many other observers.

For many decades the West lived in the shadow of the Soviet threat. With the end of the Cold War, this threat is there no more but now there is a cloud of a second Soviet threat on the horizon: nuclear weapons not properly attended to, or in the wrong hands as a result of upheavals; the danger of regional conflicts to escalate, and so on; the danger of dictatorship which may need an external enemy to fight against, for its own survival. From this point of view, the money spent on us is a kind of sound insurance policy. A good example is the Pentagon's decision to spend $400 million on the destruction of Soviet nuclear weapons. Imagine the cost of this destruction in case of war.

Now, from security considerations to economic ones. Business opportunities arise from new market conditions which one of the biggest countries in the world is trying to create. We still need to establish definite and stable rules of the game: tax laws, investment guarantees and so on. We admit that. But many companies are already discovering and exploring this new land of opportunity. Yesterday, when I was sitting at Heathrow Airport for three hours because of British Airways and British weather and a bomb scare here in Edinburgh, quite by chance I read in a newspaper that the Trade Advisory Service of Scotland had secured a $25 million contract to revamp a hotel in Moscow, just one of Moscow's ordinary hotels, with 10,000 beds. It's a good start for Scottish business. Well, we need this kind of investment and we need 'knowhow', we need advice and that's why we re-discovered Adam Smith among others.

I think the West has here self-interest, business opportunities but also responsibility. The responsibility, in my view, arises from the fact of Western victory in the Cold War. Many politicians say some people on our side don't see it like that;

some people on our side say that both sides are victors, that victory belongs to common sense. But looking from the Western side to the empire in ruins, people may find reason to think that their side prevailed, and after the magic moment of victory comes a certain period of responsibility of the victor for the vanquished. It explains the Marshall Plan for a devastated Europe after the Second World War. It explains the new constitution in post-war Japan, written with the help of the occupying power. It is the same today: the West cannot afford to tell Russia just to 'drop dead'.

Now, there are many suggestions as to how the west can help Russia. One of them is from George Soros. He suggests, as I read in the *Wall Street Journal* recently, that the West can offer a social safety net to unemployed pensioners and the needy in Russia at a rate of $6 a month which, with the existing exchange rate, is just enough to survive (incredibly, $6 a month is enough to survive in Russia, making tourists feel extremely rich). This will help to avoid a social explosion but, overall, $10 billion is needed to help to save us. As Soros says in the *Wall Street Journal*: 'I have discussed my idea with key policy makers in Russia, and they agree, but tell me it's an idle dream. Western governments are apparently too busy with their own problems.'

Of course there are problems and some of them will be addressed or just aired in this city at the Summit. Still it is my duty to state our case, which we think is also the case for the West because of possible grave consequences. While President Yeltsin's recent visit to Britain was very important, we think, and extremely useful (and as happens with this kind of visit, a lot will depend on follow-ups), we are improving our ties with Italy and with Portugal and, as an Ambassador, I try to do this. We are not satisfied with Peter the Great's 'window to Europe', we need wide open gates. Even more, we need all the walls coming down. The metaphor from Perestroika days of the 'common European home' is not used any more, but the strategy aim remains. Eventually, at some time in the future, in the next century, we hope to be a normal member of Europe or, if possible, to join the European Community. We are not ready and we know that, but we want to stand in line and wait. Meanwhile, we want an agreement with the European Community for the duration of this – as we call it – transitory period. We ask for certain preferences. But, for my last quotation, let me cite Edward Mortimer in the *Financial Times*, 18 November 1992. He says 'Domestic vested interests oppose opening the European market to competitive goods from the east. We look like selfish children squabbling among ourselves.' It is an irony of the situation that my Foreign Minister is strongly criticised back home in the press, and in the Parliament, and elsewhere for being too Westernised, looking too much to the West in his foreign policy, even to the point that many papers predict he is going to step down.

A few words now on our debt, which is actually the debt of the Soviet Union. It is estimated to be $70–80 billion. Our export earnings are not enough to pay the interest, and we are asking for this debt to be rescheduled. Yeltsin says that the problem would be solved more easily if the West moved quickly to allow Russia into the West European Economic Community, opened its markets to Russian goods and scrapped technology export controls.

Now to several final remarks, which I think are necessary for the record. Russia is active in the diplomatic process called the Conference on Security and Co-operation in Europe. The members are now busy preparing for a meeting in Stockholm where institutionalisation of this process and also a code of conduct of members will be discussed. We want this conference to be an active actor on the international scene. I think the new American administration may look at Europe as a single continent, without the old great divide between East and West and I think Washington will be less involved in European affairs interpreting the emergence, or re-emergence, of nationalism as the return to old European ways.

In conclusion, I must show that I am more optimistic than pessimistic. I am sure of the future of my country. We have all the resources we need. We have everything. It is, perhaps, the richest country in the world. We have the resources, we have talented people, we shall overcome.

Gennady Gerasimov's lecture was sponsored by Lothian Regional Council and the National Museums of Scotland with assistance from Royal Mail Scotland and Northern Ireland. It was delivered at the Royal Museum of Scotland on 4 December 1992.

The lecture was chaired by Helen Liddell, journalist, and a response was given by Neal Ascherson, writer and journalist.

HELENA KENNEDY

12   *Europe and our rights*

I CAME TO EDINBURGH KNOWING THERE WAS TO BE THE
European Summit and wishing to take the opportunity of
speaking about Europe and our rights which, I believe, we
have to set in the whole context of the current debate about
sovereignty.

British sovereignty is being revolutionised by membership of
the European Community and it seems to me important to get
back to base and talk about what 'sovereignty' really means.
Sovereignty is really about who makes decisions, who runs
communities, who has power over whom, and where authority
lies. Opponents of the Maastricht Treaty say that we are
surrendering British sovereignty to the European Community
and the centralised bureaucracy in Brussels. But to many of the
critics of the Treaty, particularly many on the right, sovereignty
means the sovereignty of the Westminster Parliament, which is
supposed to embody liberty and democracy. But what does
British sovereignty amount to?

In Britain, power is concentrated in the power of the Prime
Minister and his ministers: it is not Parliament that is sovereign,
but the executive. What results is executive sovereignty, as the
executive dominates Parliament. It does so through a number
of factors such as an undemocratic electoral system, which can
give a majority of seats to a party with a minority of the
vote. Another important factor is the Whip system and party
patronage which enable the party leaders to keep others in line:
a third of Conservative MPs, for example, hold some position
in government. They know they will sacrifice any knighthood

that might be in the offing, or any peerage, if they do not vote 'the right way'. That is one of the chief powers of the Whip system. Then there are the Crown prerogatives. The executive exercises powers of the Royal Prerogative to declare war, to appoint judges and bishops of the established church, to make treaties, without any mechanism of accountability. So when the Government ordered the security forces to shoot suspects in Gibraltar, they could later prevent an inquiry on the grounds of Crown immunity. The very fact that Crown immunity could be used as a means of opposition to an inquiry seemed something of alarm to me. The GCHQ ban was also carried out under the Royal Prerogative. Perhaps we can understand, therefore, why some people give vent to their anger, calling this elected dictatorship.

Across parts of Europe, there are the seeds of a different principle, which date from the French Revolution, and Tom Paine's *Rights of Man*: the idea that the people should be sovereign; that we should have inalienable rights, rights that defend minorities; and that we should participate in decision-making at every level, on the basis of equality. We should run our own communities; we should have power over politicians, and judges, not the other way around. Authority should come from us, from below, not from above. Edmund Burke, who opposed Paine, said that this would undermine 'the deference and hierarchy on which the British constitution was necessarily based'. In my view, there has been too much deference and hierarchy; we have had that for hundreds of years, and it is time now to do something different.

It is this, in my view, that Lord Tebbit and his companions are afraid of: that European union might actually encourage people to take that control, and act like citizens, rather than subjects. More and more people are asking whether the sovereignty we had is worth salvaging. The old form of sovereignty is already slipping away. While the Single European Act did not arouse much debate, the controversies over Maastricht are due to the fact that people are not prepared to have their consent to the

Treaty taken for granted, and quite right. They're not clear what it is about; what it is they're supposed to be giving up; what it means to their lives and their liberties.

So what has been happening? Being a member of the European Community has, from the very beginning, entailed pooling our sovereignty with our European neighbours. It meant national parliaments could no longer go on formulating policy on the economy, on the environment, on foreign policy in their own sweet way. They would have to take decisions in common with other nations and agree a joint strategy. This was not just a political decision; it was a recognition that very few things fall neatly within the boundaries of nation states. Capital is international; communications have been revolutionised; the fallout from Chernobyl spread across many Western European states. If citizens are not to be subjected to these impersonal forces, there must be an effective layer of decision-making and government at European level.

European law now has a superior status to United Kingdom law and we have to recognise that. British judges give effect to this on a daily basis. Whenever there is a conflict in the courts between the two, the courts have to bow to European rulings. Thus, what the British Parliament says and does in a number of key areas is becoming increasingly irrelevant. The idea that we are suddenly losing our sovereignty is, therefore, an enormous deception. It is not just suddenly happening; it has been happening. We, the people, have had little sovereignty to give away. The executive is having to adapt to changed times. In Europe, they can't have it all their own way, which is why Britain has been at the forefront of attempts to prevent much closer political and monetary union.

It is our task now, as citizens, to reclaim control of our Government, and our communities, to assert our rights; and our deepening involvement in Europe is a powerful force for that kind of change. But we must recognise that all is not perfect in Europe: the unaccountability of the institutions within the European Community has still to be confronted. Europe must not be held up as a Utopia. Despite the inadequacies of Britain's legislation on race, the rest of Europe is even worse. We have also seen in recent months the appalling contempt for the plight of refugees.

As well as the story that 'we are sovereign people', Conservative governments like to peddle other fictions about the United Kingdom. One is that Thatcherism got the state 'off our backs'; that Mrs T. limited government and redistributed power. This does not bear examination. Since 1979 this Government has been *on* our backs. There have been serious erosions of civil liberties with little opportunity to challenge the authorities, except by means of the tortuously long process of taking a case to Strasbourg, under the European Convention. We have seen racist immigration laws, the extension of police powers with the Public Order Act (1986) and the misuse of these powers during the miners' strike, with the setting up of road blocks, the making of whole counties 'no-go' areas. We've seen the abolition of the Right to Silence in Northern Ireland. We've seen clause 28 which prohibited schools from presenting positive images of homosexuality. We've seen unauthorised phone tapping and surveillance of such figures as trade unionists, peace activists and the former National Council for Civil Liberties officers, Patricia Hewitt and Harriet Harman – they were all under surveillance by the security services. This was revealed when the former MI5 officer, Cathy Massiter, went public. We have also seen political censorship of the media and MI5 vetting of journalists for jobs at the BBC; some people were refused jobs on the basis of incorrect information. One of these examples was the Scottish journalist Isobel Hilton, refused a job in the BBC because of her involvement with a Scottish-Chinese organisation.

Further examples include the erosion of trade union rights in the GCHQ case, amongst others, and the prosecution of Clive Ponting, a civil servant, for leaking to an MP information on the sinking of the *Belgrano* during the Falklands war. Ponting was prosecuted under the Official Secrets Act and acquitted by a jury who believed the public had a right to know the truth, but the Government's response was to legislate against the possibility of such a defence ever being used again with the new Official Secrets Act. This was also the case where the trial judged declared that the interests of the state were synonymous with the interests of the Government of the day: if this is an example of the judiciary's appreciation of our constitutional arrangements, then we have cause to worry.

Charter 88, the citizens' movement for constitutional reform, of which I am the Chair, is highlighting some of the most worrying violations of rights in Britain in a series of pamphlets that are currently being produced. Graham Pink, a nurse working in the National Health Service, writes about how health workers are being gagged, and sacked for speaking out about against unsatisfactory staffing levels, or the effects of the spending cuts on hospitals. Ken Follett, the author, has been writing about Abbas Shiblak, an Arab and one of the people arrested and threatened with deportation during the Gulf War, on unspecified charges. He was in no way a supporter of Saddam, yet he was tried before a court of three men whose identities were concealed – this is the 'three blind mice' issue – and he was not given legal representation. It is deeply disturbing to think of this happening in contemporary Britain. Future papers will be looking at the family of a Falklands soldier, killed in an accident, who fought for years to see the records which would explain why he died, yet they have not been given that information. The use and abuse of official statistics by government is the subject of another paper being written by a *Guardian* journalist.

What all these cases reveal is a system which is rotting form the inside, a complete lack of respect for civil liberties and due process. It is cases like these which should make us question the way we are governed, and wholly refute Thatcher's claim that our current constitutional arrangements serve us well. What she really meant was that current constitutional arrangements served *her* well.

The only thing standing between us and the erosion of civil

liberties has been the European Convention on Human Rights. British civil servants helped to draft the convention, and Britain signed it in 1951. But it wasn't until the late 1960s that the UK accepted that British citizens had the right of individual petition to the European Commission and the European Court in Strasbourg, a right that has been renewed regularly by governments since then. Complaints under the convention can be made by one state against the other, as the Irish Government did against the British Government over the treatment of IRA suspects, but it also can be brought by individuals against the state. It is by no means a perfect document, and the process of taking a case to the European Court is lengthy and expensive, sometimes taking as long as five or six years. Remedies frequently come too late: when prisoners bring an action which goes to Europe, they can frequently already be released before the judgement can give them any benefit. However, it has made a positive contribution to rights in Britain.

In response to successful applications to the European Court, the Government has agreed not to reintroduce interrogation techniques, such as sleep deprivation, which had been used in Northern Ireland. Mental patients under compulsory confinement now as the result of an action have more rights and a fairer procedure to review their confinement. Homosexuality for consenting adults has been legalised in Northern Ireland. There is no further birching of juveniles in the Isle of Man. Prisoners whose rights of access to a lawyer were being denied and whose correspondence was being interfered with are now entitled to access to a lawyer and to the protection of correspondence with their families as a result of action taken in Europe. 200,000 African Asians, deprived of their right to British citizenship by Parliament in 1968 had the right restored, because of the Convention. Laws of Contempt have been tested: a ban was imposed on the *Sunday Times* thalidomide article and this became one of the first cases to go to Europe, when the Government was held to be in violation of the Convention and the ban had to be amended. A judge's order imposing reporting restrictions, or restricting the public's access to a court, is now subject to a review by a higher court. MI5 has been put on a statutory basis and it has all been done in anticipation of a ruling, in Europe, on a case brought by the employees of the National Council for Civil Liberties, who were being classified as subversives and whose phones were being tapped. Nearly 100 British laws or regulations have been repealed or amended as a result of proceedings under the Convention. No country has been found guilty of so many violations of rights. Thus, paradoxically, the years of right-wing, Conservative rule have put rights on the public agenda precisely because of their demise. This is one feather we did not expect Baroness Thatcher to be able to put in her bunnett.

But rights are not part of our legal and political traditions. Traditionally we have had 'permissions' doled out to us from on high, and denied to us at whim. Our liberties exist in the silence of the law. We are not citizens with inalienable rights. In the same way that people are now looking at a different type of sovereignty, rather than harking back to an authoritarian and élitist past, rather than demanding the Government restore their liberties, we are arguing for rights. But the idea of talking about our rights as citizens is new; we are still grappling with what it means.

So why have rights become important? What's it all about? Increasingly in the post-war period the idea of human rights has gained prominence. Initially this was signalled with the United Nations declaration, the idea being to prevent Nazism and Fascism from raising their heads again and to protect vulnerable minorities from the tyranny of the majority. A key thing about human rights is that they are universal; they cross national boundaries, which is another sense in which it can never make any sense to claim that the British parliament is sovereign and all power resides in it. As far as human rights are concerned, nation states who sign international human rights treaties are voluntarily abandoning the Enoch Powell idea of sovereignty, which is that it is absolute in its very being and that sovereignty shared is sovereignty lost.

But why have rights become a new by-word in Britain? Lawyers in the United Kingdom, especially progressive lawyers, have traditionally been hostile to the idea of 'rights' – Bills of Rights and written constitutions have been anathema to us, and I confess to having previous convictions on this score myself. But what was interesting was that the 1950s and 1960s gave us a different perspective. We saw that what United States lawyers could do with the tool of the United States Constitution was to make considerable challenge to the courts and to government on issues like civil rights or Vietnam. They were using the Constitution creatively and we saw an amazing use of the Constitution which, before that, had not been particularly used by lawyers. That experience and seeing how US lawyers were able to use the Constitution in relation to civil liberties fired many of us in Britain with enthusiasm, and we began to wonder if we could do the same thing here with cases on issues of civil liberties, on race, on terrorism, on sexuality.

But the tools did not exist. From the late 1960s we were able to take cases of infringements of civil liberties to Europe, under the Convention. Even then not many lawyers knew how to go about it, or considered doing it. In recent years, committed lawyers have begun sharing knowledge and we have started meeting together to identify what cases should go to Europe, and how we can take those issues there. We see the convention as a useful tool for civil liberties. The violations of rights and abuses of power which have occurred over the last decade or more have aroused people to look at just how little power they have in their own lives and in their communities, and have encouraged them to look at their power in relation to the Government. There is a developing feeling that people want their rights, they want institutions to be accountable, to feel that the law belongs to them. They are much more knowledgeable than before. They're not tugging their forelocks to lawyers, and thank God for that. They don't agree there are some areas that are impenetrable to people, and they are more critical of the failure of some of our institutions.

You will have seen the Lord Chief Justice, coming out, rolling up his sleeves and attempting to get back in touch with 'the people'. He has responded to this growing unease and the public loss of confidence in the law. One of the things he's advocating is the incorporation now of the European Convention into UK law, both north and south of the border. This is necessary for people to be able to gain justice and to claim their rights more quickly and effectively, but it should not just be recommended to appease people who are unhappy with the legal system. It's also necessary to change the whole ethos and culture of the British Constitution and it's here that Lord Taylor fails to grasp the extent of the problem. Sadly, he is complacent about the level of public mistrust of the judiciary, suggesting that no thorough review of appointment procedures is necessary, and he is totally dismissive of the need for accountability. Many will know the way in which our judges are appointed by the method of taking soundings from the judges who are presently *in situ*, and asking for their opinions as to who the next person should be to join their number.

If the judges are going to seize greater political power, which is undoubtedly the case with the incorporation of the European Convention, they have to recognise that the old self-appointing processes will have to go. The *quid pro quo* must be an appointments commission, not merely a lay observer as Lord Taylor suggests, someone to watch over the judges' shoulder as they're taking soundings and hearing the gossip about who should join them. Who is it that he has in mind, who should have the role of the lay observer? Someone presumably not too different from himself, someone like Marmaduke Hussey perhaps, but certainly not my mum!

Similarly, he is complacent about changing the complexion of the bench, thinking it is enough to talk about appointments being based on merit. It's very important we realise that 'merit' is not a simple objective criterion. In fact, there are subjective elements within it, and it depends very much who the gate-keepers are. If the criteria being applied are heavily biased against women and against black people and against people from working-class backgrounds, then we can't expect very much change. He says that because he was a grammar school boy, this means that the judiciary is no longer élitist and is somehow changing its nature. What he does not say is that he's from a professional family, went to Cambridge, and went through the same system as his colleagues.

I am afraid the beneficiaries of a system are those who are most loathe to change anything. His adding his voice, however, to the call to incorporate the European Convention into British law is welcome. It's an essential first step, but what we really need is a Bill of Rights. The UK is the only country in Europe and the Commonwealth without such a Bill, yet in a MORI poll in 1991 conducted throughout the whole of the United Kingdom 79% agreed that their rights would be most effectively protected if they were written down in a single document and most people thought adjudication would be best left to a reformed judiciary.

A Bill of Rights would establish legally enforceable and readily accessible civil, political and human rights for everyone resident in the UK. More specifically it would enshrine the right to life, to liberty and security of the person; protection from torture, inhuman treatment, slavery, enforced labour; the right to a fair trial; the right to respect for private and family life; freedom of thought, conscience and religion; freedom of expression; the right to peaceful assembly and association; the right to marry; the right to effective remedies for infringement of civil liberties; the right to non-discrimination; and the right to equality. It would have a special status above other law and all subsequent legislation would have to be interpreted in the light of the Bill. It would provide a backdrop of principle for all other law. It would mean that temporary majorities in Parliament could not ride rough-shod over fundamental human rights and freedoms, especially those of vulnerable minorities. It would curb the overpowerful executive and bring about a much-needed shift of power from the state to the citizenry. People would know their rights and be able to enforce them in any court, from the highest to the lowest. If at first they got an unfavourable ruling, they could appeal, and what happens in other countries, certainly where there is active political life, is that governments often are forced by the publicity surrounding a case to change laws voluntarily. All public officials, MPs, ministers, civil servants, police, judges and administrators would have to respect these values and take them into account in all decisions, so that legal action is a last resort. The state would have a duty to see that private organisations, like privatised electricity or water companies or individuals, do not violate the rights in the Bill.

This legislation would have a marked effect on the training and attitudes of lawyers and judges because if in their 'lawyering' they are having to consider rights, then I think we would find that the product of the courts would be somewhat different. Government could be held to account for its actions; an argument it might otherwise have ignored must be addressed. It can't ignore what it finds inconvenient or unpalatable. It must produce its arguments in open court, and the arguments must be significantly strong to convince the court that a breach of someone's rights has *not* occurred. The burden of proof must be on the Government, and it's interesting to speculate on the effect that this might have had on the Matrix Churchill case or miscarriages of justice cases, where there was non-disclosure by the authorities.

A Bill of Rights would create a new popular awareness of human rights. Learning about the principles enshrined in the Bill would become part of the school curriculum and adult education, encouraging students and pupils to debate the importance of protecting human rights and the difficulties that arise when they conflict. This would encourage a more informed public, more sensitive to the implications of restricting civil liberties, and of extending them. This is absolutely key.

Human rights do not live in laws and constitutions, but in the hearts and minds of people. It would need to be part of a much wider constitutional settlement, and this is a far cry from what Lord Justice Taylor has envisaged so far. People are suspicious of rights, because they fear that a Bill of Rights would be a field day for judges and lawyers. This must not happen, but the suspicion is not without reason. However, it is not in itself a good reason for rejecting rights-based law. Rights are for every person, so we need a Human Rights Commission which would then in turn point out to the Government where legislation is infringing the Bill of Rights. It would bring test cases to court, and provide a tool for those who couldn't afford to take a case on their own. We need wholesale reform of the appointment, culture, and ethos of the judiciary, not just tinkering around the edges as has been suggested. Courts need to be made less intimidating, the law more accessible and comprehensible. Only then can people outside the courts begin to rebuild their trust in the judiciary and in the legal system.

There are two things Lord Taylor failed to grasp. The first is that rights are meaningless without knowledge and information. The other is that a Bill of Rights changes the balance of power in our Constitution, taking power away from politicians and ministers and putting it into the hands of the people.

To take first the need for knowledge, the right to know. People in the United Kingdom can't find out from the Government what pesticides are being put into our food, what chemicals are swilling about in our rivers, whether our trains match up to safety standards. We have no access to our medical or employment records as of right, and it's only been since legislation that we are now allowed access to post-1991 medical records, but not ones that went before.

In the 'Iraqgate' scandal, we saw government contempt for the general public; we were presented with a government fearful that it could not sell the public its policy on arms trading and so it decided not to tell the public its policy on arms trading. Even when presented with the potential conviction of three men who had only been doing what they had been privately sanctioned to do by ministers, secrecy almost took precedence over the liberty of the subject. This is shocking, blatant disregard for principles which are central to our democracy. Information is power and the right to know is crucial to our democracy. It underpins all our rights. If we do not know we cannot judge, if we cannot judge we cannot make choices, and if we cannot make choices then we are hardly free.

Rot grows in dark and secret corners, and secrecy is much too much a part of British public life: we need open government and public access to information to make our rights real. But a Bill of Rights and freedom of information would also give us the opportunity to hold our Government to account and would mean a dispersal of power away from the centre, to the people.

Then we come to the issue of subsidiarity. This brings me to the other sense in which Europe is a threat to traditional ideas about power and rights in the United Kingdom, and the relationship between the citizen and the state. Despite the rhetoric of the United Kingdom Government about how centralised and unaccountable the Brussels lot are, I'm afraid we're just as bad, if not worse. We are one of the most centralised, secretive and unaccountable states in Western Europe.

The Maastricht Treaty talks about subsidiarity, as does the British Government, *ad nauseam*. Subsidiarity means that power should be exercised at the lowest possible level, so if something can be done more effectively by local government, that is who should exercise that power, not regional, national or European government. But equally, there will be some decisions best taken at regional, national or European level, but always the assumption must be that it should be taken as close to the people as possible. This means devolving power as far as possible. But where do we devolve power to in the United Kingdom? Scotland is a distinctive nation, with its own institutions and legal system, yet denied its own Parliament; Wales is also a nation without a Parliament. The English regions have no structure, let alone elected assemblies, and local government has been completely emasculated.

In the UK, Whitehall and Westminster claim to know best. They know best about what liberties we should enjoy, what information we should be allowed to have, what powers our local representatives should exercise. They know best how our money should be spent, whether it's on royal castles, or footing the legal bills of Cabinet Ministers. I believe that the reverse should be true. Rights are entrenched, that is given special protection under the law. Governments should be representative and accountable; information should be free; power should be shared between two chambers of Parliament and a judiciary, and between national, regional and local government – and can I make it clear that when I speak about two chambers of Parliament I do not consider the House of Lords to qualify? Even those countries which traditionally had a very centralised system of government, such as France and Spain, are busy devolving power to regional government, establishing regional Charters of Autonomy. These regions have a more effective voice in Europe as a result of having democratically elected, accountable governments. Take the German Länder, who make up the second chamber, the Bundesrat, in Germany. They were able to threaten to veto the Maastricht Treaty unless the Committee of the Regions of the European Community were given more powers because the German Constitution recognises their rights and powers. Just think how much more influence the nations of Scotland and Wales would have, if we had such rights; think of the power it would give to Northern Ireland and the English regions, if there were a devolved system of power, if they had their own governments.

As we have come to see ourselves as Europeans, we also come to demand to be treated as citizens, not as subjects. Thanks to increasing European union but also thanks to the democracy movement in Scotland, which is putting pressure for change on the rest of the United Kingdom, we may not be too far away from a new constitutional settlement. (I always feel worried about coming to Scotland to speak about constitutional change, because I feel the Scots are so much further ahead than other parts of Britain, and I feel it is like teaching my Scottish granny to suck eggs.) But the Conservative response to this demand for citizenship, this demand for rights and democracy, has been to talk about more consumer rights, in the shape of citizens charters and name badges, and before that Douglas Hurd was encouraging us to take up 'active citizenship' as a private hobby, a sort of charity administered by the better-off to the passive citizens below. You'll remember Margaret Thatcher saying there's no such thing as society, there are only individuals and their families. The Tories argue that individual well-being can only be secured by less government and through the free market. As I have described, on the civil liberties front what that has produced is more government, not less, with a relentless erosion of rights and freedoms. But this is not the only sense in which the Conservative view is bankrupt – it is also that individuals cannot rely on the market-place to make them free. That much is evident from the rise in poverty, joblessness and the decay of inner cities. The short-term individualism we have seen wrecking our economy has also emphasised for us the needs for cooperative, long-term thinking.

In a modern, interdependent society, individual well-being can only be secured by a strong community and by accountable government. Citizenship is not just about rights, its also about responsibilities – to fellow citizens, and the community as a whole. What we need is a re-definition of the relationship between the citizen, the community and the state. We need a new balance of power. At present, the state has most of the power; communities are paralysed and citizens powerless. The state should have only as much power as is required to block large vested interests such as big corporations from dominat-ing society, and eroding democracy. Communities, whether regional or local, should have the power to determine their own priorities, and run themselves without excessive interference. Individuals need enforceable and accessible rights to enable them to play a full role in the life of their community and to protect them against abuses of public and private power.

What we need is a system of checks and balances which allows freedom to flourish but not at the expense of equality, social cohesion and the rights of others, particularly minorities. The only way of achieving this is a new constitutional settlement. This is not inevitable, but we could be heading along the right path. Scotland is leading the way; it could be a model for other parts of Britain. Charter 88 is working towards a new constitutional settlement for the whole of the UK. This would mean a break with the authoritarianism and the deference of the past. It would mean a society coming of age and becoming a mature democracy, but I am afraid that, before that happens, we have to get really angry.

Helena Kennedy's lecture was sponsored by Lothian Regional Council and delivered at the Signet Library, Edinburgh, on 4 December 1992.

The lecture was chaired by Ruth Wishart, journalist and broadcaster, and a response was given by John Mulvey, Director, Pilton Partnership, the EC's third anti-poverty programme.

CRISPIN TICKELL

13 *Europe: the environmental dimension*

UNLIKE OTHERS GATHERING IN THIS ANCIENT CITY, I DO NOT intend to talk about the finances of the European Community, nor the GATT round, nor the timetable for the ratification of the Treaty of Maastricht, nor the enlargement of the Community, nor Bosnia, nor even the reform of the European parliament. I have a much easier role. For my theme is genuinely popular among the peoples of Europe, even if some governments and vested interests find it difficult and even embarrassing.

My theme is the environment in which we live: that geography of space and geometry of time which constitute the essential Europe beyond frontiers and cultures and institutions and history. Neglected, misunderstood and often abused, our environment is our most precious and necessary possession. It needs our tender loving care. At one time it passed almost unnoticed in a crowd of other concerns. Then it was promoted to new status alongside others. Now it has become central to everything else.

Let us look at the coordinates of space and time. First in space. As a peninsula at the far western end of Asia, Europe includes climates from arctic to hot semi-desert, from mild Atlantic to harsh continental conditions. The variety of landscape from region to region, and the culture each supports, depend on patterns of climate that seem immutable through history. For longer than any saga can tell, Laplanders have been herding their reindeer in northern Scandinavia, while smallholders have been tending their vines on the shores of the Mediterranean.

Next in time. The further we look back and the more

compressed time becomes, the easier it is to see that the frontiers between zones are in constant movement, and that nothing stays still. Ice ages have dominated for around two and a half million years. During the last 850,000 years there were roughly nine advances of the ice, which covered much of Western Europe, and nine relatively brief intermissions or interglacials, each lasting between 10,000 and 15,000 years.

Our present interglacial – the time frame for all human civilisation – began about 14,000 years ago, and, after a brief reversal to ice age conditions, reached its peak around 6,000 years ago. In general there was more precipitation and a movement polewards of climatic belts, with average temperatures warmer than now. Sea levels were correspondingly higher. Cooling followed, causing glacial advance and more aridity from 4,800 to around 2,000 years ago. Then conditions warmed again, rising to a peak in certain areas between 900 and 1300 AD. This was followed by the so-called little ice age, which continued with certain fluctuations until the late nineteenth century. On average, temperatures were about 1 to 2 °C less than now. Then came a warming period from 1880 to 1940, levelling off between 1940 and 1970. More recently has come marked warming, with 1990 the warmest year since accurate records began.

Enter the human species into Europe in numbers and in a manner to cause environmental change of a kind no other animal species had done before. Muscle (human and animal) and water power on land, and at sea wind power, were the principal sources of energy. First came hunters, gatherers and scavengers. They were in broad balance with the environment provided numbers remained relatively low (10 million or so at the end of the ice age): but they were probable exterminators of the mega-fauna (the creatures shown on the walls of caves diminish in variety over time). Next came farmers and peasants, and the movement of peoples and their languages from the East and Southeast into a deeply forested continent. Forests were drastically reduced for agricultural purposes. Evidence of the resulting soil erosion lies in some of the Dutch islands of the North Sea.

Then came the builders of the first towns and of such monuments as the megaliths along the Atlantic coast, thereby demonstrating oceanic transport and increasing population in a rapidly changing environment. Then, with the rise of the Mediterranean civilisations of Egypt, Crete, Greece and Rome, came the citizens. They produced even more drastic changes in the environment with particular effects around the Mediterranean. The old breadbaskets of Sicily and North Africa were turned to desert as soils eroded.

Moving towards our own times some major markers have been as follows: the fall in population but ecological recovery of late Roman times and the Dark Ages; the economic expansion of the tenth to the thirteenth centuries under a warmer climate and with a steadily increasing population; the crash of the fourteenth century with drastic cooling and the Black Death, leading to a fall in population and change in the European landscape (as was said later, sheep farming became so profitable that 'sheep were eating men'); the European maritime expansion overseas from the end of the sixteenth century onwards exercising a form of ecological imperialism worldwide with colonies not only of people, but also of their animals and plants.

Then came the most extraordinary event in human history: the switch to new energy sources in the form of fossil fuels, the further extension and application of technology in Europe, and the assertion and dominance of European civilization through its children overseas ever since. The first industrial revolution in Europe was followed by other industrial revolutions in Europe and elsewhere. Such new devices as solid state electronics and biotechnology now enable us to do and produce much more from much less.

Look first at the upside of the industrial revolution. Global gross net product was around US$600 billion in 1900. It grew to US$5 trillion by 1960 and US$17 trillion by 1988 (of which 14.7 trillion – or more than five sixths – came from industrial countries, accounting for less than a quarter of the world's population, and 2.3 trillion – or less than one sixth – from the rest of the world, accounting for over three quarters of it). The results are plain. Europeans, once on a level with Indians or Chinese are now on average some 200 times richer. They and their counterparts in North America and Japan lead longer healthier lives than they ever did before, with access to a greater range of knowledge and opportunity than their ancestors could have dreamed of. The vast majority of the world's people want to live like them.

We have the bad luck to be the first generation to see the global effects of the downside. Of course we have coped with local effects before but we now face a downside of unimaginable proportions.

First, we face the consequences of population increase world-wide. As an animal species we were less than 10 million 10,000 years ago; but we were 2 billion in 1930, the year of my birth, and are 5.5 billion now. The human population is increasing at around 93 million every year. That is about a quarter of a million new people every day – the equivalent of the population of London in a month, and a new China every ten years. Europe, which now has a broadly static population, exported millions of people during its phase of rapid growth, which was not nearly as fast as it is in some other regions today. Population in those regions has grown, thanks in part to sanitation and healthcare developed in industrial countries; but there is a widening gap between population and resources.

Second, there is land deterioration linked to human prolifer-ation. The World Resources Institute in Washington recently estimated that 10% of the vegetation bearing surface of the Earth was suffering moderate to extreme degradation due to human activity since 1945. World-wide, enough productive top soil to cover almost the whole of France is washed away or degraded beyond reasonable use every year. In Europe, over-intensive use of land and the excessive application of fertilisers (a near doubling of their use within the Community in the last 20 years) and herbicides, and ground drainage and clearance are (in the words of the European Commission) causing deterioration of soils including contamination, acidification, desertification and erosion in many areas of the European Community. In England 6% of soil is already at high risk, and 37% potentially at risk of degradation or erosion due to agricultural activities. The same is probably true of Scotland.

Third, there are the effects of industry. In Britain's Black Country and in the old Silesia (from which I believe German immigrants from the United States derived the word 'sleaze'), Europe created the world's first industrially polluted landscapes. Industrialization in Western Europe bred cruelly mutated grand-children in Eastern Europe and the former Soviet Union. In some cities it has left nine out of ten children suffering from pollution-related diseases and the highest rates of lung cancer in the world. Within the vast land mass of the former Soviet Union some 16% was recently judged to be an ecological disaster area by the Academy of Sciences.

Fourth, there is the particular problem of fresh water. The global use of water doubled between 1940 and 1980, and is expected to double again by 2000. Many countries already suffer severe shortages, droughts and pollution. In Britain the National Rivers Authority has just announced the creation of hundreds of protection zones to ensure the purity of underground supplies. Competition for water was a prime source of conflict in the past, and will be in future. In some places water is already more valuable than oil.

Fifth, there is the state of the world's seas. Marine pollution is already serious in some areas. Fish stocks are depleted by overfishing, while the rivers that feed the seas are often affected by chemical waste. For the first time now, human activity could exterminate the life of an entire sea. The rivers that once gave the Black Sea life are now killing it. Discharges of phosphates and other pollutants from the Danube alone have multiplied 21 times in 15 years.

Sixth, there is the unbalancing of atmospheric chemistry.

Acid precipitation is a problem for those downwind of industry. It damages trees, rivers and lakes, and reduces fertility. But it is essentially local in character and can be managed with political will. Depletion of the ozone layer, through the processes initiated by chloroflourocarbons, halons, methyl bromide and other man-made molecules is more serious. The deepest and widest Antarctic ozone hole was recorded this year. Even with the rapid phasing-out of some of the modest potent ozone depleters, damage to the ozone layer will continue for decades. The resulting increase of UVB radiation could damage human and plant health.

Seventh, there is the prospect of global warming. Through enhancing the natural – and indispensable – greenhouse effect it could affect almost every aspect of human society. The main conclusions of the Inter governmental Panel on Climate Change of 1990, updated in 1992, represented a broad scientific consensus. On the assumption that we maintain present trends and continue to pump carbon dioxide, methane, nitrous oxide, and other greenhouse gases into the atmosphere, there is likely to be: a rise of global mean temperature of around 1°C by 2025, and around 3°C by the end of the century (compare a drop of around 5°C during the last glacial episode); a rise of global sea levels of around 30 cm by 2030 and 65 cm by the end of the century. There will be marked regional differences. For example, Europe will have greater changes than average, with less summer precipitation and lower soil moisture, particularly south of the Alps and in the Mediterranean. There will be more precipitation worldwide and a general redistribution of weather patterns with drastic local effects, including deluges and droughts. There will also be a time lag between cause and effect due to the stabilising effect of oceans. Of course many uncertainties remain but the broad trends are clear.

Last, there is the threat to biodiversity. Human population increase has led to a destruction of other species on a scale comparable to that caused by the probable collision of an asteroid with the Earth 65 million years ago. As a species we already consume some 40% of total photosynthetic production on land. There will be pressure to convert at least 4.5 million square kilometres of additional wild life habitat to human uses in the future. This is equivalent to four-fifths of the total area of nature reserves in the world today or considerably more than the area of India. On a conservative estimate human encroachment will wipe out 20% of extant species, especially those in tropical forests and coral reefs, in the next 30 years. We are likely to lose whole ecosystems which cannot move or adapt. Some life forms are likely to benefit from global warming, in particular new strains of bacteria and virus.

I turn to the rise of awareness of the problem, and efforts to deal with it.

Local responses came first: rivers like the London Thames were once open sewers, and their cleansing and management were an achievement of Victorian local authorities from the 1860s and 70s onwards. Effective water management passed to local river authorities in 1951, to river basin authorities in 1972 and a National Rivers Authority in 1989 as the benefits of a more strategic approach were recognized. There is likewise the story of London fogs. The 'pea-souper' in 1952 contributed to the deaths of some 4,000 people. Action in Britain to cope with these problems was matched elsewhere in Europe.

President Roosevelt included an environmental element in his pre-war New Deal, but truly national environmental plans are post war creations. In Britain the Town and Country Planning Act of 1947, which established the green belts around cities, was one of the first attempts to look at a country as a whole. Other countries had similar plans. In 1990 the Department of the Environment published a White Paper on the environment. The 1992 supplement, entitled 'This Common Inheritance,' seeks to integrate energy, business, land use, water and conservation policy in a fashion intended to keep the environment at the centre of decision making. Dutch national environment planning goes even further.

Regional response tends to be slower, and treaty agreements

can look fine on paper. So far there has been little coordinated effort to give effect to them. The Barcelona Convention on the Protection of the Mediterranean was signed in 1975 by all states contiguous to the sea, including the Israelis and the Arabs. It was a triumph of diplomacy and good intentions, but progress has since been slow. There is a better story to tell on acidification. Its causes and effects were broadly understood by Scandinavian scientists by the early 1970s, but for many years there were continuing arguments about the science and responsibility for the problem. West German concern about forest death was the spur to a concerted national programme to reduce emissions of sulphur dioxide. In 1980 all parties to the UN Economic Commission for Europe (which includes East European countries) signed a Convention on Long Range Transboundary Air Pollution. The most effective action was the result of German pressure within the European Community. In 1988 the Community directed Member States to reduce sulphur dioxide emissions by as much as 60% by 2010. It is unfortunate – and I hope unfair – that this country should usually be seen as playing a negative role.

The global response is a major factor over the last 20 years. Principal milestones have been: UN Conference on the Environment in 1972; the creation of the United Nations Environment Program in the same year; the Global 2000 report in 1980; the Brundtland Commission report in 1987; the two World Climate Conferences in 1979 and 1990; and the UN Conference on Environment and Development at Rio in June 1992.

A good example of what can be done was over the damage to the ozone layer. The discoveries of the 1970s led directly to the signing of the Vienna Convention of 1985. This was further strengthened by the Montreal Protocol of 1987 and subsequent meetings leading to that in Copenhagen in November 1992 to tighten up procedures to eliminate the manufacture and use of the offending chemicals. On 7 December 1992 the Environment Ministers of the European Community accelerated the timetable for eliminating the manufacture of chlorofluorocarbons.

For all its shortcomings, the Rio conference marked a high point of public awareness, and five documents were agreed: a Declaration of Principles, Conventions on Climate Change and Biodiversity, Forestry Principles and Agenda 21. Work at the current session of the UN General Assembly has continued. Perhaps the most important achievement has been the creation of a Sustainable Development Commission to monitor the achievements of Rio and to make sure that each national government respects the obligations it has undertaken.

In some countries governments have been ahead of public opinion, and in others public opinion has been ahead of governments. In Europe the growth of popular pressure has been enormous. For example in Britain there are more members of environmental pressure groups and organisations than there are members of political parties. Environment remains among top concerns, even in times of recession, and there are indications that children feel more involved in – and sometimes better informed about – the issues than most of their parents or teachers.

Catastrophes often act as a spur, whether droughts or hurricanes or accidents as at Chernobyl and Bhopal. They concentrate the mind wonderfully, sometimes with good effect, but do not necessarily make us wiser. When a disaster, such as the extinction of millions of species, is happening in comparatively slow motion it can pass almost unnoticed. We need something more.

Feelings of helplessness remain because the prevailing structure of thought, the model in our minds, remains wrong. We need flexibility of mind. This is painful. It means abandoning assumptions, changing hallowed habits, creating new models of thought, accepting different values, and seeing the world through other eyes, and still knowing how little we know.

We need to recast our vocabulary. Words are not only a means of expression but also the building blocks of thought.

The instruments of economic analysis are blunt and rusty. Such words as 'growth', 'development', 'cost benefit analysis', even 'gross national product', all require redefinition. We need to introduce the notion of capital stock.

We must realize that conventional wisdom is often a contradiction in terms. There are no universal answers to anything. The closer we are to those who exercise power, the better we realize how uncertain they are of what they are doing.

We have to change the culture. Many have lamented the division between the cultures of science and the arts. They are right to do so. But neither is now in charge. Our real bosses are the business managers, and they are not known for their ability to think long term. We should recast our educational system to promote better understanding of broad issues and lateral thinking between them. Specialisation is the bane of wisdom.

We need a value system which enshrines the principle of sustainability over generations. Sustainable development may mean different things to different people, but the idea itself is simple. We must work out models for a relatively steady state society, with population in broad balance with resources and the environment.

The whole ethos of the European Community reflects old ways of thinking that we must transcend. The fathers and founders of the Community had an implicit underlying notion of the United States of Europe on the model of the United States of America: their model of the United States was wrong in a number of ways, and they accepted from the beginning that Europe would evolve differently in accordance with a robust dirigiste tradition. But some entertained ideas which still run.

Those ideas include a belief in ill-defined notions of development and growth as catch-all answers to economic and social problems, exploitation of resources without regard to the future, and almost total neglect of environmental costs. It is not surprising that there was no reference to the environment in the Treaty of Rome.

There is also the implicit notion that such ideas are applicable to the rest of the world, as made manifest in the report of the Brandt Commission, and in the Community's overseas aid programmes (under bilateral agreements as well as the Lomé Convention).

Inevitably the Community reflected the fashionable ideas of the mid-1950s. The structure of the European Commission and its Directorate Generals, and the various Councils of Ministers, all followed national patterns. In this way policies on transport, agriculture, energy and industry were worked out in virtual isolation from each other.

With the rise of environmental awareness, the first instincts of the Community were to create another Directorate General in the Commission and another specialised Council of Ministers in addition to what already existed. Perhaps inevitably environmental issues were dealt with in a patchwork way as each arose. Seldom were they related to the more fundamental policies of the Community. It was nevertheless understood that the Community was the right unit for dealing with major environmental issues which by their nature transcended the frontiers of Member States.

It is now clearer that environmental issues affect everything, and reach into every aspect of national and international life. The reason why Green parties have not succeeded is that greenery is the property of all political parties, and all political parties need to be green. Concern for the environment is not something to be bolted on to other policies. It is an integral part of all policies and must be seen as such from the beginning. In fairness, most concerned with environmental issues within the Community have realised this for a long time. This is not so with most politicians, administrators, business people, economists, and academics.

The first achievements of the Community were of the bolt-on variety. Over the last twenty years a broad range of measures has been jointly agreed by Member States. These regulations and directives cover water, waste, noise, control of harmful substances and protection of habitat. In 1973 five measures were adopted; in 1991 the number was thirty-eight. In the last year Community agreements on the environment have included: a Community-wide scheme for environmental labelling of products; a habitats directive to protect Europe's most threatened species and habitats; and a 'LIFE' fund to finance European environmental projects.

A more integrated approach was implicit from the beginning in the Commission's successive Action Plans. The first such Plan was in 1973. Each succeeding Plan has recognized that its predecessor was inadequate and ineffective in many aspects. The 5th Action Plan goes much further than it's predecessors. It requires the full integration of the environmental dimension. Entitled 'Towards Sustainability' it recognises a 'slow but relentless deterioration' of the 'general state of the European environment', and states that pressures for further deterioration are increasing. Like other plans elsewhere it would like to square the circle by creating a framework for continued economic and social development without detriment to the environment. Whether this can be done, or is just a play of words, remains to be seen.

Among the objectives of the UK Presidency in 1992 was to entrench the environmental element in just this sense. It was a central theme at a meeting of Community Environment Ministers in September 1992, but the discussion was apparently more of an amiable exchange of ideas than any call for action. The theme was introduced at no fewer than 11 specialised Ministers' Councils, and at meetings and conferences at other levels. The prime targets were transport, energy, industry, agriculture, trade and development. Obviously some people were more receptive than others. Many must have resented what they saw as an intrusion on their territory.

All the more important is the 5th Action Plan. The plan has four objectives: to preserve, protect and improve the quality of the environment; to protect human health; to promote the careful and rational use of natural resources; and to promote international action to tackle global and regional problems.

Action to achieve them is to be shaped by seven principles: aim for the highest possible level of participation; prevention is better than cure; environmental effects should be taken into account from the earliest possible stage of any project; environmental considerations must form an integral part of other Community policies; the polluter should pay for the damage he causes, in short 'the polluter pays principle'; where there are uncertainties the good of the environment should prevail, in short 'the precautionary principle'; environmental problems should be tackled by the tier of government that can be most effective, in short 'the principle of subsidiarity'.

The 5th Action Plan is more than a wish list. The changes in the Single European Act of 1987 gave environmental policy explicit legal backing for the first time. The Treaty of Maastricht has introduced as a principal objective the promotion of sustainable growth respecting the environment. It sets out the need for the integration of environmental policy into other policies, and attaches special value to the principle of subsidiarity.

The general popularity of environmental legislation is not only good in itself but also a catalyst to governments to do what they should within their areas of responsibility. The new directive for open access to information on environmental matters will be valuable in this sense.

But these gradual moves in the right direction should not be allowed to obscure the deterioration that is taking place, nor the Community's inadequacies and failures so far. Everyone with eyes to see has observed greater river and marine pollution; continuing industrial hazards (including nuclear ones); inner city decay; continuing degradation of the soils and damage to forests; and the mounting problem of waste disposal.

More specifically, the intensification and specialization of farming stimulated by the Common Agricultural Policy have drastically affected wildlife habitats and created serious problems of pollution. So far reform has failed to put the environment at the heart of the new policy, despite pressure from non-governmental organisations and the best efforts of the UK Presidency. Current set-aside policy can be no more than a temporary expedient, and anyway raises as many problems as it solves. Additional spending proposed for environmental schemes under the Common Agricultural Policy would still only amount to some 2% of all such expenditure by 1997.

Moreover, the Community's Structural Funds have supported large-scale environmental degradation: road-building, wetland drainage, fish farming, irrigation, afforestation and other development schemes have destroyed wildlife habitats in Spain, Greece, Portugal, Ireland and France, in some cases in contravention of the Community's own environmental legislation. These problems could become acute as more funds are allocated to regional development. Projects that are already going ahead with Community funding could damage the Community's environmental credibility. For example, the Missolonghi wetlands in Northern Greece, which contain two of the largest lagoons in the Mediterranean and nurture unique forms of bird life, will suffer severely from the diversion of water to a hydroelectric system, the power from which the national generating company has said it does not need, and to irrigation schemes costing more to run than the value of what they will produce. Notwithstanding promises to integrate environmental planning from the earliest stages, it is hard to change attitudes. We have a system which demands that money be spent and large projects be completed within a short space of time.

Some governments are still resisting essential undertakings (for example, Greece and other southern states in phasing out methyl bromide which molecule for molecule is sixty times more harmful to the ozone layer than chloroflourocarbons). We must watch carefully the attitude of our own government on such issues as sulphur dioxide emissions, carbon dioxide emissions and clean water standards.

Often Community environmental policies have not been put

into proper effect. The record of enforcement is patchy. Anyone listening to debates within the Community cannot but be aware that people are still thinking in the wrong terms, and carrying on with wrong policies. There is still no European Environment Agency: the plan for one was caught up in an absurd and degrading dispute over the sites for Community institutions. Let us hope that the decisions reached at the meeting of the Council of Ministers in Edinburgh in December 1992 will lead to early progress.

In my view there are five principles on which the Community and its member governments should act singly and together: do now what makes sense for reasons other than any one environmental factor – in short, a policy of no regrets; reform systems of value by introducing environmental pricing and inter-generational equity – pricing of such commodities as coal should include the cost of cleaning up the mess they make (the same goes for cars and the fuel used to drive them); re-target relevant scientific research and coordinate results on a global basis; participate in an international strategy which sets a framework for collective action; deal with environmental issues together, because isolated measures to cope with any one of them can sometimes make others worse.

In one way or another these principles are all given form in the 5th Action Plan. The challenge will come when decisions taken on these principles collide with what a nation or a powerful interest group perceives to be its self-interest.

The Community needs to act at three levels: representation of the Community at global level; undertaking the necessary measures within the Community; and ensuring, on the principle of subsidiarity, that appropriate action be taken at national or local levels.

At a global level the Community must establish coordinated policies for use outside the Community. This raises the usual delicate issues of competence. My experience in the Commission suggests that any extension of competence should come naturally as Member States recognize the need for a

Community voice rather than as a product of legal argument. The Community can play a decisive role in helping to carry through the decisions of the UN Conference at Rio. For example, it must give effect to the Climate Change Convention and the Biodiversity Convention, and support the new Sustainable Development Commission. The UK Presidency proposed an eight point plan to Member States after Rio.

The Community must set an example rather than lecturing others. For example, the new Habitats Directive, when taken with the Natura 2000 scheme (for a coherent ecological network across Europe), shares most of the principal points of the Biodiversity Convention. But a Directive is a much sharper instrument than an international convention. More important is the proposal to limit atmospheric carbon emissions through a Community-wide tax. The present draft directive is already too qualified to carry much conviction, and there are signs that some governments (I hope not our own) may start wriggling over their present extremely modest commitment to limit carbon emissions to 1990 levels by the end of the century (remember that even if we succeeded in keeping our emissions down to 1990 levels they would remain more than twice the levels recommended by the Intergovernmental Panel on Climate Change). We have yet to see exactly how each Member State intends to honour that commitment. Transport and energy policies will be the key. We heard on 2 December 1992 from the Environmental Secretary that whatever option was chosen, fuel prices would have to go up.

Worldwide everyone wants cars. People want to live like Europeans or Americans. Taking China alone, if the Chinese had the same number of cars per person as we do, the number of vehicles in the world would more than double: from 450 million to 900 million.

Acting on the global level the Community must also establish the environmental dimension in its dealings with its neighbours, in particular Eastern Europe and the Mediterranean countries. The Community must also exercise leadership or exert comparable weight with the United States in global policy-making. Lack of a coherent European policy compounded the weaknesses and inadequacies of American policy under President Bush.

The Community must also re-orientate its aid policies towards non-industrial countries to take better account of the environmental dimension. This should apply as much to those with whom we have bilateral agreements as to the members of the Lomé Convention.

The same must be done for trade policies: like the Community, GATT began innocent of awareness of the environment; but unlike the Community, it has done very little to mend its ways. The Community should be ready to apply environmental lessons to trade policy.

Within the Community there is a need for some internal reorganization of the Commission and the Council to ensure that environmental considerations are taken into account at all levels. Probably the best if not the only way to proceed is to make environment an invariable point on the agenda of European Councils, and restore pride of place to the Council of Foreign Ministers with a specific requirement to ensure environmental penetration of other Councils.

We also need corresponding changes to those policies where the Community has full competence, in particular agriculture, regional development (including the structural funds) and fisheries. And we need to improve the access of non-governmental organizations to the Commission and Councils.

We should take such initiatives as: creating an Inspectorate of Inspectorates; reviewing environmental impact assessment directives, eco-auditing arrangements, eco-stocktaking, and measures governing water resources, air quality and waste disposal; looking at resource consumption, particularly renewability of renewable resources, and long term needs at present met from non-renewable resources. This last point is particularly important in the field of energy. One of the mistakes in the privatization of electricity in Britain was to lay the emphasis on selling electricity rather than making its generation more efficient (as many, including most recently the Chief Executive of Scottish Power, have pointed out).

Further initiatives should include increasing public awareness of environmental issues and providing more information about them. Above all, we need to bring business into closer consultation within the Community on environmental matters. The November 1992 Brussels Conference on European Business and the Environment was one of several important steps in this direction. It has helped to coordinate national initiatives. Businesses must recognize that conflict between environmental protection and economic competitiveness often arises from a short-term view of wealth generation. Turning environmental concern into competitive advantage is one of the objectives of 'Towards Sustainability', and businesses that recognize this will prosper. Leading European companies like IBM have already given a good example. Volkswagen is planning to produce recyclable automobiles. Obviously there should be a minimum of regulation. For its part the UK Government has decided that there should in future be a presumption in favour of using economic instruments (in other words incentives and disincentives) as opposed to direct regulation.

I turn to the question of subsidiarity and environmental policy. The principle of subsidiarity is already accepted in the five Action Plans. It was formulated in 1977 as follows: 'in each category of pollution, it is necessary to establish the level of action (local, regional, national, Community, international) best suited to the type of pollution and to the geographical zone to be protected. Actions likely to be most affected at Community level should be concentrated at that level; priorities should be determined wth special care'.

Subsidiarity was emphasized in the Single European Act of 1987, and again in the Treaty of Maastricht. But there is a danger of governments pleading subsidiarity to continue in bad old ways. We need to look particularly at transport policy. In transport and energy each Member State tends to pursue its own policy (or blunder along for the lack of one). Work has hardly begun in bringing them together. No doubt the UK Government was acting on what it saw as a short-term requirement to help an industry in trouble when it cut the tax on new cars. This was a small move in itself, but it was surely in the wrong direction. Was it part of a long-term transport policy incorporating environmental considerations? So far we show no sign of weaning ourselves from the cult of the petrol driven car with all it implies for our transport system, our cities, our countryside, and the air we breathe.

There was a good definition of a subsidiarity in a paper published by the European Environmental Bureau (EEB): 'Subsidiarity in the environmental field should mean that decisions are made at the level which will secure the highest environmental standards'.

In applying subsidiarity, it is important not to overdo the role of the market. The market is an artificial construct. There is no totally free market in the world. Markets are efficient – the most efficient – mechanisms for exchange, but all operate according to ground rules set by authorities at whatever level. The problem is to fix the ground rules. Sustainability is more important than profitability in this as in other respects. This is particularly important when giving directives to local and municipal authorities. As has been well said, 'the responsibility of business is to profits, not to public welfare'.

My conclusions are as follows.

Thinking differently is always painful. The Community, like national governments, has to contend with a rich variety of vested interests as well as the power of inertia in resisting change. These forces cannot be overcome overnight. It is a long process in which patience and persistence are essential.

The Community is the natural unit for coping with major environmental issues, and only a unit the size of the Community can hope to carry weight in international affairs, in particular with the United States. European endorsement of the precautionary principle, for example, would carry great authority around the world.

The process of environmental policy-making needs to cover all economic sectors and disciplines, to draw strength from ordinary citizens, local communities and non-governmental organisations, and to be more visibly accountable. It has to be flexible to take account of new circumstances and the advance of scientific understanding.

There is a real risk that if persuasion fails, the Community could, like other parts of the world, be faced with creeping ecological catastrophe. The earlier we initiate change, the less the dangers will be, and the better we will be able to cope with them.

Yet in the last resort we may not be able to cope. Neither the world, nor the Community, nor still less any nation state is in real control of events. We live at a time when governments of East, West, North and South seem unable to manage their affairs and operate by sufficient consensus.

I end with a couple of quotations. The first comes from John Reader. He has well said:

> In the brief space of time that civilization has been a feature of human existence, it has not demonstrated any tendency to produce a well regulated steady state whereby people are well fed and secure, generation after generation. Civilization is distinguished more by its erratic cycles . . . Time and again it has risen dramatically from the field of human endeavour, then collapsed and fallen. Human inability to impose adequate restraints brings it down. Inventions provide the initial impetus, intellect supplies methods of application and solutions to problems that arise as the system swells and grows, but in every instance so far, the uncontrolled growth of civilization has ultimately thrown up more problems than human intellect can solve.

My second quotation comes from the new book by the authors of *The Limits to Growth*. This book on the twentieth anniversary of its predecessor is entitled *Beyond the Limits*. Building on their 1972 models, the authors show that the world economy tends to overshoot capacity because of expanding population and continuing economic growth. To sustain this growth people draw down resources below certain thresholds at which the whole economy behaves differently. This is because of the steplike – non-linear – character of change: in jumps not curves. The author wrote that

> Any population-economy-environment system that has feed-back delays and slow physical responses, that has thresholds and erosive mechanisms, is literally unmanageable. In most [of our computer] runs . . . the world system does not run out of land or food or resources or pollution absorption capability, it runs out of the ability to cope.

Let us make sure we do not do so.

Sir Crispin Tickell's lecture was the third IBM/Scottish Science Library Annual Lecture. It was delivered at the Royal Museum of Scotland, Edinburgh, on 8 December 1992.

The lecture was chaired by the Rt Hon the Earl of Crawford and Balcarres and a response was given by John Bartholomew, FRSE, FRGS, President, Royal Scottish Geographical Society. The text for publication was prepared by the National Library of Scotland ©.

14   *At the heart of Europe*

IT WAS A GREAT HONOUR TO BE INVITED TO GIVE THE FINAL
lecture in what I understand has been a very successful series and
I wish to express the hope that Heads of Government meeting
in Edinburgh will be just as successful as those involved with
the Lothian European Lectures have been.

It was kind of you to quote my Maiden Speech of 26 June
1950; it was obviously rather a good speech and I must re-read it.[1]
But I am afraid, as so often has happened, the Government of the
day refused to take any notice of what I said and the result cost
us 20 years' membership of the European Community. Today,
I have to remind myself constantly that anybody under the
age of 65 has no direct recollection of how the Community
began, what brought it about and how it has developed and I
think the occasional Summit meeting in Britain does give us an
opportunity to put this into perspective. The press commentary
and the broadcast commentaries about this meeting have been
far too localised to do credit to today's events; we should rather
see this meeting in the context both of what has gone before
and of what we want to happen in the future.

Some would say that it began in 1950, but in fact it began long
before that. In 1940, in the darkest days of the war, Churchill,
who had just become Prime Minister, put forward a proposal
which even then was surprising, and today seems astonishing.
He was to go to Paris and say to the French Government
'We will become one country, one people, one nation, one
parliament', and not just in order to try to win the war and
do so more quickly. 'It will be an indissoluble union.' It was

a startling suggestion and you can imagine the effect it had on his high officials in Whitehall. 'Well, Prime Minister, this is a very imaginative proposal. It is something we could never have thought of ourselves. I am sure you deserve the highest praise. But of course there may be one or two technical difficulties. You must give us a chance to examine it for just 48 hours before you go to Paris.' They got their 48 hours to look at it, and then they would have come back and said 'Prime Minister, this is an even more powerful proposition than even we had thought when you explained it to us. It really is a tremendous effort and of course, Prime Minister, history will always remember it. But these little technical difficulties: now, the first one is that we are going to be one country and one people. If we are going to do that, we have to have one passport and what is this to be? The British are very proud of the fact that they have a large, dark blue, leather bound passport. The French – I am sorry, Prime Minister, I mean our friends in France – have a very small, brown paper, rather scruffy passport and this will have to be sorted out, Prime Minister, if you are going to make us into one country and one nation.'

Churchill, fortunately, was not influenced by that sort of thing but a few weeks ago, walking across the market square in Salisbury where I live, three young people spotted me and came running up to me, brandishing in the fingers their documents. They said, 'Our European passports, you see we're all Europeans now, real Europeans.' That is what it means to the younger generation today, I am delighted to say, that they see that we are one, we are Europeans.

After the war Churchill made another extraordinary speech in Zurich in which he declared he would say 'something which will astonish you, it is that France and Germany must immediately become friends', and that, only a year after the end of the Second World War. He went on to describe how it could be brought about, how Britain would play her part, and even went so far as to talk about a sort of United States of Europe. He took, of course, a major part in the conference at The Hague in

1948 which created the Council of Europe which still exists in Strasbourg.

It is very important to put all this into context because the Council of Europe was created to improve cooperation between governments. It still exists and is a valuable forum for discussion for the countries which belong, but it is not a machine for action. That was the Council's great drawback. In its discussion process it is also not very democratic because the members are all appointed by the government of their country, some in consultation with the opposition parties and some not. I was Chief Whip for four years so I know how it's done.

I mention this because there are still people today who ask why can't we just have a Council of Europe? The answer is that it cannot achieve what is necessary in the modern world. Looking today at the European Community it is one of the great success stories, if not *the* greatest success story of this century. Why do countries like Sweden, Austria and Finland want to become members of the Community? Not because we are just a talking shop but because we are successful. With the collapse of the Soviet Empire they see that they have no longer to worry about Soviet power and so they wish to become members of a community, in fact *the* Community.

You may argue that Switzerland has just had a referendum in which the people have declined to join, but anybody who knows Switzerland and the Swiss could have anticipated that – that result is in their nature, it's in their centuries of history. Switzerland is not even a member of the United Nations and in their referendum some four or five years ago they turned membership down flat. Who could blame the Swiss? They are a very canny people; they've got all the United Nations organisations in Geneva bringing in all the United Nations' money; they've got all the highly paid United Nations' officials, bringing in money and spending it there; they've got all the visitors to the United Nations organisations, bringing in money, filling the hotels. If you've got that already why should you pay a subscription to the United Nations in New

York? What is more, the Foreign Minister knew what it was all about because he didn't want to be telephoned at 2 o'clock in the morning by his representative in New York saying 'Minister you will recollect that at the moment we are debating Resolution 1394 and we have got to paragraph 15 and, of course, you will remember Minister that sub-paragraph 9d half-way through has the word "not" and they now want to remove "not". What I want to know is should we not, not, not or should we not?' Well, being woken up at 2 o'clock in the morning is not much fun, and so the Swiss turned it all down. I anticipated that, as far as the Community is concerned, because the Swiss do very well out of the arrangements I negotiated for them and therefore they see no real need for full membership.

We then come to the stage of the Schuman Plan which I talked about in my maiden speech. It was the plan really of Jean Monnet who had great experience on both sides of the Atlantic. The Convener of Lothian Regional Council has mentioned the comparison between Edinburgh and Lothian and Massachusetts, but I am not sure it is, after all, a very sound comparison. I have always thought of Edinburgh as being one of the best informed places in the country, if not in Europe, and the most full of understanding. But there was an opinion poll recently in the United States which showed that whereas 2% of the population have heard of Europe, only 1% in fact knows where it is. I well recall a great meeting we had in Edinburgh in the first negotiations for EC membership. The meeting was absolutely packed, and went on for well over an hour and a half until finally the Chairman called for positively the last question. He pointed to a gentleman standing right at the back against the wall and said 'Your question Sir'. The man got up and he said 'I want to ask Mr Heath this: if you can't get the whole lot into Europe will you make sure you get the Scots in for the sake of the auld alliance?' Well, unfortunately, I didn't get anybody in that time, and it took until 1971 to get the whole country in.

In 1950, Jean Monnet produced his plan and took it to the

French Prime Minister. A few days later Schuman, the Foreign Minister, came to him, saying he was to meet Adenauer, the Chancellor of Germany and needed a plan to put to him which would serve to go on improving Franco-German relations. Monnet said he had prepared the plan and taken it to the Prime Minister. 'Well' Schuman said, 'He hasn't shown it to me'. So Monnet went to the Prime Minister, asked the private secretary for the plan, which the Prime Minister hadn't read, retrieved the plan and handed it to Schuman. It became the Schuman Plan and it was this that the Germans accepted. From that moment on, the Community was created as a Community to deal with post-war problems.

The point I wish to make here is that the Community was created for a *political* purpose, to prevent France and Germany ever fighting each other again. Those of my generation who fought through the Second World War and survived wanted just this.

But what were the means to be used? The means were economic, to put the two raw materials needed to create weapons of war under a supranational power which would stop them being abused by either of the major countries or by any other country which joined the Community. So it has had from the beginning a political purpose while the means were economic, and so it remains to this day: the Community is, and always will be, political. People sometimes say that we shouldn't have anything to do with supranationality, but we've got it. It was in the first Community and when we became a member I signed the Treaty, which produced supranationality.

European momentum continued with the Economic Community in 1956 and the Common Agricultural Policy in 1962, with British membership along with Eire and Denmark in 1973 followed by Greece in 1979, and Spain and Portugal in 1984, and now the Great Single Market starting on 1 January 1993. The point here is that the Community always moves forward in a great leap. It doesn't shuffle, and say let's try this or let's try that, then we might do something. Not at all. It examines the issue, thrashes it out, takes a decision and gets on with it. Those who want to change this are not going to match up with what is required in the Community. They say we are trying to go too fast; my view is that in this world you can't go too fast. The great danger is that you hang around and never catch up with events, a fact which applies particularly to the other things that I hope to discuss later on. Having taken, in 1986, the leap forward, to create the Single Market for 1992, we now take another great leap forward with Maastricht – and it should never be forgotten that all the governments agreed to Maastricht. Then we can start on the the next great leap forward: the movement towards the single currency, towards more power for the European Parliament and the other measures which are in the Maastricht Treaty.

What then? We have produced a Community which is economically successful and has political influence, and the rest of the world listens to what we say. This is true of Japan, it is true of the United States and both of them see great opportunities in the Community. There are those who talk about the selfish Community, but we are not selfish in the least. We have one of the lowest external tariffs in the world. When I became Prime Minister and took the UK into the Community I had to explain to industrialists that they would have to drop their tariffs speedily to the level of the rest of the Community. Look at the help we give to countries outside the Community, to the former colonies of the major powers in the Community – the British, the French, the Italians, the Dutch and the Belgians. We provide them with a large amount of assistance and the negotiations go so smoothly that they don't criticise the Community for not helping the Third World enough in the activities which we carry through. So, in that respect, we can see how the Community has developed and the process which it will continue to follow.

Which brings us to being 'at the heart of Europe'. When the present Prime Minister took over he used this phrase saying 'I want Britain to be at the heart of Europe.' Of course it is where we should be, but it does involve certain attitudes and actions as far as the Community is concerned. It's no secret that, for the ten years of the eighties, no good word was ever said by the then Prime Minister in Britain about the Community and, as the members of the Government knew she didn't want it, they didn't say any good words either. As a result, the people of the United Kingdom have never been told about the work of the Community, either for the UK or for Europe as a whole and this is one of the missing links which now has got to be discussed. This is the very big task facing the European Movement which is meeting in Edinburgh and which has a role to play in keeping our people informed about what is going on.

As far as Maastricht is concerned, I'm afraid that a very poor job has been made of explaining what the Treaty is about, so I would like to add something on this. In many ways I think the most important aspect of it is the decision to have a single currency in the Community. What is the benefit of this and what are the disadvantages? First of all, to anybody who says we should stay with twelve different currencies, I say to them name any single market in the world which has more than one currency. Can you imagine the United States with a currency for each state, fifty different coins? Can you imagine Japan, a great single market, with more than one currency, one for the islands, one for the middle island and so on? It is not a workable proposition. What is more, it is extremely costly. Businessmen realise this and I wish they would speak up more. It's time that businessmen had their say and it's time that the Government listened to their views.

The business community recently arranged for a gentleman to go round the Community. He was given £100 and told not to buy anything, just to change the currency in each of the twelve countries that he visited. When he returned, he had left just £66, with nothing to show for it. £34 had gone to the bankers and the brokers in exchange charges. If he is doing business, think of all the invoicing this attracts. This is extremely costly, but the result of the introduction of a single currency would mean that a great deal of money would be saved, which means cheaper goods for the consumer.

That is why a single currency is very important as far as the people of Britain are concerned. But they say 'yes, but what about the dear Queen's head'. Well, the dear Queen has kept her head and will continue to do so and there will be a coin in the single currency on which we can have the Queen's head and the other monarchies in Europe. It's not beyond the ingenuity of man to have a coin with all the Royal heads round it at one go, that could be done as well. When they talk about these things, they don't seem to remember that the monarch's head never appeared on our bank notes until the Bank of England was nationalised in 1948. It is a very recent introduction, but these are the arguments that are being used against the vital ones of the advantage to business and to the consumer.

How can a single currency be achieved? What Maastricht does is to set out a timetable. People say this is far too short, but in fact it is far too long and the most dramatic example of that was given in September 1992 with the concerted attack by speculators on individual currencies. They attacked sterling and it fell. It showed, I am afraid, that we haven't got many friends at the moment and we ought to realise this because it is very important to make friends who will back us up when there are difficulties. The French were backed because they've got friends and the franc was saved.

The only way in which we can deal with this situation overall is to have one currency which is strong enough to defy all their weight of speculation. There was basically nothing wrong with the UK economy when they speculated against us. There was nothing wrong with the French economy which is even stronger than ours was, but they made the attempt and they will continue to make the attempt. I remember that in 1972 I happened to be staying with the German Chancellor Herr Brandt when the speculators attacked the dollar. He said to me on the Thursday night 'We can't go on taking in dollars like this, because of the effect on the mark.' I said 'You have got to go on, take them all, then they will burn their hands, and then we shall get ten years of financial peace.' He called a cabinet meeting, delaying dinner, and came back to me saying 'I couldn't carry it, I'm sorry. We have got to take action to stop the dollars coming in.'

We have still not mastered this problem of speculation. When I was bemoaning 'Black Wednesday' and the collapse of sterling, a friend said 'I understand your point of view but you can't expect me to share it.' I said, 'Why not.' 'Well you know that I am not connected with the city but I made a million out of that and that was very useful.' That's speculation and you have got to have a single currency which is strong enough to stand up against all the weight of speculation which the modern world can now produce.

There is only one way in which you make currency adjustments and that is for the Ministers of Finance to meet on a Saturday night at five to midnight, and at five past midnight they tell the world we are now going to have one single currency and the rate of exchange existing today will be the rate at which you transfer your currency into the single currency. That is the only way in which it can be done to avoid all the speculation that has done so much damage in autumn 1992. It is not beyond human power to do that, if you have the will and the courage, and it's what we shall find will happen, and much sooner than people think, under Maastricht.

The next thing that Maastricht does is to increase the powers of the European Parliament, not greatly but to a certain extent. I am in favour of this; both in the first negotiations in 1960 onwards and again in 1970, European leaders said to me they wanted Britain in because we have more experience of how to run a parliamentary system than any of them. But we failed them. We haven't tried to build a European Parliament which is on the UK model or capable of doing what the British Parliament does and has done for so long and they feel we have let them down. The European Parliament ought to have more powers, but the people in the House of Commons who criticise the European Parliament and say it's not democratic are the very people who refuse to grant it more powers. This is sheer hypocrisy! And this is the mark of so much of what is said by the European 'septics'. I say 'septics' because they are poisoning politics.

We ought to strengthen the European Parliament and at the same time we ought to do more to understand the European structure. The European Community is *sui generis*, it is 'of its own'. There has never been anything like it before, there is nothing else like it in the world today. It may be that some others will in time copy us, but they will have to understand what it is all about. It was very largely the creation of Jean Monnet and the intellectual body he had around him. What did they do?

They created the Commission and the Commission was given its job of making constructive proposals. The British Civil Service wasn't intended to do that. It has the highest reputation for integrity of almost any Civil Service in the world; in all the years I have been concerned I have known of only one case where a civil servant was accused of a lack of integrity. That is remarkable. But it wasn't put there to create proposals and to say this is what the country needs. That's been the job of the politicians. The civil servants get four weeks' holiday every five years while we have an election and they sit back and reflect and they look at the party manifesto. They say 'well, if we get the same lot, we carry on as before, they've got the same things in their manifesto. If we get a new lot, they'll tell us what to do according to the manifesto so we'll be ready to do it.' But it's not their job and they don't conceive it as their job to put forward positive proposals. The Community Commission was created quite deliberately for that purpose; and it has been very successful.

Now there are some who say 'look at all the bureaucrats'. Well, look at the bureaucrats. In Brussels there are 9,200 bureaucrats, excluding interpreters, who are responsible for 340 million people. Now in Edinburgh there is also a sizeable bureaucracy. There was an argument about exactly how large it is. There were originally said to be 11,800 employees but some of the services have been taken out and there are now said to be 6,900, responsible for five and half million people. What a contrast! Now, with great respect, we know the Scots can be difficult, but to have a difference of that sort is very instructive.

There is an attitude which wants to stop the bureaucracy in Brussels doing this and doing that. The fact is that the decisions are taken by the ministers or the Prime Ministers and President. They have to agree the measures which will then be implemented by the Commission and the weakness of this system is that, having taken the decisions in Brussels, so many of the ministers are not prepared to come and stand at their boxes in their parliaments and say 'Don't criticise Jacques Delors, I took this decision, I am responsible for it together with the other ministers.' They are responsible and they won't accept their responsibilities. If you ever get within reach of a minister, which I know is difficult, then say to him 'Did you take responsibility for this or not? And if not, why not?' This needs badly to be done.

What is the next stage of the organisation? It is, of course, what is going to happen here at the Summit, the meeting of the Heads of Government. I remember very well the first one. It took place in October 1972 after the UK had signed the Treaty and before we actually went into the Community. The nine of us met in Paris and President Pompidou was in the Chair. He produced the first half of the declaration, which was one of the best international declarations which I have ever come across, and we settled everything. But there were a lot of very good Europeans who said 'Why have you got a meeting of Heads of Government, you have no right to have this, you don't appear in any of the Treaties and if you are not in the Treaties you don't exist, and if you don't exist you can't have a meeting.' President Pompidou ignored this Cartesian logic and said 'Well here we are, and we are having a meeting.' We set out there everything we were going to do for the Community by 1980, eight years away, and it covered a far wider field than is covered now.

One of things which I ensured was included was regional development, very largely based on my experience in Scotland in 1963, as Secretary of State for Regional Development. It wasn't all that easy but we had made our plans and set out our proposals and I went to Herr Brandt, then still Chancellor, before our meeting, and asked him to back me on it. He said 'I'll back you. You've also asked for something else.' I said 'Yes I've asked for special treatment for the Commonwealth.' He said 'I can't back you on that, the Germans won't have it, but I'll back you on Regional Development if you will back me on one thing.' I said 'What is that?' 'Well' he said 'we have joint boards, two level boards and on one level the trade unionists are allowed to have representation and so are the managers and I want this to be accepted in the Community'. I said 'I am quite prepared to accept that provided that you don't say that it must take a particular form.' 'Very well' he said 'then we do business'. So I then went to see President Pompidou and I said, 'I want your backing on this.' He said 'I don't see why I should back you. We don't need it in France, no need for it at all' and I said 'Well we do need it as an old industrial country to bring about change.' 'Well' he said 'even if that is true I don't like your proposals'. I said 'why not?' 'Well' he said 'you have sent me this map and I look at it and I come from Auvergne . . When I look at the map, you haven't put any black spots for money on Auvergne at all. Why should I have anything to do with a silly thing like this?' I said 'Well don't worry just give me that map back and tomorrow when we have the meeting you will have another map and when you look at Auvergne you will see it smothered with black spots and back me!' Well, he did back me and, as a result, we got the funds for regional development.

That all came about because of that Summit, and I remember so well that we worked until 10 o'clock the next evening and agreed that we had settled everything up till 1980. One of the ministers, I think he was Dutch, said 'Do you think we ought to have a meeting in 1980 just to celebrate?' We said, 'what a good idea, we'll have a celebration' and then somebody said, I think one of the Commission, that 'Perhaps we ought to meet half-way through 1976 to check that everything is going in the right direction and correct anything if necessary but I'm sure that it'll be all right and we will celebrate in 1980.' Look at the faith and confidence we had then, complete confidence in bringing everything about.

What went wrong? What went wrong was the Yom Kippur War in the Middle East, the establishment and growth of OPEC which quadrupled oil prices with one blow, and then, in 1979, trebled them again. As a result, the money flowed out of the Community countries and into the Arab world, which had no plans to use it for their own development and so we went into a recession. In that recession, each country said we must find a way of dealing with this ourselves, but we failed. We couldn't do it on our own in the modern world and it wasn't until the mid 1980s that the Community countries said that the way to get out of this is to do it as a Community. Now we have the Community countries hit by recession or depression. We mustn't make the same mistake of saying we will retract into our own shells and solve each problem on our own. It can't be done and this is why I hope that at this EC Summit meeting they will concentrate on the economic solutions to the problems within the Community. That must be the first priority and they have no reason why they shouldn't do it.

There is one difficulty however, and this joins up with what I was saying previously. These meetings last for two days. As those responsible know, a great deal of time is taken up with lunching, dining, wining and music and so on. This is an enormous burden which they are carrying. How can they deal with it in two days? At Commonwealth Conferences we used to have fourteen days and didn't have to reach agreement on anything. All we had to do was exchange views and tell each other what jolly good fellows we all were. Then it was cut down to ten days, and we still have ten days in a Commonwealth Conference but these European Heads of Government are expected to deal with these enormous burdens in just two days. It is asking and expecting far too much of them. They have got to face reality. To deal with a Community like this and its place in the world, including the GATT Agreements and so on, you have got to have the time and the proper advice in order to work out between the Heads of Government themselves what the solutions can be. This is now urgently required as part of a review of the structure of the Community.

I remember that, as I have said, we were only proposing to have one meeting half-way through our programme, in 1976, but after the oil crisis President Pompidou argued that we ought to have a get together, not with hordes of civil servants but just with the Heads of Governments and, as Denmark was in the Chair, he suggested that we meet in Copenhagen, which we did. It was the worst international meeting I have ever attended because, having planned to have just our own closed talks, suddenly the oil countries said they were sending six Foreign Ministers to discuss the oil problems with us. We spent the morning of the first day discussing whether or not anybody should see the Arab Foreign Ministers and by lunchtime we had decided that we should. We then spent the afternoon discussing who should see them and it was finally decided that our Foreign Ministers should meet the Arab Foreign Ministers. So they went to the airport and waited there for the plane. We had a quiet dinner. After dinner we decided what they should say to the Arabs when they met them and we decided they should only listen and say nothing.

The Arab Foreign Ministers arrived late, about 2 o'clock in the morning, and the result was that, when we met the next morning at 10 o'clock, the European Foreign Ministers all arrived having been kept up all night and told by the Arabs what they ought to think. They were hardly in a position to communicate what they had been told, but they managed to finish telling us by lunchtime. By this time, 2,000 of the world's press had arrived. Everybody said we needed a communiqué which we hadn't been intending to produce, we spent the afternoon and the evening working out the communiqué. It was a disastrous conference.

After that, however, we got Summit conferences organised properly, as this one will be, but they still now don't take account of the real situation of the Community and what is required of its leaders. That is a positive step which needs to be taken.

When I mention positive steps, I believe that if you are at the heart of Europe you have got to have positive proposals. Any suggestion that we can withdraw into a different sort of organisation is simply not possible for the very simple reason that the rest of the Community and the basic six members who formed it don't want any other form of organisation because they have had so many years of success with the curent one. They realised that if you tried to spread things so that there is no central arrangement you get so many exemptions that the system becomes unworkable.

I don't like the fact that in Maastricht we have the economic developments I have been describing, but a separate foreign policy and a separate defence policy and separate organisation for them. Could you imagine the Government of Britain saying that in Westminster we'll keep the economic side of things but we'll put foreign policy in Liverpool with a different body, and we'll put defence in Glasgow with another body? It just wouldn't work and this won't work either. The only consolation to me is that when it doesn't work people will come to their senses and say that this Community has to act as one because defence policy depends on foreign policy. You have to know who your enemies are in order to be prepared against them. This, I am sure, is bound to come and it would be much better if we saw Community development in that context instead of trying to break it up.

This brings me to the other question which is going to be discussed in Edinburgh, with a ghastly word – subsidiarity – which I can never remember. I wouldn't propose to join an organisation or a club or a business and say to the members that

I was coming in order to do as little as possible. They would say perhaps you had better not join us at all – we'd rather have somebody who is coming to do as *much* as he possibly can. That should be our positive approach to the Community.

Together we can do so much more than we can do individually and that is why subsidiarity is a false doctrine. I know it's fashionable at the moment but there are those, like Jacques Delors, who say that in fact it is going to be impossible to work in practice and that's what we shall find. Hours are spent by officials trying to define whether something is best done in a country or best done by the Community as a whole and we know that, in most cases, it will be better done by the Community because so much in the modern world isn't limited to countries and nations, it's cross-border, it's cross-boundary, it's cross-channel, it's cross-sea and that can be handled best by the Community. The Commission is a very effective body. I know a lot of the members and I always made it a point that we should send our top people to Brussels, to become Commissioners and officials. I said to Whitehall that, as far as I was concerned, you must say to your people that unless they come out top in every respect they will never get to Brussels; we will only send the top people there and that is a policy which, I am glad to say, has been carried on by successive governments.

Why is there this criticism, very much limited to Britain, of Jacques Delors, the President of the Commission? I think that a lot of it is sheer envy of what the man has been able to do. Take the Single Market and all the effort which was needed to examine that, to decide how it could be created amongst twelve different countries. It was agreed in 1986 and at the end of 1992 it's in operation. I am sad to see reports that we seem to be lagging in putting into effect all the regulations we have agreed but we can still catch up. That is what M. Delors has achieved with his fellow Commissioners and with the agreement of the governments concerned.

We have often lagged behind. One of the things which

concerns me, because of my former home where I was born and because of my constituency, is the Channel Tunnel. We started discussing the Channel Tunnel in the 1850s. I agreed it with President Pompidou in 1972 and we started work which the Labour Government stopped in 1974. Then it was agreed again in 1984, started again in 1986, with constant rows from this side – not from the French side – about money, and it'll be finished some time in the future. With it we ought to have what the French and the Germans and the others have planned, which is fast railroads and certainly a fast link.

What has happened about that? We started discussing it five years ago in 1987 and still have no decision. No decision at all and, as I said, although it comes up from Dover, we haven't even decided what side of the Thames it's going to end. The first proposal put forward went slap through the middle of my constituency and my constituents strongly objected because no action was being taken to look after the surrounding country-side or the surrounding houses. The argument given by the Government then was that these provisions must be covered by the railway. But you can't get any railway, whether it's private or not, to say we are going to spend this amount of money on protecting the environment; that's not our job, they say, and if you want that then I'm sorry but we are not going to produce a railroad at all. There is still no decision on this issue.

When I found they wanted to put it straight through my constituency I went to the chap who was responsible and pointed out that it was undesirable and he very kindly agreed and as a result they then published another plan which put the railway round the boundary of my constituency. It is just a little unfortunate, because the boundary of my constituency has one little bulge which comes out and he was so thorough that he actually made the railway go all the way round this little bulge as well. This made some people suspicious that something was up! However, we still have no final decisions and we are not even within sight of a fast link. That is the contrast with what goes on from the Commission in Brussels under the instructions of the Ministers themselves.

What about the widening of the Community, because that also will be under discussion in Edinburgh? There are two aspects to this. First, concerning those who want to join us as members of the Community, such as Sweden and Austria in particular. There is also Norway, but Norway will have to have another referendum. I brought Norway into the Community, they had a referendum and they said no, we propose to live on oil and fish, which is what they have done successfully ever since and they may say and do the same thing again. That's their affair and I am not grumbling in the least. But the other two, Sweden and Austria, want to come in and I think that a referendum in those two countries will succeed.

But there is one point I must put here and it applies also to our friends the Danes; part of the Community is going to be common defence. In this situation we are bound to see the Americans withdrawing forces. It's understandable. They have a terrible financial problem, an enormous budget deficit, enormous trade deficit and, with the collapse of the Soviet empire, they will withdraw forces. It is then incumbent on us in Europe to make sure that our defence is all right. Who can tell what is going to happen with the Soviet Empire now that it has collapsed?

I suppose we shall never know why Mr Gorbachev brought about its collapse or why the military let him bring about the collapse. Now, how long is his successor going to survive? We have seen an attempt to get rid of him and, if he does get pushed out, who is going to take over? If Mr Yeltsin goes, are the military going to step in and run the whole show? I would have thought there was quite a likelihood of that because there is nobody politically there capable of doing it, whereas the military are always prepared to take over.

Therefore, we have to be sure that our defences are prepared. One only has to look at what has happened in Europe and in many other Russian states to see that nationalism has taken over.

That should be a solemn warning to us about the Community. Those people who are worried about Germany's developing strength, far from praising the country for what it has achieved after being defeated in the war, those who are worried about it, should recognise that the only answer is to bind Germany tighter and tighter into the Community, to bind Germany with us and keep nationalism down. Chancellor Kohl has taken very strong action against those people who are on the frontier between what was East Germany and West Germany, who are extremely right wing. That's quite right and if we are going to deal with these problems of nationalism, then we have to bind them more and more tightly together in the Community. I suppose the French, almost more than any, realise how important that is.

But I say to my Danish friends what justification have you for saying you want to be 'excused' any action on defence? If something happens you would expect us to defend you, why then shouldn't you accept your proper responsibilities under Maastricht as far as defence is concerned? I think that they should and the same thing will apply to a single currency. The Danes have done extremely well out of membership of the Community, and if they are not going to be prepared to give that up, then there are certain obligations which they ought to accept. We can say that the Government of the day didn't explain it sufficiently well to the people to get their support. I am prepared to accept that, because, it has happened elsewhere but now is the time when they can explain what the future is as far as Denmark is concerned.

As far as the aspects of other countries wanting to join us are concerned, we come then to the former Soviet states, and here we must not deceive them. It is all very well to say yes, we welcome you with open arms but the situation is such at the moment that we can't possibly welcome them. Perhaps it would be more accurate to say they can't be welcomed. I have seen almost all of them and the plain fact is that their economies are in an absolutely disastrous state and they have no idea how to recreate them, or how to get a market economy.

Let us not, however, join in the American chorus, 'do it within the year, and then we'll trust you'. After the Second World War, it took Britain 11 years before we finally abolished the last of the restrictions which were put on during the war, and they were related to rationing. I remember it well because Anthony Eden was Prime Minister and, as Chief Whip, I sat in the cabinet. He was against abolishing rationing since he said it would be politically very costly. Harold MacMillan was Chancellor and he said that the restrictions must be cancelled; MacMillan won and so the last of the restrictions went 11 years after the end of the war.

Take now Spain and Portugal after the two dictators. I didn't like Franco, in particular, and I was in Spain during the Civil War against him, but one has to give him credit for the fact that, in the 40 years he was there, the Spaniards built up a substantial economy, they built a very large tourism revenue, they built up their industry, they built up their agriculture, they built up their banking and their insurance and they built up people who knew how to run departments in the Government. They were fortunate in having, when Franco died, a King who was able to constitutionalise the whole situation and, when there was an attempted coup, he put his foot down and that was that.

It still took them ten years, however, before they came to the Community and said we now feel we are in position to ask for membership. We must make this plain to these other countries and help them with finance, with technology but don't say 'yes, you are coming in at any moment'. What would happen if they did, what do we want to buy from them? What do we want to buy from Poland? What do we want to buy from Romania? There is nothing, perhaps glass from Czechoslovakia, but that's all. What do they want to buy from us? Everything. Now they see what the Western World is like they want everything. This is true of Eastern Germany but they have now got the money from the Western Germans in order to be able to buy a very large part of the standard of living which they want.

So let us be clear about this. We can help them, though we

have to be careful on the side of defence. As far as Yugoslavia is concerned we can see what happens when you have a country which is broken up by nationalism and by religion. On two occasions I said to Marshall Tito, once when he stayed with me and once when I stayed with him in Belgrade, that 'We are worried, you are healthy and strong but you are over 80 and what is going to happen when you go?' He said 'You will have no need to worry, I have tied Yugoslavia together so tightly that they won't be able to break away. Well, you look doubtful, you must remember also that along our border we have got the Soviet countries. We are never going to allow them to come into Yugoslavia as a result of our own quarrels.' Very well, Yugoslavia lasted, it lasted beyond his death. However, he didn't foresee, any more than anybody else, the collapse of the Soviet Empire and, when that happened, Yugoslavia collapsed and broke out into civil war itself. In my view, what we must remember is that this is a ghastly, bloody civil war which is trying to wipe out the results of centuries and it is not a civil war in which we in the West should become involved. By all means we should help them with food supplies and with medical supplies as much as we possibly can, but this has not to be a war in which we take part. If we did take part it would go on for years, because these are rebels determined to get their own way, and they will go on for months and years in the mountains as they did in the Second World War. This is not the Arabian Desert, this is an entirely different situation and the Community should not tear itself apart by trying to settle a civil war of that kind.

Looking to the future, we will also have the problem of Russia, maybe with millions starving, as well as the millions starving in Africa. It sometimes strikes me as strange that, ever since Roosevelt, the Americans have been paying farmers not to produce food, and now they are putting pressure on Europe also to pay farmers not to produce food. Yet in Africa, and this winter in Russia, there are millions of starving people. This doesn't seem to make sense.

And so the problems will be there. The Russian economy is run down. In 1990 I was in St Petersburg, or Leningrad as it then was, conducting some symphony concerts and people talked very freely saying that now they had got rid of 'those ghastly people', things would be better. When I went back recently, however, they seemed to be thinking that, whilst the other lot were pretty loathsome, at least they knew that under them the people would have jobs and food – now they didn't have either. When people get into that frame of mind, things are really becoming dangerous, quite apart from the civil war in some of the former Russian territories.

Of course, the Russians have always had economic problems. I remember Mr Khrushchev talking to me on one occasion saying that I must make the British buy Russian goods. I said that I couldn't make the British buy Russian goods, because I couldn't even make them buy British goods. But he argued that I must persuade them for the sake of good relations between our countries. So I agreed but asked what I should persuade them to buy. After a pause he said 'well, persuade them to buy Russian watches'. 'Why on earth should they buy Russian watches?' I asked. 'Well', he said, 'they are better than Swiss watches and they are cheaper than Swiss watches, and also, they go faster than Swiss watches'.

Meanwhile, the Chinese economy is increasingly getting stronger and more successful, with, over the last decade, an average growth of over 12% a year. China is also alongside Japan. People *say*, of course, that they are enemies, but they aren't enemies any longer. There are 1.25 billion people in China who are now becoming very well educated and trained technically. They have all the raw materials that they could want, with coal up in the north-west, oil up in the north-east, oil in the centre, gas off Hynan Island in the South, precious metals everywhere and an enormous agricultural area which is self-supporting.

In Japan they have the most advanced technology in the world, always moving forward, and they have a sales drive stronger than anywhere else in the world. Why? Because so many of their people in industry have got contracts for life. If you have contracts for life and you get a recession, the workers can't be sacked. You have to keep on paying them and the only way to deal with that is to sell and sell and sell, and use every means to sell. That's the secret of the Japanese success. When you put those four together, the educated workforce, the raw materials, the technology and the sales drives, we are, in the next century, going to see the most powerful economic force the world has ever known.

So we come back to Europe. This is what we have to challenge and we can't do it by withdrawing further and further from the Community. The only way we can do it is by strengthening the Community, by bonding it more and more closely together, recognising what is now needed for its developments and then being prepared to face the battle across the world for trade. It isn't just a question of the GATT although I think that the figures given for the GATT have been greatly exaggerated. Of course it is a good thing to move forward with the GATT. But the real challenge is going to be from the East with powerful countries, well-educated people, advanced technology, and tremendous sales drive. That is what we have to create in the Community and in doing that the British have to be positive as to how it can be done. We should not be thinking instead how we can withdraw from those aspects which don't particularly suit us.

I am as confident as I have ever been about the future of the Community. When I hear the Community's on the razor's edge, it must be a very funny razor. Others who say that, if this Summit doesn't go well that that will be the end of the Community, are talking absolute nonsense. The Community is there and it's strong. We have problems like every organisation has, but it is up to us to overcome them and this, I believe, is what the Community will do.

You can help the Community as fellow citizens by under-standing more and more what it is about and by persuading other people what it's about, showing them how it's an advantage to them because it exists for the benefit of the citizens, not for the politicians. The politicians sit there in the House of Commons and talk about sovereignty. Sovereignty exists for the benefit of the citizens and if we use it with our fellow members of the Community then that is for the benefit of the citizens. Sovereignty isn't something you put down in the cellar and go down with a candle once a week to see if it is still there, as you do with your precious gold articles and your silver and all the rest of it. Sovereignty exists to be used, and used for the benefit of the citizens. You are the citizens, you must make sure that it is used for your benefit and I wish you well in doing so.

Sir Edward Heath's lecture was sponsored by Lothian Regional Council and delivered at the Royal College of Physicians, Edinburgh, on 9 December 1992.

The lecture was chaired by Professor William Paterson, Director, the Europa Institute, and a response was given by the Rt Hon. Sir David Steel, MP.

Councillor Eric Milligan, Convener, Lothian Regional Council, presided.

15   *Patrick Geddes: visual thinker*

I THINK IT IS SIGNIFICANT THAT THIS LECTURE SHOULD HAVE come
about as a cooperation between a poetry library and a Regional
Planning Department, for Patrick Geddes was an advocate both
of poetry and of planning. Furthermore, I have prepared this
paper as a lecturer in the Centre for Continuing Education of
the University of Edinburgh, while a key organiser of this
event is a lecturer in art history. Again, Patrick Geddes was
a strong advocate of both adult education and the visual arts.
So my first point is that the diverse combination of people
involved in bringing about this event tells one something
about Patrick Geddes himself, for he took it for granted
that people of different specialisations should work together.
For him, it would have been natural that the Scottish Poetry
Library should work with Lothian Regional Council Planning
Department to present a lecture, and that that lecture should
be given by someone involved in adult education. In addition,
it would have delighted him that this event was taking place
under a European banner. It was once written of him: 'Geddes'
Scotland embraced Europe and his Europe embraced the world.'
And it would be difficult to better express Geddes' concern for
Scotland as an active and integral part of Europe. He would
however have been scornful of the non–democratic nature of
the present government of Scotland where 'subsidiarity' is held
to apply to London *vis-à-vis* Brussels, but not to Edinburgh or
Glasgow *vis-à-vis* London.

I wish in this lecture to put the work of Patrick Geddes into a wider context than that in which it is normally seen. He is often referred to as a pioneer of town planning and this is fair enough, but I want to make clear that his town-planning abilities were just one expression of a polymathic genius. Furthermore, I want to suggest that his refusal to be pigeonholed and specialised, far from simply being a maverick intellectual attribute, is in fact directly related to the generalist tradition of thought in Scotland which has, this century, been explored under the title of 'democratic intellectualism'. Hugh MacDiarmid summed this up well when he said,

> . . . Geddes's constant effort was 'to help people to think for themselves, and to think round the whole circle, not in scraps and bits.' He knew that watertight compartments are useful only to a sinking ship, and traversed all the boundaries of separate subjects.

Related to this generalism, is the little-discussed, but culturally potent, tradition of visual thinking in Scotland, which finds its expression, on the one hand in the commitment of nineteenth-century Scottish mathematicians to geometry as against algebra and, on the other, in the achievements of, among many others, Thomas Telford, James Watt, Robert Adam and James Clerk Maxwell. Again, Geddes only makes sense if one sees him as a visual thinker, born into a culture in which visual thinking was taken for granted.

Introduction: a multiplicity of activity

How can we get some idea of Geddes' achievements? He is one of the most obscured, though at the same time one of the most influential, of thinkers. Many of his ideas come down to us today through the works of his follower, the American theorist of city planning Lewis Mumford, and a reading of Mumford can be a good introduction to some aspects of Geddes. For example, in his book *The Culture of Cities* published in 1938, Mumford cites Geddes considerably more often than any other person mentioned in the book. In the classic summation of Mumford's thought, *The City in History* from 1961, Geddes is not top of the citation list, but the only persons more cited than he are Socrates, Plato, Aristotle, Aristophanes and Herodotus. To find Mumford inadvertently placing Geddes in company with these Classical Greek thinkers is an unexpected, but appropriate, compliment to Geddes. In *The Condition of Man,* published in 1944, Mumford devotes several thousand words to Geddes and gives what is still a very accurate, if somewhat enigmatic, assessment of Geddes' significance as follows: 'What he was, what he stood for, what he pointed towards will become increasingly important as the world grows to understand both his philosophy and his example.' This lecture is an attempt to begin to understand that philosophy and that theory.

Brief biography

Patrick Geddes was born in Ballater, Aberdeenshire, in 1854 and died in the Scots College he had founded in Montpellier, in the South of France, in 1932. In between times, he had studied evolution with T.H. Huxley in London, helped to found the Sociological Society and been appointed Professor of Botany in Dundee in 1888. He had also become a pioneer of town planning, and in that sphere carried out work on the conservation of urban environments, as well as developing an evolutionary analysis of the growth and decline of cities. Much of his important work in urban conservation and planning was carried out in India and it was there, in 1919, that he was appointed the first Professor of Civics and Sociology at the University of Bombay. As if that wasn't enough, there is much more – for example, his initiation of student-run university residences (Patrick Geddes Hall on the Mound in Edinburgh marks this achievement) in which he revitalised the medieval tradition of universities as, at least in part, democratic, student-run bodies. Or again, one might mention his pioneering of Summer Meetings in Edinburgh, early examples of the Summer Schools that are now so much a part of educational life throughout the world. One can say all this without even mentioning what is perhaps his best known achievement, the Outlook Tower in Edinburgh, which marked its centenary in 1992.

It was here, along with nearby Riddles Court, that these Summer Meetings were based. This Outlook Tower was one of Geddes' great educational statements. Through it, one could learn, not just through words and images, but from direct experience, about a multiplicity of aspects of Edinburgh, Scotland, Europe, the world and the cosmos, all of which had a bearing on how people made their lives through their work in a particular place. The Outlook Tower was described in its heyday as 'the world's first sociological laboratory' , but it was more than that. It was a solid assertion of the importance of all areas of knowledge, all arts, all sciences, all religions, within the context of a real place. Knowledge was not split off from doing: as Geddes said in his 1888 pamphlet on cooperation 'it is only by thinking things out as one lives them, and living things out as one thinks them, that a man or a society can really be said to think or even live at all'. Geddes summed this idea up in his educational motto 'Vivendo Discimus', which translates as 'By Living We Learn', a motto emblazoned not only on his Scots College in Montpellier but also on an archway in Riddles Court, open for anyone to see today. Not surprisingly, in this context, Geddes was also a powerful advocate for the unity of the intellectual and the practical found in the arts, both in drama – his dramatisations of history ranged from the earliest time to the present – and in the visual arts, in particular the work of Celtic Revival painters such as John Duncan and Phoebe Traquair.

But having briefly described some of Geddes' achievements and interests, how can we begin to get a handle on the multiplicity of activity which characterised his life? A useful beginning is to reflect on the experiences of his childhood and

youth, which he spent living overlooking the city of Perth. For
the most part, he ignored his formal schooling, preferring to
absorb an education in the natural world offered to him by his
father, a Gaelic-speaking Highland soldier, retired from serving
the interests of the British Empire to cultivate his garden on
Kinnoull Hill. From this hill young Patrick could see not only
Perth, but the rich agricultural lands of Strathearn and Strathtay,
tucked between the Grampians and the Ochils. For Geddes, this
gardener – his father – and this place – a hill overlooking a
region of diverse human activity and natural features – were
key experiences. They became tools for thought which were
to play a large part in his later thinking. This later thinking,
as it relates to his early experience of living overlooking a city
from a hill, can be seen not only in his commitment to the
Outlook Tower – standing as it does at almost the highest point
in the City of Edinburgh – but also in the simple, but powerful,
visual thinking device of what Geddes called the Valley Section
diagram.

In his diagram, Geddes can be seen making sense of basic
human activities. The hunter is shown in the forest, the shepherd
on the hill, the miner within the hill, the crofter or peasant on the
lowland, the market gardener on the outskirts of the city, the
fisher in the sea. All are given symbolic reality within a highly
stylised version of the city which Geddes used as a living symbol
of his ideas, namely Edinburgh in the shadow of Arthur's Seat.
Geddes shows that, by attending to a real environment, real
people and real work, in a symbolic but organised way, one
can begin to be in a position to understand that environment
in its fullness and therefore to be able to plan it, or simply to be
able to live constructively within it. Geddes does not, of course,
expect everyone to be able to fit into the categories of the simple
Valley Section. The point of the Valley Section diagram is that
it is a symbol of how a situation begins to make sense when you
look at it from a holistic perspective and this holistic, generalist
message of Geddes is applicable in all situations. The Valley
Section diagram is a visual reminder, a symbol of the need to

analyse an environment, not a full prescription for that analysis. The deceptive simplicity of the Valley Section diagram is linked to another of Geddes' deceptively simple devices for thinking, namely the three interacting categories of Place, Work and Folk which are discussed below.

One of the most beautiful, but also the most informative, of all the representations of the Valley Section is the stained glass version, made for the Outlook Tower, which can now be seen at Cannonball House on Castlehill in Edinburgh, just across the road from the Tower itself. In that depiction, the basic diagram is seen as before, but produced in a wonderfully accessible way, and (typically for Geddes) making use of a local craft. At the time the window was produced, at the end of the last century, domestic as well as religious stained glass was a commonplace in Scotland, and much of it can still be seen today. This use of stained glass is interesting because it shows Geddes making an educational point, that is to say illustrating one of the basic analytic tools of what he called the Regional Survey, while at the same time ensuring that the medium through which the ideas are presented was as popularly accessible as possible. He doesn't compromise his ideas, he simply makes a representation which allows interested viewers to go as far in to the ideas as they like and to stop where they like. On one level, this is simply an attractive image. Alternatively, it can be seen as a careful classification of Place, Work and Folk with reference to nature. Again, he shows the miner in the hill, the shepherd and the forester on the hill, arable and cattle farming on the low ground, and the City with its port and its trade.

But on yet another level, the Valley Section is a multiple representation of what the physical and social world is at the moment and could be in the future. Looking at the Latin wording which appears below this window – 'Microcosmos Naturae. Sedes Hominum. Theatrum Historiae. Eutopia Futuris' – one sees Geddes insisting on a set of, at first sight, contrasting, and yet mutually illuminating, views of the valley. The valley is first a 'microcosm of nature', but also the 'sedes hominum', the seat of men, or as we might say, the place where human beings make their lives. Linked to this is the dramatic 'theatrum historiae', the theatre of history. Finally, it is the 'eutopia' or 'good place' of the future, not 'utopia' with a 'u' ,which means an idealised 'no place', but 'eutopia' with an 'eu', a good place that Geddes believed could be achieved through local and international cooperation.

Geddes doesn't stop there, however. Looking at the window, one can see that the 'theatre of history', for the present, is represented by fighting birds of prey. But the good place of the future, the 'eutopia', is symbolised by three peaceful doves. For Geddes, this was symbolic of a transition from a crudely mechanised capitalist society based on unfettered competition (what he called the paleotechnic world), to his dream of a new society which made use of sophisticated, environmentally friendly technologies, based on a local cooperation (which he called the neotechnic world). This would, he thought, succeed the centralised and hierarchical power structure of his, and our, present. (In the context of the European Summit in Edinburgh, these notions might even put some meaning back into the word 'subsidiarity'.) These are anarchist ideas, in the most constructive sense of that description, and it's interesting to note here that Geddes numbered among his friends the influential anarchist thinker Peter Kropotkin.

The image of three doves runs throughout Geddes' work. They appear unexpectedly at first, not least in another window preserved at Cannonball House, but then you start to look for them on book covers or information sheets. They are found again on the inside cover of his *Masque of Ancient Learning,* a text for performance and reading, which brought the participant into contact with Geddes' view of the evolution of culture. For Geddes, they were not just symbolic birds, they were also three stylised versions of the letter S. These three Ss stand for Sympathy, Synthesis, and Synergy and this message is thus also part of the Valley Section window, as it is part of the *Masque of Ancient Learning.* What Geddes meant by sympathy was the Enlightenment use of this word, closer today to what we might call empathy, the ability accurately to imagine oneself in another's place. From this emotional engagement with other people, he proceeds to the intellectual power of comparing and synthesising different ideas. And finally, having emphasised first the emotional and secondly the intellectual, he moves to the social notion of synergy, that is to say of acting together to solve problems and create opportunities – in other words, Geddes' primary principle of successful human society, cooperation.

Thus in one image, the stained-glass version of the Valley Section diagram, Geddes provides the basis of a philosophy for thinking about human ecology, not only by drawing attention to the necessity of exploring any environment in terms of its natural characteristics and the way in which those characteristics relate to the folk who live there and the work done, but also by specifying the psychological attitude necessary for any such analysis, that is to say an emotional, intellectual and cooperative engagement with that place, those folk and their work. If we look back over the twentieth century it becomes obvious that in terms of planning, whether we look north, south, east or west, this simple interdependence of Place, Work and Folk, and the engagement with these categories in terms of sympathy, synthesis and synergy, have for the most part been ignored, to the detriment of us all. Had Geddes' essentially simple, but well-analysed, ideas been borne in mind, any number of twentieth-century planning disasters could have been avoided.

The analytical framework of Place, Work and Folk is derived from the thinking of the French sociological pioneer Le Play. Whereas Le Play used the words Lieu, Travail, Famille, however, Geddes (despite an enduring respect for Le Play) provides what is, in my view, a much more flexible framework, by substituting for 'Famille' the word 'Folk', which immediately brings in the notion of a wider, potentially supportive community (synergistic and cooperative, as Geddes might say), as against a smaller kinship group.

Thus, for those of us trying to understand Geddes' work

today, an appreciation of the importance of his ecologically inspiring childhood experience of a garden overlooking a region, helps us to make sense of the continuity between two poles of his work: first, the garden, which is both a symbol of creative interaction between person and nature and a place of contemplation, and secondly, the Regional Survey, Geddes' method of total social analysis, in the generation of which the Valley Section, the categories of Place, Work and Folk, and the attitudes of Sympathy, Synthesis and Synergy were key tools. Geddes pioneered the Regional Survey in order to be able to plan an environment in which human beings and nature could exist in a dynamic and creative harmony, and a hundred years later, it is becoming very obvious that such an approach is not just desirable, but a necessity. Mumford, writing in America 1922, describes the Regional Survey thus:

> [Its] aim . . . is to take a geographic region and explore it in every aspect. It differs from the social survey with which we are acquainted in America in that it is not chiefly a survey of evils; it is rather a survey of existing conditions in all their aspects; and it emphasises to a much greater extent than the social survey the natural characteristics of the environment, as they are discovered by the geologist, the zoologist, the ecologist – in addition to the development of the natural and human conditions in the historic past, as presented by the anthropologist, the archaeologist, and the historian. In short, the regional survey attempts a local synthesis of all the specialist 'knowledges'.

Perhaps it was this insistence on the importance of all 'knowledges', rather than the safe commitment to one specialist area, that made Geddes so much at odds with academic institutions throughout his life, whether at school in Perth, or applying for university posts later on. He has never been given the recognition due to him by the academic establishment, of which he was so suspicious during his life, and yet to say that he is neglected may give the wrong impression. There are few thinkers who have had three biographies devoted to them in the last two decades (by Paddy Kitchen, Phillip Boardman and Helen Meller). It's as though his thinking lies just beneath the surface of what we take to be our culture. At first glance, he is seen nowhere, but with a little digging he's hard to miss. This would not have surprised Geddes at all. Another diagram, this time of the 'Arbor Saeculorum', first published in his magazine *The Evergreen* in spring 1895 is Geddes' own version of the tree of life. It shows the growth of civilisation and is accompanied by the following description:

> A great tree and its branches, spreading right and left, suggests the twofold aspects of each historic era, temporal on one side, spiritual on the other. The tree has its roofs amid the fires of life, and is perpetually renewed from them, but the spirals of smoke which curl among its branches blind the thinkers and workers of each successive age to the thought and work of their precursors. While the branches symbolise the past and passing developments of society, the bud at the tree-top suggests the hope of the opening future. Two sphinxes guard the tree and gaze upward in eternal questioning; their lion bodies recalling man's origin in the animal world, their human faces the ascent of man. Issuing from the smoke-wreaths at the top of the tree are the phoenix of the ever-renewed body, and the butterfly (Psyche) of the deathless soul of humanity. On either side of the window rises a series of symbols, those on the right hand indicating the dominating spiritual forces of the great historic periods, those on the left the corresponding temporal powers.

Recall the phrase he uses – 'the spirals of smoke which curl among its branches blind the thinkers and workers of each successive age to the thought and work of their precursors'. If ever any comment described our own blindness to Geddes, it is this one. Geddes has been obscured for long enough, so let us blow away some of the smoke.

In trying to make sense of Geddes' intellectual history, a

consideration of his strongly Calvinist background is revealing, not simply because of the highly democratic values of Calvinism, at least within the structure of the church itself, but because of the influence of his father, who, though fundamentalist in outlook, was also Geddes' most valued teacher.

This is an interesting point because the tension between fundamentalist belief and wide-ranging intellectual questioning is a key aspect of Scottish intellectual history, often expressed within the same individual. It seems paradoxical, but in fact the two approaches are strongly linked in that they both recognise the importance of first principles. The difference is that for the fundamentalist the first principles are given, for the questioner they have not yet been discovered.

When the conflict is expressed too strongly in one individual, the result can be catastrophic. For example, the pioneering nineteenth-century geologist Hugh Miller is thought to have killed himself because he could not reconcile his geological discoveries with his faith. The relevance of this for Geddes is that he made what might be described as the classic Scottish intellectual move. That is to say, he became a generalist. So in a sense he didn't reject his religious background, he simply took seriously the religions of other folk, too, so that Christianity became one of many alternatives. In the Arbor Saeculorum, what Geddes sees as religious and spiritual contexts are presented in a historicist manner, beginning with Judaism and culminating in the anarchism and cooperation with which Geddes himself identified. As an example of visual thinking which is at the same time a fine educational tool, the Arbor Saeculorum is fair enough, but in fact Geddes' interest in the ways of the human soul extended much further than the Arbor would imply. For example, around 1900 one finds him a strong advocate of Bahai'ism which is a faith that insists on the real significance of other faiths, and insists on the unity of truth within all religions. It's interesting to note that Geddes shared his advocacy of Bahai'ism with a number of those on the liberal wing of the Free Church, notably Jane Whyte, wife of Alexander

Whyte, sometime Principal of New College and Moderator of
the Free Church, an aspect of Geddes elucidated by *The Seven
Candles of Unity,* Anjam Khursheed's account of the early days
of Bahai'ism in Edinburgh. An aspect of the Bahai faith which
must have appealed to Geddes was the notion that religion and
science were not in opposition to one another, but were necessary
complements. For Geddes, all human activities had their truth,
so all religions had relevance, all science had relevance, all art
had relevance. What had to be questioned were not these human
insights, but the way they related to one another and the way they
made sense with reference to Place, to Work, and to Folk.

Place, Work, Folk

Turning to these ideas of Place, Work, and Folk in a little
more detail, how did Geddes think about these terms and their
interactions? Philip Boardman tells how Geddes lost his sight
briefly on a visit to Mexico in 1879-80, and that this experience,
combined with – as I've suggested – the Scottish culture of visual
thinking which Geddes found in his background, led Geddes to
a deep reflection on the nature of the visual. This, in turn, led
to his creation of diagrammatic 'thinking machines'. According
to Boardman, these matrices are in part based on the window
frames which Geddes used as imaginary classification devices
while he was convalescing, but he soon adapted these to folded
paper form to explore the inter-relationship of the ideas more
deeply. Geddes used the combinations yielded within these
matrices as a way of thinking about the manner in which
elements of a situation combined with different emphases. It's
interesting to note that Lewis Mumford, who, it seems, was not
a visual thinker to the same extent as Geddes, rejected this side of
Geddes' thought. Yet Geddes' own description of his diagram,
and its relation to academia on the one hand, and planning on the
other, is worth quoting.

Here the study of place grows into Geography; that of Work

into Economics; that of Folk into Anthropology. But these are commonly studies apart, or in separate squares, touching only at a point. Witness the separate Chairs and Institutes and Learned Societies of each name. But here we have to bring them into a living unison. Place studies without Work or Folk is a matter of atlases and maps. Folk without Place and Work are dead – hence anthropological collections and books contain too much of mere skulls and weapons. So too for economics, the study of Work, when apart from definite Place and definite Folk, comes down to mere abstractions.

But what do these side squares mean? Below our maps of Place we can now add pictures of the human Work-places, ie of field or factory; next of Folk-place of all kinds, from farmhouse or cottage in the country to homes or slums in the modern manufacturing town. Our geography is now fuller and our town planning of better Work-places, better Folk-places, can begin.

So again for Folk, Place-folk are natives or neighbours; and Work-folk are too familiar on all levels to need explanation. Our anthropology thus becomes living and humanised and surveys the living town.

Work too becomes clearer. For Place-work is a name for the 'natural advantages' which determine work of each kind at the right place for it; and Folk-work is our occupation, often tending to accumulate into a caste, not just in India. [This latter comment reflects the great amount of work Geddes did in India and this piece was written there.]

Our geography, economics and anthropology are thus not simply enlarged and vivified; they are now united into a compact outline of Sociology.

From these separate notes of life we thus get a central unified Chord of Life, with its minor chords as well.

This is an outstanding visual attempt both to unify different areas of knowledge and to make them useful in what, today, we might call a human-ecological sense. It's also worth noting that Geddes sees the diagram simply as a starting point for further visual thinking 'below our maps of place we can add pictures of the human–Work places' that is, the situation being analysed becomes real through visual means not through abstractions. The diagram is the most abstract level. All other moves take one nearer to the reality.

It is likely that what Mumford really objected to were the more complex levels of Geddes' visual thought, in which he tries to unify absolutely everything. The primary example of this is the diagram he called the Chart or Notation of Life in which the simple Place, Work, Folk diagram appears as the very useful analytical tool we have seen it to be. But the rest of the diagram seems to be much less an analytical tool than a highly imaginative attempt to describe all human behaviour. It can be used almost as a creativity exercise, a sort of guided brainstorming session. But whatever it is, it is an extraordinarily intellectually fertile piece of work. Travelling anti–clockwise, quadrant by quadrant, one can move from what Geddes calls the simple practical life of Place, Work, and Folk (top left) to the simple mental life of Sense, Experience, and Feeling (bottom left) to the full inner life of Imagery, Ideation, and Emotion (bottom right) to the full effective life of Achievement, Synergy, and what Geddes called Etho–Polity (top right). While this is not exactly easy to understand, in fact it's a terminological minefield, what Geddes is putting forward here is a way of beginning to understand human behaviour, and mental life, within the same framework as cultural evolution. For this diagram never stops. The results of the full, effective life of one generation make a difference to the simple, practical life of the next. And suddenly, the Notation of Life can be seen as an amazingly stimulating attempt to come to terms with the evolution of human history in which art, science and religion all play their parts. Geddes does, however, tacitly admit that his Notation is less than clear. At one point he comments gleefully with reference to the top right quadrant '. . . our diagram next turns out to be that of Parnassus, the home of the nine Muses; and their very names and their symbolisms will be found to answer to the nine squares above, and to connect them with those below, and this more and more precisely as the scheme is studied. Not indeed that there are not one or two difficulties at first sight, but these can easily be cleared away by a little psychological and social reflection.' This final comment, that there may be 'one or two difficulties', is perhaps the understatement of the century, but whatever difficulties it may have got him into, I admire Geddes for pushing his ideas this far. What's important here is not that he's right or that he's wrong, but that he's prepared to push it; that he's prepared to try to integrate human experience over a wide, wide canvas, for the wide canvas is, after all, the only one that exists. This is the crucial, holistic truth that powers all Geddes' work. As such, the Notation of Life is a diagram that deserves to be taken seriously. Like all great works, it rewards the attention you are prepared to give it.

Constructive generalism

If Patrick Geddes is characterised by anything, it is by his conviction that one area of knowledge or experience can be illuminated from the perspective of another and vice versa; religion can illuminate science, thought can illuminate action, and so on. In this constructive generalism, Geddes is very much part of that Scottish philosophical tradition which has been explored by George Davie under the heading of 'democratic intellectualism' and this sense of the importance of a general, but integrated, perspective is an enduring feature of the intellectual character of Scotland. It was strong in Geddes' day and typical is this comment from John Burnet, Professor of Greek at St Andrews around the time of the First World War: 'The most important side of any department of knowledge is the side on which it comes into touch with every other department. To insist on this is the true function of humanism.'

This quotation seems to sum up a quintessentially Geddesian position, but in fact shows just how closely related his thought was to an essential generalist current in Scottish culture. Another example of this commitment to a general, but integrated, approach to knowledge from Geddes' time can be seen in the efforts of the then Professor of Education at the University of Edinburgh, S. S. Laurie, to rekindle interest in the pansophism of the seventeenth-century educational pioneer from Moravia, John Amos Comenius, with whose thinking that of Geddes often resonates. Like Geddes, Comenius had a high regard for the practical, as well as for ideas. Indeed, the following, from his *Pansophiae Praeludium* of 1637, with its profoundly ecological symbolism, could almost have been written by Geddes:

> We see that the branches of a tree cannot live unless they all alike suck their juices from a common trunk with common roots. And can we hope that the branches of wisdom can be torn asunder with safety to their life, that is to truth? Can one be a natural philosopher who is not also a metaphysician? or an ethical thinker who does not know something of physical science? or a logician who has no knowledge of real matters? or a theologian, a juriconsult, or a physician who is not first a philosopher? or an orator or poet, who is not all these at once? He deprives himself of light, of hand and of regulation, who pushes away from him any shred of the knowable.

Typically enough, Geddes' own view of Comenius emerges in his book *Cities in Evolution* during his analysis of the district of Chelsea in London:

> . . . it is but a step in thought . . . from the quite little Moravian meeting house with its austere cemetery, to one of the greatest and best Puritan movements in history. Even their tiny disused schoolhouse, dingy though it be, is more than a mere surviving landmark for progress. It has a tradition of its own, older than that of any of our schools and colleges: for among the educators of history there are few more significant and perhaps none at this moment more vividly modern, more directly indicative

of the twofold meeds of progress in the sciences and the humanities together, than the Moravian pedagogue and bishop Comenius . . .

This comment, 'none at this moment more vividly modern', can, I think, be used by us today to describe Geddes himself. Just as Comenius' message reached Geddes, so does Geddes' message reach us.

The garden

I want now to turn back again to Geddes' commitment to the idea and actuality of the garden. Geddes placed the strongly visual symbol of the garden at the heart of his work, as a model of creative interaction between human beings and nature. What others saw as urban wasteland, he saw as an environmental opportunity. Critical to his thinking was the insight that in an urban environment, a modest change – even if it didn't look like much to a visiting dignitary – might make a big difference to a local community. What concerned Geddes was not to create perfect places, but to create places that were good enough. His wasteland garden in West Port, Edinburgh (recently restored by the Patrick Geddes Memorial Trust), isn't much, it doesn't get much light and never will, but it's good enough to make a difference to the environment of that street. And that's what counts. During the 1990 Edinburgh Science Festival the importance of the garden for Geddes (both as a symbol and as a practical fact) was made clear in a small-scale, but significant, exhibition organised by Sofia Leonard of the Patrick Geddes Centre. This was subtitled appropriately 'The Green Pioneer', for it must now be clear that Geddes was a profound ecological thinker in the most general sense, a century ahead of his time in his understanding of the dynamic relationships between human beings and their environment. For him, the city was an evolving entity open to decay, but also to regeneration. Indeed the whole notion of building conservation owes much to the initiative he took to rehabilitate the slum tenements of Edinburgh's Old Town in a process he referred to as 'conservative surgery'. With this phrase he emphasises the need to preserve on the one hand, but to be prepared to remove and build anew when need be. Not for Geddes the gutless facadism which is so popular today. He began his conservation work with James Court, where he lived with his wife Anna from the mid 1880s. A consequence of this revitalisation of the Old Town was the building of new buildings (of panache, not imitation) side by side with the old, for example Wardrop's Court; and, from the early 1890s onwards, Ramsay Garden, just beneath Edinburgh Castle, in which architects Stewart Henbest Capper and Sidney Mitchell extended and adapted older structures to create a completely new complex.

In the intervening century, Geddes' vision of restoring to the Old Town of Edinburgh a locally valid mixture of social classes and activities has been superseded by gentrification and the many-headed monster of the tourist-cum-heritage industry, but his vision of a multifaceted community of thinkers and doers is as valid and necessary now as it was then. Ramsay Garden was a kind of condominium for the intellectual class, built to attract them back from the New Town of Edinburgh and place them side by side with the working-class folk of the Old Town, an intention summed up in the principles of the Edinburgh Social Union, founded by Geddes in the mid 1880s. Some of Geddes' most cogent statements about planning – which emphasise its essence as primarily a social, not a spatial, activity – were made in his Indian reports. The following is from the report on the town of Madura in the Madras area:

Town-planning is not mere place-planning, nor even work-planning. If it is to be successful it must be folk-planning. This means that its task is not to coerce people into new places against their associations, wishes and interests – as we find bad schemes trying to do. Instead its task is to find the right places for each sort of people; places where they will flourish. To give people in fact the same care that we give when transplanting flowers, instead of harsh evictions and arbitrary instructions to 'move on', delivered in the manner of the officious amateur policeman.

If ever there was a manifesto for the proper treatment of people and places, that in my view is it.

The Outlook Tower and visual thinking in Scotland

I'd now like to move from Ramsay Garden and turn again to that most concrete of all Geddes' devices for education and thinking, the Outlook Tower. It is 100 years since Geddes adapted this building, already developed as a viewpoint for the city by Maria Teresa Short. What Geddes added was a set of ideas which turned an instructive viewpoint into a integral part of his philosophy of teaching, in which the theory and application of knowledge were united. As we have seen, the interdependence of knowledge and perception, knowledge and action, were fundamental to Geddes' thinking and in the Outlook Tower the physical and the cognitive were brought into explicit relation. Every physical step on the way down the Tower (top to bottom was the preferred route by which Geddes would conduct the interested student) was also a cognitive step towards the integration of the local and the global. From the top of the Tower was the view of the City and its Region in two versions, the concentrated and projected view within the Camera Obscura, which Geddes likened to the synoptic vision of the artist, and the broad sweeping view from the balcony and terrace outside. Geddes compared the latter, which has to be selected from to make sense, to the necessarily analytical view of the scientist. The Outlook Tower is located at a key point within the psychogeography of the city of Edinburgh, between the symbol of state power, the castle, and the then symbol of rejection of the authority of that state in matters spiritual, the Free Church College (now New College of the University of Edinburgh). Furthermore, it is on a ridge of rock coextensive with the remains of an extinct volcano which we now call Arthur's Seat: truly an outlook with which to begin thinking about the evolution of cities, regions and cultures.

Below the terrace was a floor devoted to the consideration of Edinburgh, then Scotland. Below again were floors devoted to the consideration of English-speaking cultures, Europe and, finally, the world as a whole. But today, apart from the old Edinburgh Room, where some of Geddes' work is still preserved, but not open to public view, it's just a tourist attraction. A brilliant description of the Tower, in which its modern role as no more than this is juxtaposed with its intellectual role in the past, can be found in Elspeth Davie's novel *Coming to Light*:

Now they went down another stair to the ground floor [of the Outlook Tower] and waited at the counter for the others. This place was full of books, pamphlets, postcards and gadgets for tourists. But not a word here about the extraordinary man – Patrick Geddes – who began it all, a man thought of by many from that day to this as a genius. When he acquired the old Outlook Tower nobody knew what he wanted it for, except perhaps, it was thought, for some devilish ploy. In fact, he saw it as becoming a museum which would bring together the problems of workers in all fields – educational, social and industrial. It was also to be a laboratory where he himself would express and gather in the thought of all ages. People in his time were hugely divided about it. Most visitors were none the wiser about the place when they left it. Others thought it a triumph of intellectual experiment . . .

Davie goes on:

Geddes himself wished for a Tower with a view over everything in life. He had ideas on Townplanning, Botany, Geology. He had plans for an Art Institute, and Outdoor Theatre and a Concert Hall . . . Geddes . . . could be satiric, not to say savage in his utterances. It would be interesting to know which of these expressions would come uppermost had he foreseen that there would be now simply a very small picture of him on the dark stairs of his Camera Obscura.

It would interesting indeed. What characterises the Outlook Tower is the linking of immediate perception with the distantly known in a network of dynamic and changing knowledge. This is distinctively Geddesian, but it should be stressed that here Geddes is again very much part of the intellectual tradition of Scotland, for the link between the perceptual and the conceptual is a commonplace of Scottish philosophy. As I indicated in the introduction, it found its expression in the nineteenth century not only in Geddes' work but in the geometrical underpinning of James Clerk Maxwell's mathematics (it's no coincidence that Maxwell wrote the entry on 'Diagrams' for the ninth edition of the *Encyclopaedia Britannica*) and in Sir William Hamilton's philosophical defence of geometry against algebra. This has relevance not only to the study of Geddes' ways of thinking, but also for the growing recognition today of the advantages of perceptual methods of mathematical teaching with which Patrick Geddes would have been very much at home.

This is what Sir William Hamilton says:

> The mathematical process in the symbolical method (ie the algebraic) is like running a rail-road through a tunnelled mountain; that in the ostensive (ie the geometrical) like crossing the mountain on foot. The former carries us, by a short and easy transit, to our destined point, but in miasma, darkness and torpidity, whereas the latter allows us to reach it only after time and trouble, but feasting us at each turn with glances of the earth and heavens, while we inhale health with the pleasant breeze, and gather new strength at every effort we put forth.

One should also mention here, as points of departure for further thought, the visual intuitions of architects such as Robert Adam and engineers such as Thomas Telford, and the visual insights in the biological work of Geddes' younger professorial colleague in Dundee, D'Arcy Thompson, as expounded in his classic book *On Growth and Form*, and it's not surprising to read in Boardman's biography that Thompson had a very high opinion of Geddes. What we are looking at here is a culture of visual thinking in all fields, and Geddes must be considered with respect to this Scottish tradition, if we are to grasp one of the essential strands that brings unity to his thought.

The point should be made here that Geddes' commitment to visual thinking extends throughout his activities. His advocacy of Celtic Revival artists such as John Duncan, Helen Hay and Phoebe Traquair was not some sort of detached act of patronage; it was a close involvement in art as visual thinking. Close to the Outlook Tower and Ramsay Garden, John Duncan designed a fountain marking the spot where witches were burned outside the Castle. Typically for anything associated with Geddes, it gives one pause for thought about cultural history. The central serpent is transformed into a serpent of wisdom. But Duncan is better known for his highly illustrative work such as 'Tristan and Isolde' which can be seen in the City Art Centre in Edinburgh, not so far as I know commissioned by Geddes, but typical of the kind of Celtic Revival work Geddes encouraged to illuminate the history and mythology which he regarded as fundamental to any satisfactory appreciation of one's own, or anyone else's, culture. As one would expect, he was often subtly ecological in his engagement with art. There is, for example, a work by Helen Hay entitled 'Tak Tent'. It works on both a cultural and an ecological level and is from an issue of Geddes' magazine, *The Evergreen,* which unlike most magazines intentionally only had four issues, one for each season. Here, a Scots language proverb, 'Tak tent ere time be tint' resonates with the passing of the seasons (the image represents the period from the autumn equinox to the winter solstice) and draws attention to the importance of getting on and doing things, both notions close to Geddes' heart. So what Geddes was, in fact, doing was recognising art as a key form of visual thinking, and making use of it as such. This can be seen very clearly if we go back to the

Arbor Saeculorum. It is worth drawing attention to the fact that there was once a stained-glass version of this, too. I hope it still survives somewhere. The Arbor is, at one and the same time, an intriguing work of art and an educational resource, uniting areas of knowledge in visual form.

An interesting aside is the increasing effect Geddes is having on contemporary Scottish artists. At the time of writing, there is a Geddes-inspired installation by sculptor George Wyllie in the Tron Kirk. Another sculptor involved here is Kenny Munro, of the Edinburgh Sculpture Workshop, and the show as a whole has been organised by Gillespies, the Glasgow Design firm. Geddes is the informing presence.

Similarly Geddes-inspired is the 'Niches' project on Calton Road in Edinburgh. The centre niche is a collaborative construction, primarily the work of Kenny Munro, but also involving George Wyllie and Stan Bonnar. It is a real piece of visual thinking in a Geddesian tradition. Not only is the work itself strongly influenced by Geddes, but the whole project involving all the niches, placed in an urban environment and involving work from various interest groups and schools, has a cooperative nature which is very much in the spirit of Geddes.

It is difficult to decide what Geddes' most extraordinary contribution to visual thinking was. Sometimes, I think it is the Outlook Tower, sometimes the Valley Section, sometimes the Notation of Life, sometimes the fact that he made such good use of the artists of his day, sometimes the fact that he is directly influencing teachers, artists, architects and planners 100 years later. But what makes one realise his real significance as a visual thinker is all of these things together. Perhaps his most profound piece of visual thinking was in fact to draw attention to the exceptional visual properties of Edinburgh itself. Exposed geology, palaces, church and state, medieval growth versus Enlightenment plans, are all relevant to Geddes' meditation on the city in terms of Place, Work and Folk.

Another tool for Geddes' visual thinking was photography. At the end of the last century Geddes and his colleagues made very effective use of the camera as an instrument of town planning. Each picture records a critical urban relationship: the rise of street, a road forking (one fork following a contour), a trade route surrounded by tenements and public buildings. These images help the viewer to understand how people relate to specific parts of a built environment and how that built environment relates to them. As such, they give an immediate insight into Geddes' profound concern for the spaces we live in, their history and their potential for the future. For Geddes: 'the process of planning is like a complicated and never finished game of chess . . . in both, you have to study existing situations carefully before making any move and then try to turn difficulties into opportunities'. It's interesting to note (and that's all I want to do here) that the earliest photographic analysis of what Geddes would have called Place, Work and Folk was in fact carried out in Edinburgh: it was, of course, Hill and Adamson's great Newhaven project, from 1845, a few years before Geddes' birth. Whether it influenced Geddes directly I don't know. What I can say, with certainty, is that it was part of the same visual thinking tradition.

But back to the Outlook Tower: Philip Boardman notes that at the heart of the Outlook Tower was its necessary complement: an Inlook Tower. In *The Worlds of Patrick Geddes* Boardman reconstructs a teaching session with Geddes:

> At this point our heads are reeling from the rapidity with which we have journeyed from prehistory to the future and from Edinburgh to the limits of the universe and back again. As PG motions us towards a corner of the room we protest we cannot cope with anything more just now. 'Come, come!' he insists. 'Here is the needed complement to all those outlooks on the external world'. Behind a curtained doorway is a tiny bare-walled cell containing nothing but a single chair: the beginning of an Inlook Tower. This is to symbolise the solitary meditation with which every observer must complete his studies of the outside world.

Geddes himself explored another sort of inlook in a letter to Victor Branford:

> The Tower of Thought and Action needs a corresponding basement and not merely that of Arts and Sciences in general as hitherto but a sub-basement or catacomb proper in which the life of feeling is similarly to be recognised. Is there any escape from this argument? and if not where does it lead? Do not imagine that I have in any way lapsed into a Quietist or delirious mood. This is only a clearer development of what has been more or less incipient all along.

Conclusion: the need for generalism: back to the garden

In closing, I want to refer again to Geddes' three Ss: Sympathy, Synthesis, and Synergy. Geddes' comprehensive vision, of which these three Ss are symbolic, has an increasingly obvious relevance today as we face problems of pollution, on the one hand, and educational impoverishment on the other. Both these problems stem from an industrial culture which 'specialises' in production, on the one hand neglecting environmental consequences, on the other neglecting the broad educational needs of those who work in that society. It advocates narrow knowledge which can be seen to have immediate relevance to this or that, instead of enabling the development of broad appreciation of the context within which such knowledge finds its expression.

Thus Geddes must be seen as an ecologist of the mind (to use Bateson's phrase), as well as of the planet. Like Adam Smith, he recognised that the division of labour leads to the mental impoverishment of the worker, unless a good general education is provided as a matter of course. So, the complement to Geddes the environmentalist is Geddes the educator and, for Geddes, these two interdependent parts met in the symbol and fact of the garden, a planned environment in microcosm.

Throughout his life, Geddes resisted the fragmentation of

knowledge consequent on misguided notions of specialisation in education that took as their model the production-line rather than the person. This was not, of course, a denial of the value of specialisation; rather it was an assertion that specialisation, without the recognition of the importance of the context within which that specialisation takes place, was a social disaster. Boardman illuminates Geddes' generalism with reference to his pioneering Summer Meetings:

> . . . he held constantly before both teachers and students the single goal of reuniting the separate studies of art, of literature, and of science into a related cultural whole which should serve as an example to the universities still mainly engaged in breaking knowledge up into particles unconnected with each other or with life. His project can be called the first real summer school in Europe to combine art, philosophy of education, and science.

Geddes advocated such breadth of vision at a time (the end of the nineteenth century) when specialisation was getting into its mechanical stride. The consequences for restriction of thought and action, and environmental degradation are things with which we are all now familiar. But Geddes saw these educational and environmental problems with clarity, when few others could see them, and this, combined with his untimely generalism, may explain his relative neglect. For me, Geddes' philosophy is summed up in these lines by his friend, the great Bengali poet Rabindranath Tagore, a reference made particularly relevant by the involvement of the Poetry Library with this lecture:

> The same stream of life that runs through my veins night and day runs through the world and dances in rhythmic measures. / It is the same life that shoots in joy through the dust of the earth in / numberless blades of grass and breaks into tumultuous waves of leaves and flowers.

Geddes himself put this more concisely in a statement which

one might invoke as a motto for a successful and sustainable environment. It also conjures up a wonderful visual image, worthy of this extraordinary visual thinker. What Patrick Geddes said was this: 'By Leaves We Live'.

In conclusion I want to quote Hugh MacDiarmid again:

> Prophets are proverbially without honour in their own country, but even so the neglect or ignorance of Sir Patrick Geddes in Scotland goes to an uncommon degree and throws a very disconcerting light on our whole national condition, since he was one of the outstanding thinkers of his generation, not merely in Britain but in the world, and not only one of the great Scotsman of the past century but in our entire history.

I agree with MacDiarmid here. I don't think he's exaggerating Geddes' significance. But he wrote this 25 years ago and still Geddes has not received the recognition he deserves. Yet Geddes' thought has never been more obviously relevant than in the present. I think his time has come.

Murdo Macdonald's lecture was sponsored by the Scottish Poetry Library and Lothian Regional Council and presented as a 'Lothian in Europe' event.

The lecture was chaired by Councillor David Costello, Chair of the Planning Committee, Lothian Regional Council, and a response was given by Sofia Leonard, Director, the Patrick Geddes Centre, Edinburgh.

The 'Lothian in Europe' lecture was delivered at Old College, the University of Edinburgh, on 27 November 1992.

It was developed as a 'Lothian in Europe' event by Tessa Ransford, Director of the Scottish Poetry Library, and by Norman Ireland, Principal, EC and Corporate Affairs, Lothian Regional Council, and Geraldine Prince, Co-ordinator of the Lothian European Lectures and lecturer in the Humanities Department, Edinburgh College of Art.

JACQUES DELORS

16 *Address to the
University of Edinburgh*

MY PRIDE AND GRATITUDE FOR THE GREAT HONOUR
conferred on me by the University of Edinburgh stems from
my knowledge that Scottish excellence in education is a constant
theme whenever experts get together to compare the world's
education systems. The Scottish people were quick to make
education one of their top priorities which explains the influential role Scottish universities have played over the centuries.
In the sixteenth century, they invented medical teaching; in
the seventeenth century, the mathematical concepts which still
form the basis for computers; in the eighteenth century, the
market economy; in the nineteenth, the physical laws which
govern modern microprocessors. And today the University
of Edinburgh leads the field in artificial intelligence, genetic
engineering and, indeed, European Community Studies in the
Europa Institute.

Educational standards are now widely recognised as a vital
element in new forms of competitiveness but, beyond that,
as a factor contributing to mutual understanding between
nations. Scotland, which holds the European record for the
highest number of university degrees per head of population,
is a shining example to us all.

I am well aware, of course, that the award of an honorary
degree is made to me as an intermediary, that it is the process of
European integration that is being honoured through me. I also
realise that, through me, a link with Europe is being reaffirmed
– a link which has been a constant feature of Scottish history,
both before and after the Treaty of Union in 1707. Scotland's

universities, for example, did not wait for the ERASMUS programme to arrange large-scale student exchanges: before and after the Reformation, young Scots left to take up religious studies at the Sorbonne, Leiden, Padua and Utrecht. This spirit of openness helps to explain why there are more than 20 million people of Scottish descent worldwide.

Compared with Scotland's ancient links, and the University of Edinburgh's history of more than 400 years, the European Community's 35-year adventure hardly amounts to much. The Community has therefore every reason to be modest. But this should not prevent us – rightly or wrongly – from attaching importance to certain dates which will have a direct impact on our daily lives.

Reference has been made to the Single European Market as the 'Big Idea' of my Presidency. It would be impossible for me to ignore it with the deadline we set ourselves in 1984 now imminent. Before I began my term of office in January 1985, I made a 'Grand Tour of the Capitals', to look at the prospects for breathing new life into what had become a lethargic community. I discounted three possibilities:

• the first was European defence: the time was not ripe and there were too many obstacles;

• the second was institutional reform: the Member States were too hesitant, although they recognised the need to abandon unanimous voting for many decisions;

• the third was a stronger European monetary system, but at least two countries wanted the liberalisation of capital movements to come first.

So the objective I chose was the abolition of the Community's internal frontiers and the creation of a Single Market comparable to the United States or Japan. There was no other way of restoring the dynamism of Europe's economy. But there was nothing new about the idea. I was merely asking the Member States to honour the commitments they had given 35 years previously in the Treaty of Rome.

We had come a long way since 1957. Everyone realised in

1985 how serious the crisis was and how little could be done with purely national resources. But a timetable was needed to concentrate minds and instill a sense that the process was irreversible. It was a gamble, but we took it and set 1992 as our deadline. We adopted a programme setting out a method – qualified majority voting, cooperation with Parliament – and instruments – the famous set of almost 300 proposals to do away with physical, technical and fiscal barriers.

Have we succeeded? The answer is a ringing 'yes'. Perhaps the brasses could do with a little spit and polish, but Europe's Single Market will be open for business on New Year's Day 1993. There will be no big bang, of course, because the business community has anticipated events. Yesterday's blueprint – involving the harmonisation of technical rules, the opening up of public procurement, the liberalisation of services, the mutual recognition of qualifications, free movement of goods, services and capital – has become tomorrow's, if not today's, reality. Only one major problem remains. There are still two divergent approaches to the question of checks on individuals. They may eventually be reconciled. But the question is a tricky one, because national sensitivities differ and because the issue is being handled for the most part in an intergovernmental context and this complicates matters.

Were we right to take this approach to treating Europe's lethargy? The world crisis has shown how vulnerable Europe's economy still is. But who could deny that 1992 and the Single Market has stimulated our economies, boosted investment and transformed attitudes?

Everyone has benefited from unification of the European Market and our combined strength has grown. More than 60% of Scotland's exports now go to Community countries, compared with a mere 23% in the early 1970s. There is no better illustration of Europe's new lease of life than Scotland's Silicon Glen. It is a symbol of an innovative Europe, confident of what it has to offer, but attractive and open to foreign investment. It should be remembered that Scotland absorbs more than

one-tenth of all American investment in Europe. There are
other examples, too. Since I have mentioned free movement
of capital and services, it should be recalled that Edinburgh
ranks sixth among the world's financial centres. Far be it from
me to claim that the 1992 exercise deserves all the credit, but I do
believe that it has made a major contribution to the far-reaching
modernisation of Europe's economy in recent years.

Europe is more competitive today, but it has not lost its
sense of solidarity. Another important decision, though less
spectacular and more difficult to implement, dates from February 1988. Then the Community set its budgetary framework
up to the end of 1992 and gave itself the means to work towards
greater economic and social cohesion. Cohesion does not catch
the imagination in the same way as the Single Market. The two
projects are, of course, quite different. Cohesion needs time –
there are no short cuts. But the two go together; as the old song
says, 'You can't have one without the other'. Competition gives
us vitality, but cooperation gives us strength, and solidarity
binds us together.

Cooperation and solidarity are no abstractions for the people
of Strathclyde or the Western Isles, or for your neighbours down
the road in Pilton.[1] The Single Market would mean little to them
if there were no flanking policies. Something had to be done to
compensate for the cost of adapting shipbuilding and the coal
and steel industries, to create an environment in which the new
high-technology industries could grow, to stem the flight from
the land. This is precisely what the structural policies set out
to do. They will have provided 675 million ecus in aid for
this purpose in Scotland over the five years to 1993. We have
a long road ahead of us but the distance already covered should
encourage us to keep going, to lengthen our stride.

The Single Market would serve little purpose if Scotland
remained isolated, which is why there has been investment in
transport and telecommunications networks. These should help
Shetland fishermen, at the northernmost tip of the Community,
to feel that they too are part of the great European adventure.

This is also why there is an infrastructure policy concerned not only with the modernisation of major ports and motorways but also with the electrification of secondary railway lines and with facilities at Dundee and Cumbernauld airports.

These examples are proof, if proof were needed, that we are creating more than a free-trade area. What we want is an economic area that is organised and caring; an area where the old Scottish merchant tradition can thrive, where new forms of cooperation can develop.

But why am I concentrating on trade at the expense of culture in Edinburgh, the 'Athens of the North'? Quite simply because trade, for all its selfishness and ruthlessness, is one of the main vectors of civilisation. Witness the Athenians against the Spartans; the Lombard, Venetian and Florentine traders; the Champagne fairs and the Flemish cloth merchants; the Hanseatic League and the Scots of the First Industrial Revolution.

Trade in goods often precedes trade in ideas in the development of a civilisation. Similarly, financial speculation has never been a bar to speculation of the philosophical kind. The age of Scottish Enlightenment, the age of David Hume, is proof of this. So when we speak of the four freedoms of the Single Market – goods, services, capital and persons – we must not forget the fifth which is implicit but still fundamental: the freedom of ideas.

The ERASMUS, COMETT and ESPRIT programmes of the European Community were all designed to organise intellectual exchange and re-create the network of the first mediaeval universities. The reputation of Scotland's universities attracts many Community students and post-graduates today. They may play an even bigger role tomorrow.

In a general climate of doom and gloom, clear thinking is vital. And where better to find it than in a university as celebrated as Edinburgh – for its past, its culture, its analytical capacity and its powers of invention. It is important that we take the broad view, ignoring ups and downs and passing disputes. The real issue is the historical role of a revitalised Europe on the world stage. We began with the foundations: the freedom to think, to move and to trade. And from this will come the confidence, the strength, at the Edinburgh Summit, to rise above present difficulties, to transcend real differences, to create unity in diversity – the essence of our Europe, where everyone has a place.

Jacques Delors' address was delivered in the McEwan Hall, Edinburgh, on 10 December 1992 on the occasion of the award of the degree of Doctor *honoris causa* by the University of Edinburgh. Professor R. E. Asher, Vice-Principal, gave the Laureation Address.

Notes and further reading

Chapter 1 (Europe undivided)

1. Ian Davidson, 'Europe Between Nostalgia and Utopia' in J. Story (Ed.) *The New Europe: Politics, Government and Economy since 1945*, Blackwells, Oxford 1993, pp.475–92 at p.480.
2. Timothy Garton Ash, *The Uses of Adversity: Essays on the Fate of Central Europe*, Granta, London 1991, p.266.

Further reading

F. Fukuyama, 'The End of History?' The National Interest, No. 16, 1989, pp.3–18

T. Garton Ash, *The Uses of Adversity: Essays on the Fate of Central Europe*, Granta, London 1991

G. Prins (Ed.), *Spring in Winter: The 1989 Revolution*, Manchester University Press, Manchester 1990

J. Story (Ed.) *The New Europe: Politics, Government and Economy since 1945*, Blackwells, Oxford 1993

Chapter 4 (Nations, states, people and commerce)

1. See William E. Paterson's *Lothian European Lecture*, 'Europe Undivided', included in this volume.
2. A large, and much-criticised housing scheme on the outskirts of Glasgow.

3. Ian Brownlie, *Principles of Public International Law*, fourth edition, Oxford, 1990, p.72ff.

4. Ibid, p.108.

5. P. Meehan, *The Unnecessary War: Whitehall and the German Resistance to Hitler*, Sinclair-Stevenson, 1992, p.6.

6. Jean Monnet, *Memoirs*, tr. Richard Mayne, Collins, 1978, pp.304–5.

7. Articles 31 ECSC, 164 EEC and 136 EURATOM.

8. Cases 26/62 Van Gend en Loos (1963) ECR 3, and 6/64 Costa *v.* ENEL (1964) ECR 1141.

9. J. Bryce, *Studies in History and Jurisprudence*, Oxford University Press, 1901, vol.1,ch.4.

10. Ibid.,vol.1,ch.3.

11. Ibid.,vol.2,ch.10.

Chapter 5 (Imperialism and after)

Note: Edward Said's lecture was drawn from his *Culture and Imperialism*, Chatto and Windus, 1993, which contains amplified footnotes and references.

1. Harry Magdoff, *Imperialism: From the Colonial Age to the Present*, Monthly Review, New York 1978, pp.29 and 35.

2. William H. McNeill, *The Pursuit of Power: Technology, Armed Forces and Society Since 1000 A.D.*, University of Chicago Press, Chicago 1983, pp.260–1.

3. Richard W. Van Alstyne, *The Rising American Empire*, Norton, New York 1974, p.1. See also Walter LaFeber, *The New Empire: An Interpretation of American Expansion*, Cornell University Press, Ithaca 1963.

4. Michael W. Doyle, *Empires*, Cornell University Press, Ithaca 1986, p.45.

5. David Landes, *The Unbound Prometheus: Technological Change and Industrial Development in Western Europe from 1750 to the Present*, Cambridge University Press, Cambridge 1969, p.37.

6. Tony Smith, *The Pattern of Imperialism: The United States, Great Britain, and the Late Industrialising World Since 1815*, Cambridge University Press, Cambridge 1981, p.52. Smith quotes Gandhi on this point.

7. Joseph Conrad, 'Heart of Darkness,' in *Youth and Two Other Stories*, Doubleday, Page, Garden City 1925, pp.50–1.

8. V.G. Kiernan, *Marxism and Imperialism*, St Martin's Press, New York 1974, p.111.

9. D.K. Fieldhouse, *The Colonial Empires: A Comparative Survey from the Eighteenth Century*, 1965; rprt. Macmillan, Houndmills 1991, p.103.

10. Frantz Fanon, *The Wretched of the Earth*, tr. Constance Farrington, 1961, rprt. Grove, New York 1968, p.101.

11. Michael Barratt-Brown, *After Imperialism*, rev. edn, Humanities, New York 1970, p.viii.

12. Arno J. Mayer, *The Resistance of the Old Regime: Europe to the Great War*, Pantheon, New York 1981.

13. *North–South: A Programme for Survival*, MIT Press, Cambridge, Mass. 1980.

14. Cheryl Payer, *The Debt Trap: The IMF and the Third World*, Monthly Review, New York 1974.

15. For a useful history of the three worlds classification, see Carl E. Pletsch, 'The Three Worlds, or the Division of Social Scientific Labor, circa 1950–1975,' *Comparative Studies in Society and History* 23, October 1981, 565–90.

16. Noam Chomsky, *Towards a New Cold War: Essays on the Current Crisis and How We Got There*, Pantheon, New York 1982, pp.84–5.

17. Ronald Steel, *Walter Lippmann and the American Century*, Little Brown, Boston 1980, p.496.

18. See Anders Stephanson, *Kennan and the Art of Foreign Policy*, Harvard University Press, Cambridge, Mass. 1989, pp.167, 173.

19. Richard J. Barnet, *The Roots of War*, Atheneum, New York 1972, p.21. See also Eqbal Ahmad, 'Political Culture and Foreign Policy: Notes on American Interventions in the

Third World', in *For Better or Worse: The American Influence in the World*, ed. Allen F. Davis, Greenwood Press, Westport 1981, pp.119–31.

20. V.G. Kiernan, *America: The New Imperialism: From White Settlement to World Hegemony*, Zed, London 1978, p.127.

21. Eqbal Ahmad, 'The Neo-Fascist State: Notes on the Pathology of Power in the Third World', *Arab Studies Quarterly*, 3, No.2, Spring 1981, 170–80.

22. Paul Virilio, *L'Insecurité du territoire*, Stock, Paris 1976, p.88ff.

23. Gilles Deleuze and Félix Guatarri, *Mille Plateaux*, Minuit, Paris 1980, p.511 (tr. Edward Said).

24. Virilio, op. cit. p.84.

25. Theodor Adorno, *Minima Moralia: Reflections from a Damaged Life*, tr. E.F.N. Jephcott, 1951; New Left, London 1974, pp.46–7.

26. Ibid., pp.67–8.

27. Ali Shariati, *On the Sociology of Islam: Lectures by Ali Shariati*, tr. Hamid Algar, Mizan Press, Berkeley 1979, pp.92–3.

28. This is discussed at length in Edward Said, *Beginnings: Intention and Method*, 1975; rprt. Columbia University Press, New York 1985.

29. John Berger and Jean Mohr, *Another Way of Telling*, Pantheon, New York 1982, p.108.

30. Immanuel Wallerstein, 'Crisis as Transition', in Samir Amin, Giovanni Arrighi, André Gunder Frank, and Immanuel Wallerstein, *Dynamics of Global Crisis*, Monthly Review, New York 1982, p.30.

31. Hugo of St Victor, *Didascalicon*, tr. Jerome Taylor, Columbia University Press, New York 1961, p.101.

Chapter 14 (At the heart of Europe)

1. In introducing the lecture, Professor William Paterson quoted from Edward Heath's Maiden Speech in the House

of Commons on 26 June 1950 in which Edward Heath argued vigorously the case for closer European union and, particularly, for the benefits to the UK of integration with Europe.

Chapter 15 The 'Lothian in Europe' lecture
Further reading

Philip Boardman, *The Worlds of Patrick Geddes*, Routledge and Kegan Paul, 1978

Peter Hall, *Cities of Tomorrow*, Basil Blackwell, 1988

Murdo Macdonald (ed.), *Patrick Geddes*, Edinburgh Review Issue no.88, Polygon, 1992

Helen Meller, *Patrick Geddes: Social Evolutionist and City Planner*, Routledge, 1990

Jacques Delors: Address

1. Strathclyde, Scotland's largest local authority, the Western Isles on Europe's periphery, and Pilton, an urban housing scheme in Edinburgh, currently all benefit from EC investment programmes.

List of European terms and acronyms

Acquis communautaire	Accumulated legislation of the European Communities
CAP	Common Agricultural Policy
CEMA	Council for Mutual Economic Assistance
CIS	Commonwealth of Independent States
COMECON	see **CEMA**
COMETT	Community Programme in Education and Training for Technology
CSCE	Conference on Security and Cooperation in Europe
EC	European Communities
EFTA	European Free Trade Association
EFTANS	Members of European Free Trade Association
EMU	Economic and Monetary Union
ERASMUS	European Community Action Scheme for the Mobility of University Students
ERDF	European Regional Development Fund
ERM	Exchange Rate Mechanism
ERNACT	The European Regions Network for the Application of Communication Technology
ESC	Economic and Social Committee
ESF	European Social Fund
ESPRIT	European Strategic Programme for Research and Development in Information Technology
EURATOM	European Atomic Energy Community
European Weeks	Initiatives to encourage focused promotion of the EC at local levels

Four Freedoms	Freedom of movement of goods, services, capital, people
GATT	General Agreement on Tariffs and Trade
GDP	Gross Domestic Product
Gemeinschaft	Community
Gesellschaft	Market–place
GNP	Gross National Product
IGC	Intergovernmental Conference
IMF	International Monetary Fund
INTERPRISE	Initiative to promote partnerships between industries and services in Europe
INTERREG	Programme to promote trans–frontier cooperation in economic development
IT	Information technology
MEP	Member of the European Parliament
NATO	North Atlantic Treaty Organisation
NGO	Non-governmental organisation
OPEC	Organisation of Petroleum Exporting Countries
RECITE	EC Community Initiative to promote cross–border cooperation between the regions and cities of Europe
SCENT	System Customs Enforcement Network
SME	Small and Medium-sized Enterprise
TEMPUS	Trans-European Mobility Scheme for University Studies (in Eastern European countries)
TREVI	Member States' Interior Ministers meeting to discuss terrorism, violence and drugs
UN	United Nations
UNDP	United Nations Development Programme
UNHCR	United Nations High Commission for Refugees
WEU	Western European Union
YES	Programme for the promotion of youth exchanges